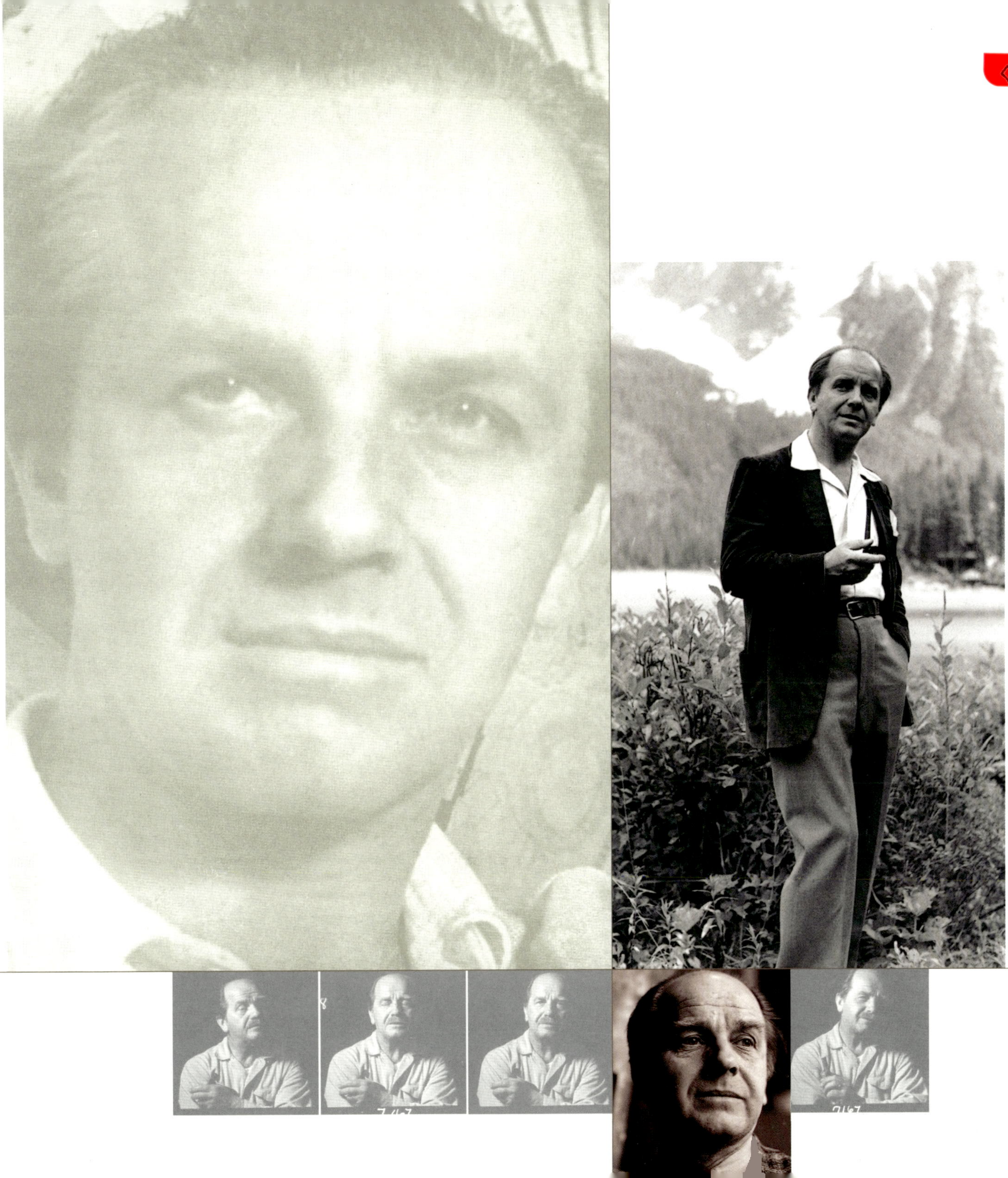

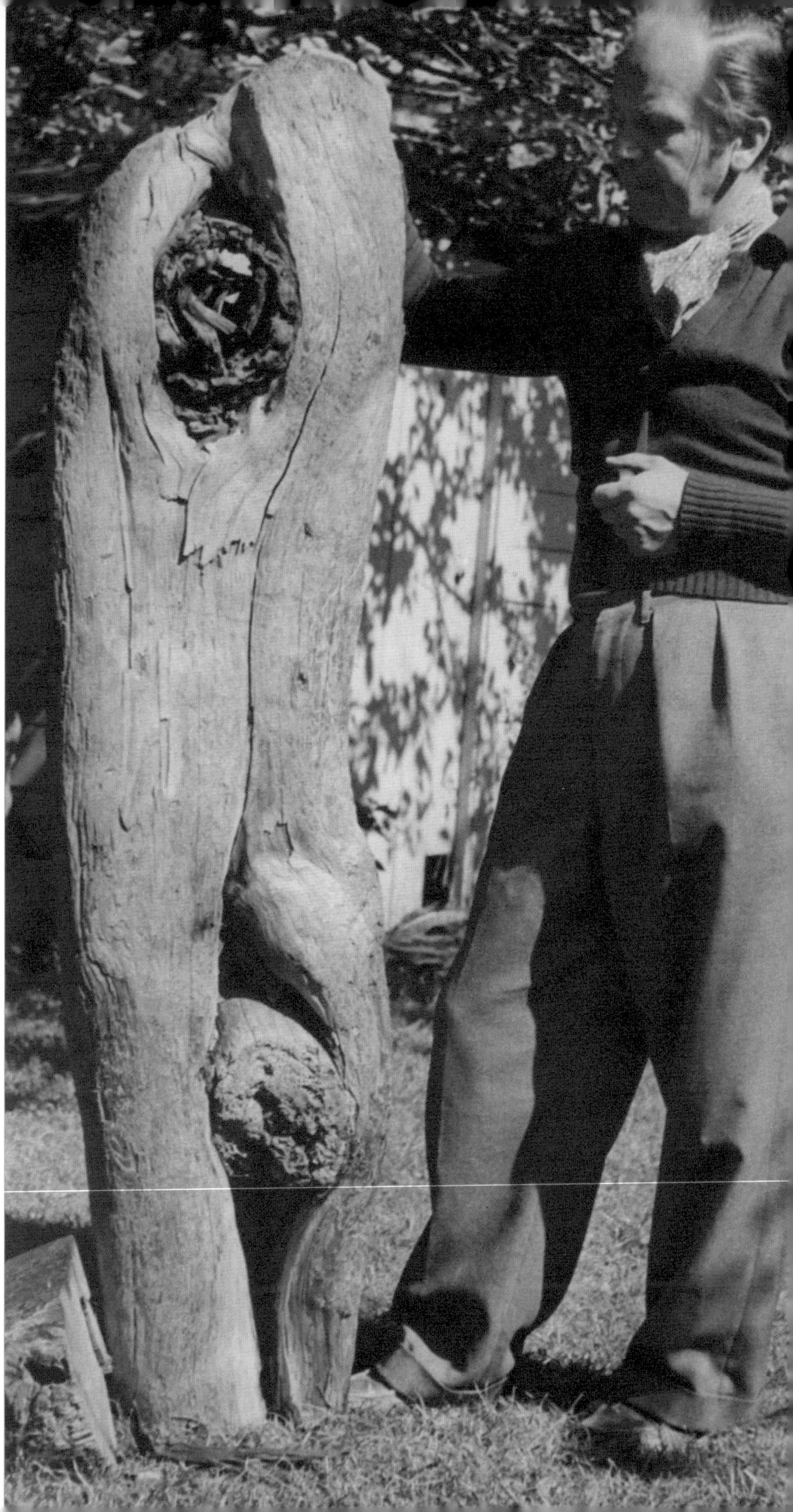

Intersections:
The Life and Art of Jan Zach

Roger Hull

INTERSECTIONS

JAN ZACH

Hallie Ford Museum of Art
Willamette University

Distributed by
University of Washington Press
Seattle and London

This book is published in connection with an exhibition arranged by the Hallie Ford Museum of Art at Willamette University entitled *Intersections: The Art of Jan Zach* (February 1 – March 29, 2003).

Financial support for the exhibition and book was provided by contributions from friends, relatives, and former students of Jan Zach, with additional support provided by the Oregon Arts Commission and the National Endowment for the Arts.

Design and typography by Acme Graphic Design, Portland, Oregon

Printing by QSL Communications, Eugene, Oregon

Bindry by Lincoln & Allen, Portland, Oregon

Front cover: *Totem* (lumino-kinetic sculpture), 1952. See Figure 34, page 43.

Page one, clockwise from upper left: Jan Zach, age 35 in Rio de Janiero, Brazil; Jan Zach, age 45 in Banff, Canada; Jan Zach, age 55 in Eugene, Oregon; Jan Zach (series), age 65 in Eugene.

Page two: Jan Zach with the log for *Venus*, 1951. See Figures 25 and 26, page 39.

Page seventy-seven: Jan Zach, age 65 in Eugene.

Photographs Hallie Ford Museum of Art, Willamette University, Salem, Oregon. Judith and Jan Zach Archives.

Library of Congress Control Number 2002115384

ISBN 1-930957-53-X

Distributed by
University of Washington Press
PO Box 50096
Seattle, Washington 98145-5096

Jan Zach (Czech-American, 1914-1986) was a highly regarded Oregon sculptor and professor of art at the University of Oregon. Born in Slaný, Czechoslovakia, in 1914, Zach trained as a painter and decorator in Prague during the 1930s and came to the United States in 1938 to work on the Czech pavilion at the New York World's Fair, never to return to Czechoslovakia because of the Nazi invasion in 1939 and the Communist takeover in 1948.

In 1940 Zach moved to Brazil and spent the next eleven years in Rio de Janiero and in the nearby Brazilian countryside. In 1951, he and his wife Judith moved to her hometown of Victoria, British Columbia, and in 1958, at the encouragement of Mark Sponenburgh, he joined the art faculty at the University of Oregon, in Eugene. Over the next twenty-one years, Zach emerged as an important teacher and mentor and trained several generations of sculptors, many of whom are still active in the region.

One of Zach's students in the 1970s was Tommy Griffin, a young graduate student from San Jose, California. Over the next dozen years, Zach and Griffin moved beyond the normal teacher-student relationship to become close personal friends. Just before Zach died in 1986, he asked Griffin if he would help find an appropriate repository for many of his sculptures and archives.

Griffin, with the assistance of Judith Zach and fellow sculptors Jerry and Lin Harpster, began a process that would culminate in the donation of a large body of work and related archives to the Hallie Ford Museum of Art in the spring of 2000. Griffin, Judith Zach, and the Harpsters were particularly impressed with our committment to the collection, preservation, exhibition, and interpretation of regional art.

At an early meeting of the Zach Advisory Committee, comprised of Griffin, Judith Zach, the Harpsters, Willamette faculty members Roger Hull and Robert Hess, Zach's niece Ruth Gilombardo, and myself, it was decided that we should organize a major exhibition that examined Zach's life and artistic career in depth. It had been at least twenty years since Griffin had organized a retrospective exhibition for Zach at the University of Oregon Museum of Art and the time seemed ripe to re-examine the artist's career.

Faculty member Roger Hull, who had written previously about Carl Hall and is keenly interrested in historic regional art, seized the opportunity to write about Zach and to organize the exhibition, and we are extremely grateful to him for his willingness to take on the project and to produce such a thoughtful and insightful essay on Zach and his work.

Jerry and Lin Harpster have been extremely supportive from the get-go and helped clean and prepare many of the pieces for exhibition. Similarly, Zach's niece Ruth Gilombardo has been a key member of the Zach Advisory Committe for the past two years and generously agreed to provide initial support for the Zach Archives and lend several pieces to the exhibition. We are further indebted to the many lenders to the exhibition for agreeing to part with their precious Zach works for the run of the exhibition.

As always, a project of this magnitude would not have been possible without the support and help of a number of key individuals. I would like to thank Greg Holly of Acme Graphic Design in Portland for his innovative design and layout of the Zach book, and QSL Communications, Inc. in Eugene for agreeing to donate their press time so that we might print the book within the limitations of our budget. I am further indebted to the many friends, relatives, and former Zach students who helped underwrite the cost of the publication. While I can't thank each donor individually, their names appear at the end of the book.

On the Hallie Ford Museum of Art staff, I would like to thank administrative assistant Carolyn Harcourt, collection curator Mary Parks, preparator Bruce Black, front desk receptionists Molly Fitzsimmons and Megan Jensen, safety officer Frank Simons, and custodian Peggy Flores, for their help with various aspects of the project. Research assistant David Roberts was absolutely instrumental in assembling the extensive résumé on Jan Zach that appears near the end of the book.

Finally, and by no means least, I woulk like to express my thanks and appreciation to Judith Zach and Tommy Griffin. It was really their committment to the memory and legacy of Jan Zach as husband, teacher, mentor, artist, and friend that brought the collection and archives to the Hallie Ford Museum of Art in the first place and the current exhibition and accompanying book to fruition.

John Olbrantz
The Maribeth Collins Director

Jan Zach, 1985.
Photograph by
Bob Keefer.

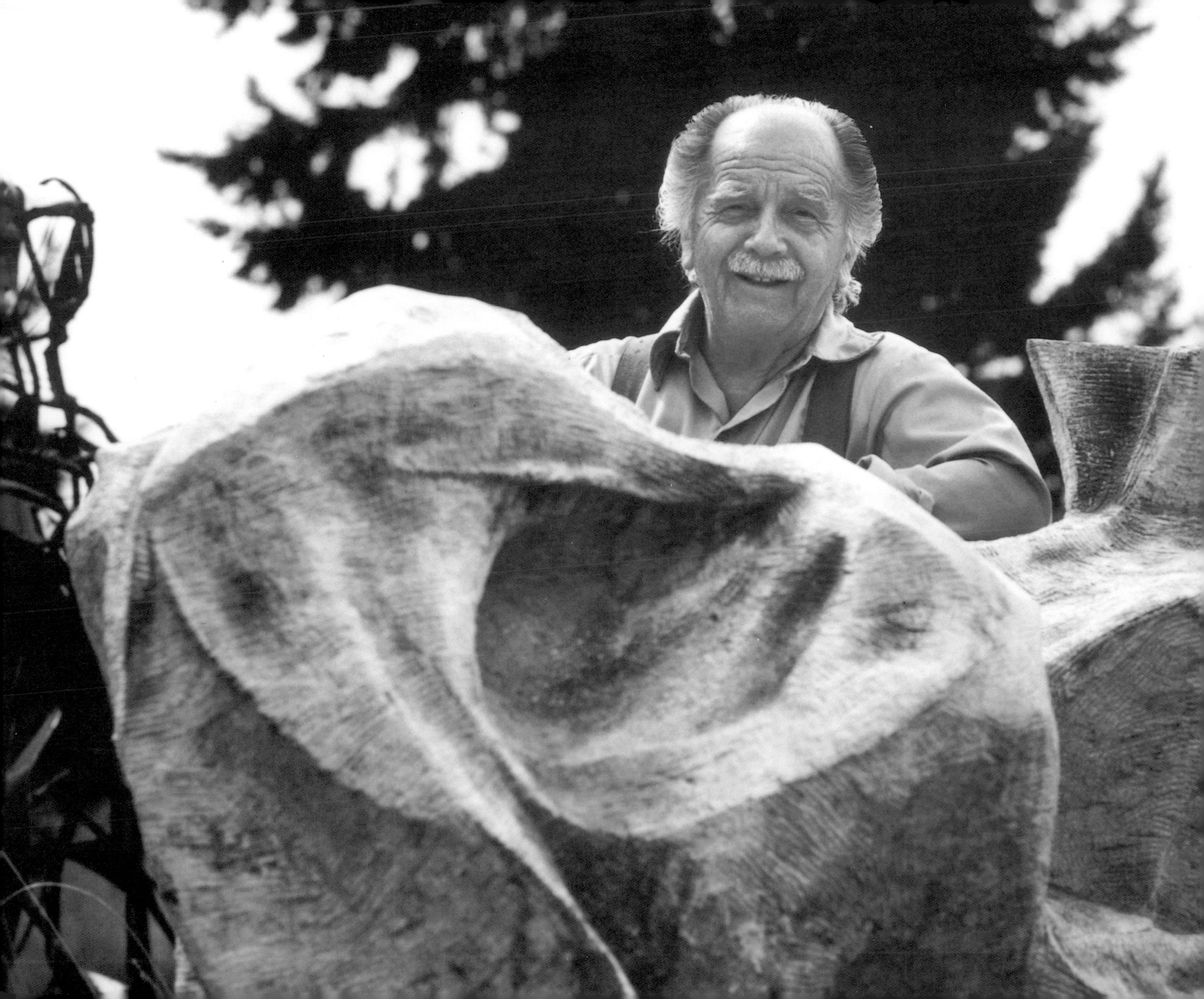

This book on the sculptor Jan Zach results from the efforts and kindnesses of many individuals–most especially Judith Zach. In 2000, she donated to the Hallie Ford Museum of Art a significant body of her late husband's work and a major collection of his letters, exhibition catalogues, manuscripts of essays, photographs of sculptures from all periods of his career, and files of news clippings and reviews documenting his life as an artist. Without these materials, a book on Jan Zach would not have been possible. Judith also spoke with me at length on a number of occasions, answering questions about her life with Jan Zach, identifying individuals in photographs, and clarifying the significance of materials in Zach's papers. The anecdotes and details that Judith was able to provide helped humanize my essay. I am most grateful to her for her generosity, assistance, and warm encouragement of the projects to establish the Judith and Jan Zach Collection and Archives at Willamette, publish this book, and organize the exhibition "Intersections: The Art of Jan Zach" at the Hallie Ford Museum of Art (February 1-March 29, 2003).

I also wish to thank Ruth Gilombardo, Jan Zach's niece, for information she provided about Jan's stay with her family in Union City, New Jersey, in 1938-1939 during the New York World's Fair and for her financial and moral support for establishing the Zach collections at Willamette. I am indebted, too, to Jan Zach's former student and friend, Tommy Griffin, who first suggested the possibility of the Zach Collection and Archives at Willamette University and has served as advisor and agent in placing these resources at the Hallie Ford Museum. Tommy has taken an active role in planning the Jan Zach exhibition and, together with Jerry Harpster and Lin Cook Harpster (two other friends and former students of Jan Zach), cleaned and repaired several of Zach's large sculptures so that they could be photographed for the book and made ready for the exhibition. I am very grateful to all these people, who knew and loved Jan Zach and have worked tirelessly to help document his life and art.

Jan Zach's international life makes his story geographically wide ranging. Luckily, I had my research representatives in Prague and Victoria. JoAnn Elizabeth Seibert spent portions of two summer vacations in Prague tracking down information about the early life and work of Zach, who had left his homeland in 1938, never to return. In July 2001, JoAnn Elizabeth spent the afternoon with Jan's last surviving sibling, Marta Źidlická, at her home in Hradec Králové, learning details about Zach's family life in Czechoslovakia in the 1920s and 1930s. That summer and again in 2002, JoAnn Elizabeth located early paintings by Jan Zach in the collections of the National Gallery in Prague and the City of Prague, gaining access to repositories and private offices because she speaks Czech and is tremendously plucky. Her photograph of Vladamír Študent in his office with Zach's painting *Stefanik Bridge* was the triumphant culmination of a particularly complex morning of detective work. I also thank JoAnn Elizabeth for her translations of letters and other documents from the Czech.

Meanwhile, our man in Victoria, Eugene, and, thanks to the Internet, much of the western world was David Roberts, researcher at the Hallie Ford Museum. During holidays in Victoria, Dave conducted highly informative interviews with Colin Graham, the former director of the Art Gallery of Greater Victoria (who arrived in that city at about the same time that Jan Zach did in 1951), and with Anne Mayhew, the daughter of the sculptor Elza Mayhew, one of Zach's most illustrious students. Both Colin Graham and Anne Mayhew spoke thoughtfully and at length about their old friend Jan Zach, and Dave Roberts' interviews with them were crucial sources of information.

In addition, Dave Roberts conducted an enormous amount of background research on countless aspects of Zach's varied and complex life and art. He supplied information on every conceivable subject–from the location of the 1939 New York World's Fair to the correct spelling of musical composers who crossed paths with Zach. He investigated the fate of certain lost or destroyed works by Zach, discovering that some thought to be lost actually exist in new locations. Further, Dave compiled the extensive "Sources and Resources" section of the book, which includes a bibliography, lists of exhibitions and commissions, and awards. I sincerely thank Dave Roberts for his enormous efforts in support of this project.

Dave Roberts, in turn, was assisted by many other interested and cooperative people, including (in addition to Colin Graham and Anne Mayhew) Pierre Arpin, director of the Art Gallery of Greater Victoria; Eileen Morales, reference librarian at the Museum of the City of New York; Jocelyn Young, curator of collections at the Anchorage Museum of History and Art; Jean Nattinger, assistant registrar at the Museum of Art at the University of Oregon; and Marya Hunsinger, who translated a number of documents from the Portuguese. "There are literally hundreds of others who could be cited," Dave has told me, and he and I are grateful to them all.

I owe a special debt of gratitude to Michael D. Hall–sculptor, collector, independent scholar, and author of books and catalogues on Midwest regionalist art. Michael Hall graciously agreed to read my manuscript (as he did my earlier manuscript for the book on Carl Hall) and made suggestions that considerably strengthened it–especially the discussions of the Styrofoam displacement process of metal casting and of Zach's relationship to American sculptural practice in the 1960s and 1970s.

Clearly, the creation of this volume was in many ways a collaborative project, and I offer my very sincere thanks to all who have helped me by fanning out across the world and remembering back through time to help make the telling of Jan Zach's story as rich as possible. I thank Zachary Hull for his sensitive editing of the manuscript. Ultimately, the responsibility for accuracy–of both fact and tone–is fully mine: errors, misinterpretations, or other inevitabilities must be attributed to me.

Books are expensive to publish, and our solicitation letter for funds to support this one resulted in generous donations from friends and admirers of Jan Zach and from others interested in the documentation of the history of art in the Pacific Northwest. Donors to the book fund are listed at the end of the volume. I thank them and Tommy Griffin, who led the effort to raise money and procure other support. Special thanks are due QSL Communications, Inc., of Eugene and Acme Graphic Design of Portland for their in-kind donations of services.

Finally, I wish to thank John Olbrantz, the Maribeth Collins Director of the Hallie Ford Museum of Art, for his good will, support, and assistance with numerous technical details associated with preparing a book and organizing an exhibition. I am grateful to him, his assistant Carolyn Harcourt, the preparator Bruce Black (who worked long and hard to prepare objects for the exhibition), the collections curator Mary Parks, and the other members of the museum staff. The Hallie Ford Museum of Art provides the context and the mission for staging exhibitions of the work of key figures in the history of Pacific Northwest art and for publishing books that explore their significance in our region and beyond.

Roger Hull
Professor of Art History
and Faculty Curator
Willamette University

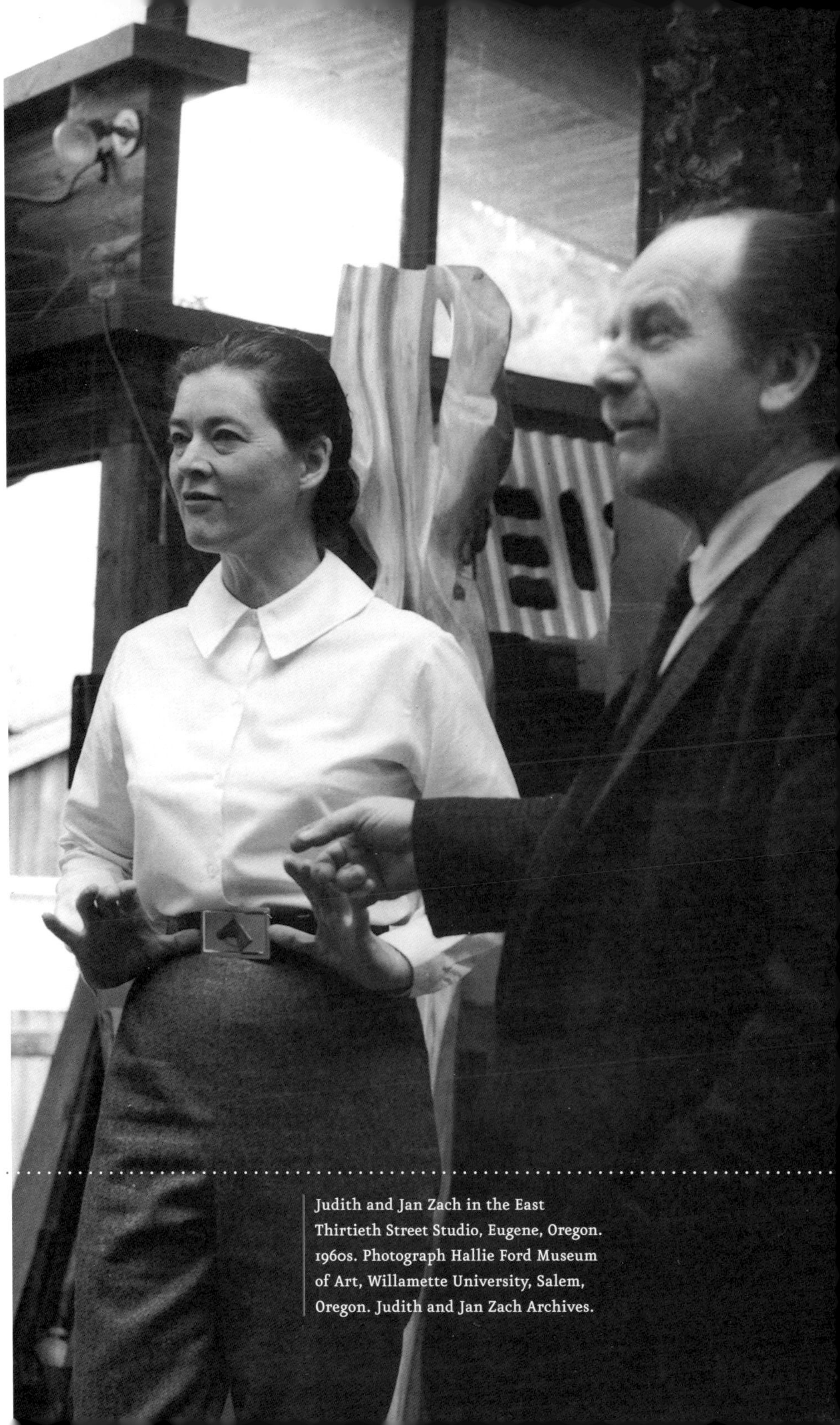

Judith and Jan Zach in the East Thirtieth Street Studio, Eugene, Oregon. 1960s. Photograph Hallie Ford Museum of Art, Willamette University, Salem, Oregon. Judith and Jan Zach Archives.

Jan Zach's story is one of a life lived large. His passion for art enlivened the communities he touched in Eastern Europe, South America, Canada, and the Pacific Northwest. As an artist and citizen of the world, his contribution will be with us for generations to come, both in the remarkable body of sculpture he created and in the inspiration that he spawned in the minds of students and fellow artists.

Like so many other students, I came to the University of Oregon to study under Jan Zach in the graduate sculpture program. I recall showing him a small clay maquette for an eight-foot tall sculpture I was planning. Jan held the maquette up to the light, studied it, and said, "Fantastic! But, why not eighty feet tall?" No matter what the size or material of a proposed sculpture, he always saw grand possibilities. For Jan Zach, art was an expression of the freedom he valued so deeply. Robert Clark, President Emeritus at the University of Oregon, wrote: "We think of Jan Zach's art as abstract, but we know that it speaks to the human condition, largely freedom, or the want of it — in *Prometheus*, on the University of Oregon Campus, the torture and agony even a god must endure when he confronts tyranny and oppression; in Flowers of Freedom; and in all of the flowing forms of his art — the joyous celebration of freedom in a democratic society."

Nature was Jan Zach's primary source of inspiration, but he did much more than document what he saw. He interpreted his observations and refined them into a visual language that was entirely his own. In his journal he wrote: "The formations of ever-changing cloud shapes interest me; also the surfaces of rivers, the ripple of the water which is so like drapery ruffled by the wind." A messenger of his time, he captured the ephemeral qualities of the rugged Northwest landscape in his sculpture. And, with years of observation and refinement, he developed a completely original visual language that can be seen throughout the diverse range of his work, from woodcarvings to stainless steel constructions.

Jan Zach died in 1986, leaving three studios filled with a significant portion of his life's work. Over one hundred sculptures and studies at various stages of development remained, along with scores of drawings and paintings. Dozens of maquettes and small sculptures lined the shelves and workbenches, in addition to shells and other found objects he saved for study and inspiration. These were his favorite children, the works he couldn't part with. In his journal he wrote: "I regret the moment when a sculpture is finished and the creative process comes to an end. It delights me to have some forms around me for years and slowly to carve them away from the mass and thus cherish the image in my mind for a length of time." For over a decade after Jan Zach's death, his works stood undisturbed in the darkness of the locked studios, as if they were waiting for his return. A note tacked to the studio door read, "I'll be back soon! Jan."

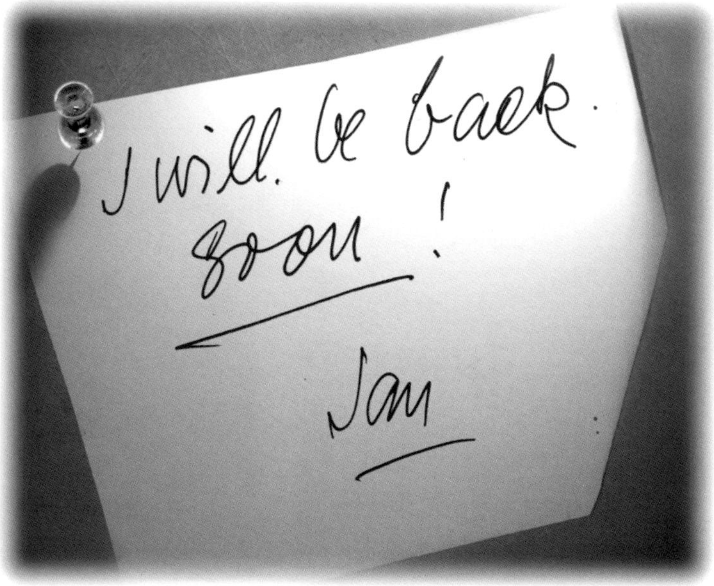

As the years passed, the question of what to do with this unique collection became more pressing. The outdoor works began to deteriorate due to the effects of, ironically, nature. Blackberry brambles damaged some of the pieces; others were nearly destroyed by wind or weather. Finding a permanent home for this remarkable collection had become critical. Now, thanks to the Hallie Ford Museum's mission to collect the work of important Northwest artists, the nucleus of Zach's work, along with his letters and drawings, will be preserved. From these archival papers, Roger Hull, Faculty Curator at the Hallie Ford Museum of Art, has written a compelling chronicle of Jan Zach's life and work in the pages that follow. It is my hope that this book, and the exhibition it accompanies, will ensure Jan Zach's place in the history of contemporary Northwest art and honor his contribution, both as an artist and as a citizen of the world.

Tommy Griffin

Jan Zach. *Windflower*, No.1. 1967. Stainless steel. Enmeshed by nature and the passage of time near the artist's studio in Elmira, Oregon. Photograph by Sean Poston, 2002.

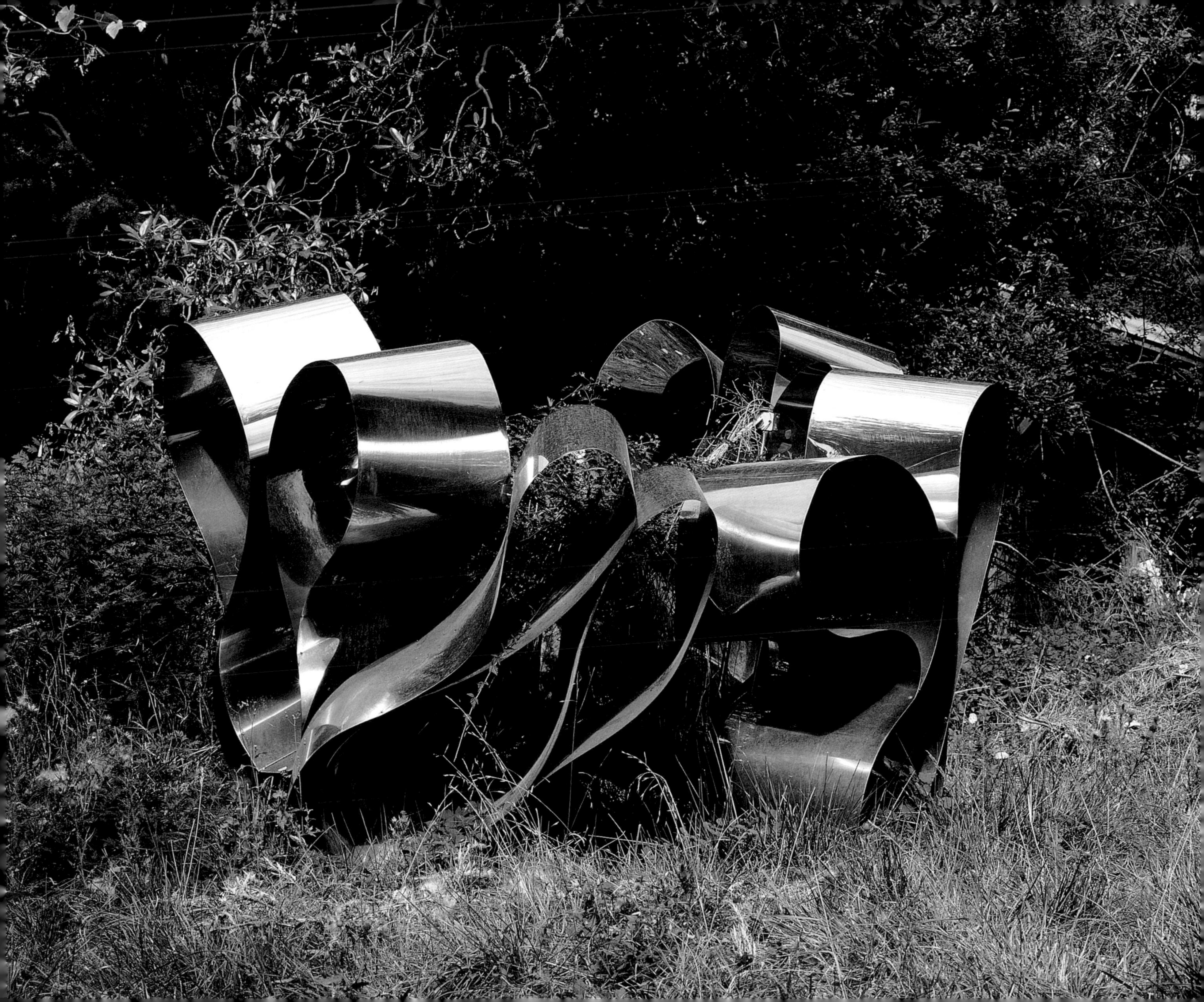

Born in central Europe on the eve of the First World War and displaced in the Americas by the eve of the Second, Jan Zach came of age in one of history's most turbulent periods. World circumstances and personal choices made Zach's life a succession of cultural intersections–with the dazzling city of Prague, where he arrived as a young boy ready to study art; with New York, where he remained for less than two years; with the international crossroads of Rio de Janeiro and then the Brazilian interior; with the quaint city of Victoria, British Columbia, where his wife had been born and where he became a Canadian citizen; and finally with Eugene, Oregon, where he settled in 1958 at the of age forty-four to become a professor of sculpture and, in due time, an American citizen. In Oregon he found his most permanent home and the opportunities he needed to create the major works of his career. He died in Oregon in 1986 at the age of seventy-two.

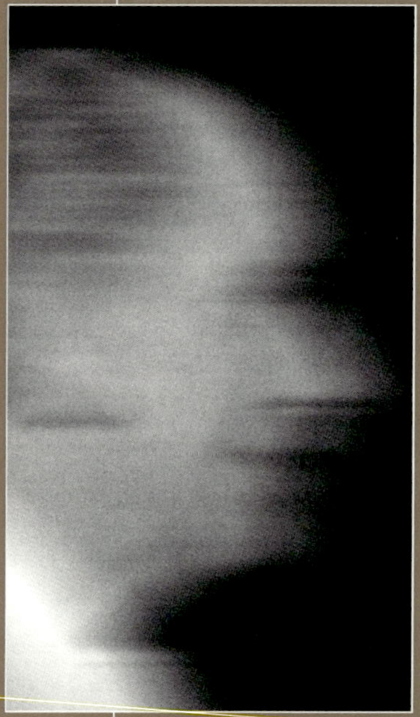

Zach grew up and established himself as an artist during Czechoslovakia's First Republic (1918-1938), a period of economic development, industrial growth, democracy, and personal freedom during which both traditional and modern art flourished in the cosmopolitan Czech community. In the spirit of the Bauhaus in Germany, artists in Prague during the inter-War period worked to integrate all the arts–fine, decorative, and applied–in terms of twentieth-century social, cultural, and economic life. While Zach was to leave Czechoslovakia a few months before the Nazi invasion of 1939, never to return, the principles of international modernism in art and design, the relevance of such historical art forms as the "Prague Baroque" to modern expression, and the belief that art could be a passionate call for human freedom all were ideas that Zach assimilated in his homeland that remained central to his thinking throughout his life.

In his intersection with Oregon, Zach brought an international perspective on culture, art, and politics that was unusual among artists in the Pacific Northwest. His importance in the art history of Oregon, in fact, is based partly on his grafting of European modernism with Northwest regionalism–an intersection that resulted in a wide range of sculpture, from rough hewn beach logs to stainless steel kinetic constructions. While the sheer variety of his work has made his sculpture difficult to classify, the diversity of his production is unified by the elements that most fascinated him: light, movement, and time. His art is also unified by his relentless call for human freedom and resistance to oppression, whether by fascism or totalitarianism. Zach's art is passionate, never ironic, and thus modern in an old-fashioned way. Art for him was a vehicle for expressing and demanding freedom and in this way was another type of intersection, of formal beauty and human values.

The idea of intersection occurs in Zach's art in still other ways, whether of art with nature, art with civic life, art with art history (in addition to Prague Baroque sculpture, Czech kinetic art, Russian Constructivism, and Dutch de Stijl are among the sources that charged Zach's imagination), or the planes of his sculptures intersecting with each other to form patterns of abstract beauty. To the extent that "intersections" suggests seams, breaks, and disjunctions, however, it fails as a metaphor for Zach's artwork even though it remains accurate as a descriptor of his multi-faceted life. Despite its variety, his oeuvre is one of remarkable unity.

Zach's life of displacement and even loss was also one of vibrant engagement with people, ideas, and possibilities. He lived his life to the fullest, sometimes in almost antic ways. "Jan didn't drive," Anne Mayhew recalled, telling of the car tour of Europe that she and her mother, the sculptor Elza Mayhew, made with Zach in 1964. "So we took turns driving him around. He was very competitive. He wanted us to be faster than any other car on the road.

Go faster! Pass him, pass him! Unbelievable. We used to get quite angry sometimes. It was really very funny. He was so joyous. He loved what he was doing. He loved going fast in the car. He loved many things.

He was a man of a very wonderful heart. He also had no problem phoning anyone to see if they had time to meet him. So we were lucky enough to visit [the sculptor Jacques] Lipchitz on the Italian Riviera. We drove up to the top of the mountain where he lived. And I'll never forget that site somewhere in Provence where Picasso was living at the time. Jan said pull over, pull over here! He went to a phone [to call] Picasso. So he had a wonderful conversation. We could see him. We said he spoke thirteen languages, most of them at once. So we never knew quite what was happening. But he came back, full of smiles. Oh, he said, he is not in town right now. But Mrs. Picasso, oh, she was so wonderful. She said we could come another time, no problem. But we didn't get any further than that. We did end up having an afternoon with Henry Moore in England, which was just wonderful, thanks to Jan. Then we went home."[1]

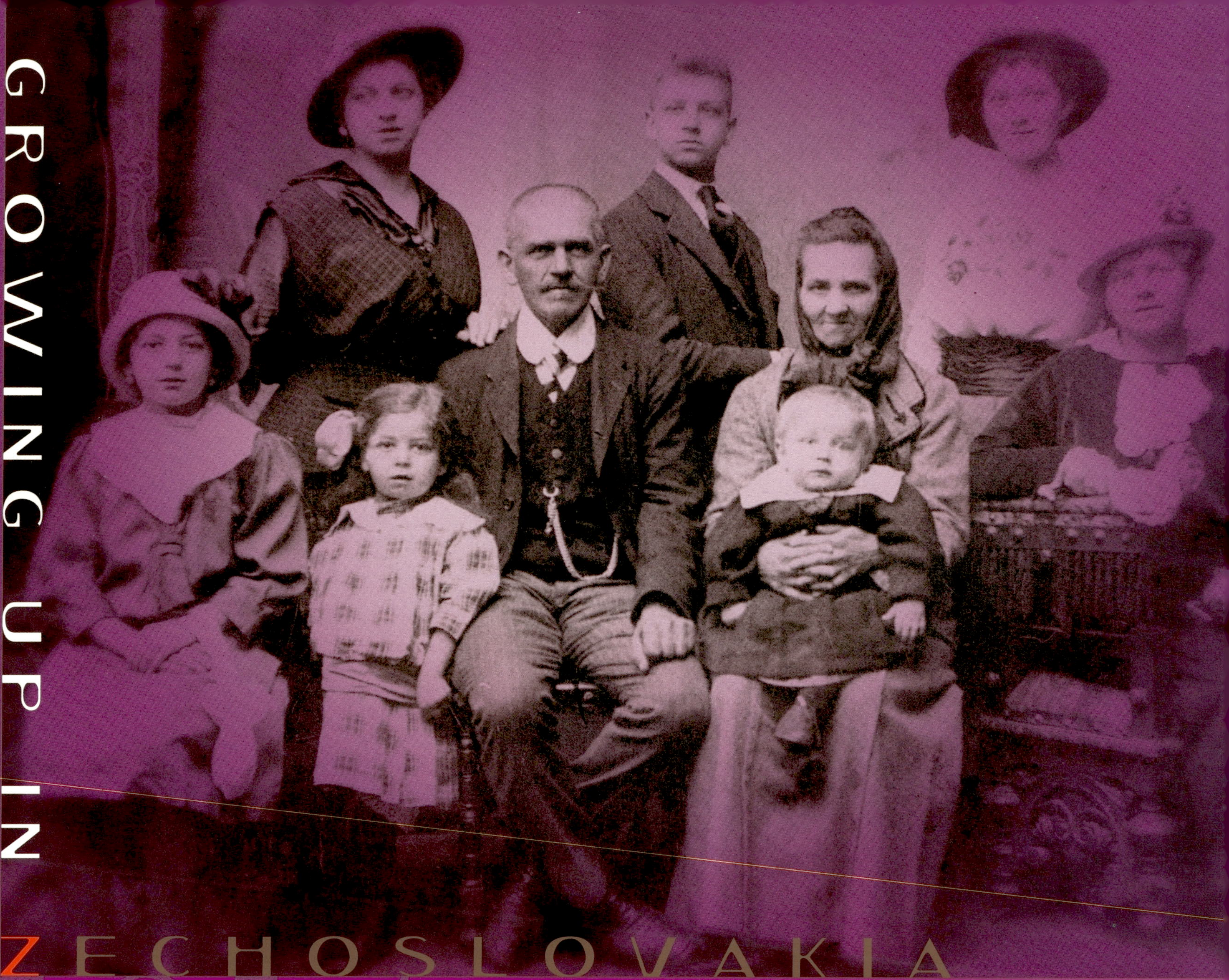

GROWING UP IN CZECHOSLOVAKIA 1914

Jan Zach was born July 27, 1914, in the medieval town of Slaný, located northwest of Prague in the Austro-Hungarian Empire. The region soon became a part of Czechoslovakia and today lies in the Czech Republic. Historically, Prague, Slaný, and surrounding territories comprised the "Czech land" of Bohemia. Jan Zach[2] was the youngest of sixteen children, over half of whom had died at birth or in infancy or, in the case of Ferdinand, by drowning at age twenty-seven. A photograph taken in Slany in about 1916 (Figure 1) records the Zach family when Jan was approximately two years old: it shows Jan seated on the lap of his mother, Rosalie Patová Zachová; his father, Vincent Zach; and their six other surviving children. From a family of saddle makers, Vincent Zach worked in this trade in his youth and early adulthood but broke from family tradition and went to work as a security guard in a chemical factory in Slaný, eventually moving the family to the Bubeneč area of Prague where he operated a gas station.[3] Vincent Zach's break from saddle making alienated him from his two brothers, and Jan never knew his uncles.[4]

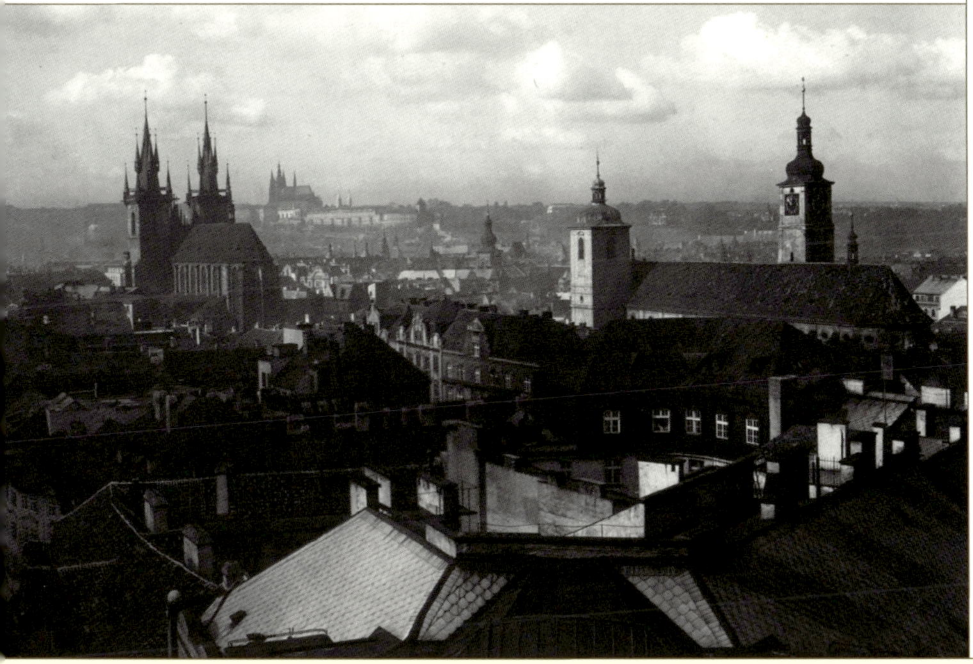

Vincent was Roman Catholic, and Jan and presumably all the children were raised Catholic. Rosalie was Hussite, a follower of John Huss, the Bohemian religious reformer. Jan attended local schools in Slaný. His family and friends called him by various pet names–Honza, Honzík, and Jenda, all common nicknames for Jan. His sister Marta remembers that he had a talent for art as a young boy and was always drawing and painting. He is said to have received his first commission for an artwork at the age of seven.[5] Zach particularly loved to draw the Gothic church in Slaný and made meticulous ink renderings of its architectural details.[6] Marta said neither their parents nor any of the other children were interested in or skilled at art (although many family members including Jan sang, sometimes with friends in groups, performing in pubs and even on the radio).[7] According to Judith Zach, "Jan became an artist *in utero*. It wasn't a matter of becoming, or deciding when; he was born an artist."[8] Zach gravitated to nearby Prague in 1929 or 1930 when he was fifteen to pursue his interest in art. He painted posters for theaters and sometimes sang with other boys in pubs and restaurants in exchange for food.[9] For a time during his Prague years, he played professional tennis. A self-portrait that Zach said he painted in 1931 shows him as a boyish youth with brown-gray eyes and prominent ears, wearing a cap, brown jacket, and blue shirt buttoned to the neck (Figure 2). Apparently painted when he was about seventeen, the portrait has the wistful, sweet gaze of a boy who appears younger.

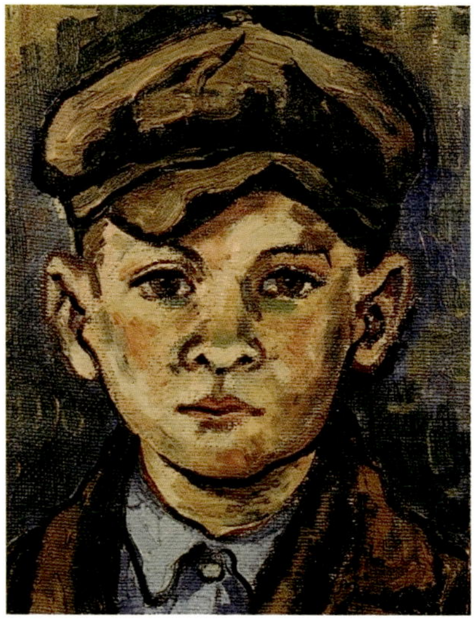

Studying in Prague, City of Art

At the age of sixteen, Zach became the student of the watercolorist and book illustrator Jan Maria Angelo Zeyer (1878-1945), traveling with Zeyer in Yugoslavia and spending time with him and other students at the ruins of Okoř, a fourteenth-century castle near Prague. One of Zach's earliest known surviving works is a colored

FIGURE 1 [OPPOSITE PAGE]

The Vincent Zach Family in Slaný, Czechoslovakia, about 1916. Vincent and his wife Rosalie Patová Zachová, with their son Jan Zach on her lap, are surrounded by their other children (counterclockwise from Vincent): Marta (born 1911), Jindřiška (1904-1981), Jaroslava (called Slávka; 1900-1977), Josef (called Pepík; 1898-1967), Marie (1901-1952), and Anička (1887-1967). Eight other children had died at birth or in infancy, and an older son had drowned in 1916. Photograph Hallie Ford Museum of Art, Willamette University, Salem, Oregon. Judith and Jan Zach Archives.

[ABOVE LEFT]

Prague, Czechoslovakia. c.1920. Photograph Hulton Archive/Getty Images.

FIGURE 2 [ABOVE RIGHT]

Jan Zach. Self-portrait. 1931. Oil on canvas. 10 x 8". Collection of Ruth Gilombardo, Belmont, California. Photograph by Dale Peterson, 2002.

pencil drawing of rooftops and church towers of a town nestled in foliage, with distant hills and a partially clouded sky in the background. Possibly executed under the influence of Zeyer's Romantic, illustrational manner, it is an accomplished example of poetic realism, blending nature and architecture in an idealized view of old Bohemia. Another early oil, said to have been painted at Kordela in Yugoslavia while traveling with Zeyer, is more simplified and "modern" with buildings massed at the edge of a lake, hills layered into the distance. It reflects Zach's awareness of Cézanne, whose work along with French modernism in general had been assimilated into Czech painting from the first years of the twentieth century. In 2002, these works by Zach remained in the collection of his sister, Marta Źidlická, in Hradec Králové. Marta also owns Zach's early still life of yellow flowers in a blue vase, which she said he painted when he was a student in Prague. Architecture, still life, and portraiture would be the recurrent subjects in Zach's paintings in the years ahead in New York, Brazil, and Canada.

In addition to studying with Angelo Zeyer, Jan Zach was the pupil of two other major figures in Czech twentieth-century art. The first was the painter František Kysela (1881-1941), with whom Zach studied in 1934-1935.[10] Kysela taught at the School of Applied Arts (also known as the School of Industrial Arts) and exemplified the Czech modernist interest in breaking down established divisions between the fine and applied arts. Kysela's paintings of the various crafts were the models for tapestries woven by Marie Teinitzerová in 1924-1925 at the tapestry workshop she established in 1910. Zach also studied with Otakar Nejedlý (1883-1957) at the Academy of Fine Arts during 1935-1937, with additional study in 1938. Nejedlý was legendary in Czech art for his paintings based on his 1909-1911 sojourns in Ceylon and southern India. Trained at the School of Landscape Painting in Prague in 1898-1901, he left Europe in 1909 in search of an exotic world in which to pursue his creativity unrestricted by conventions. In this, Nejedlý paralleled Gauguin, who spent portions of his life in Brittany and Tahiti, or the German Expressionists Emil Nolde, who joined an expedition to New Guinea in 1913, and Max Pechstein, who spent 1913-1914 on the Palau

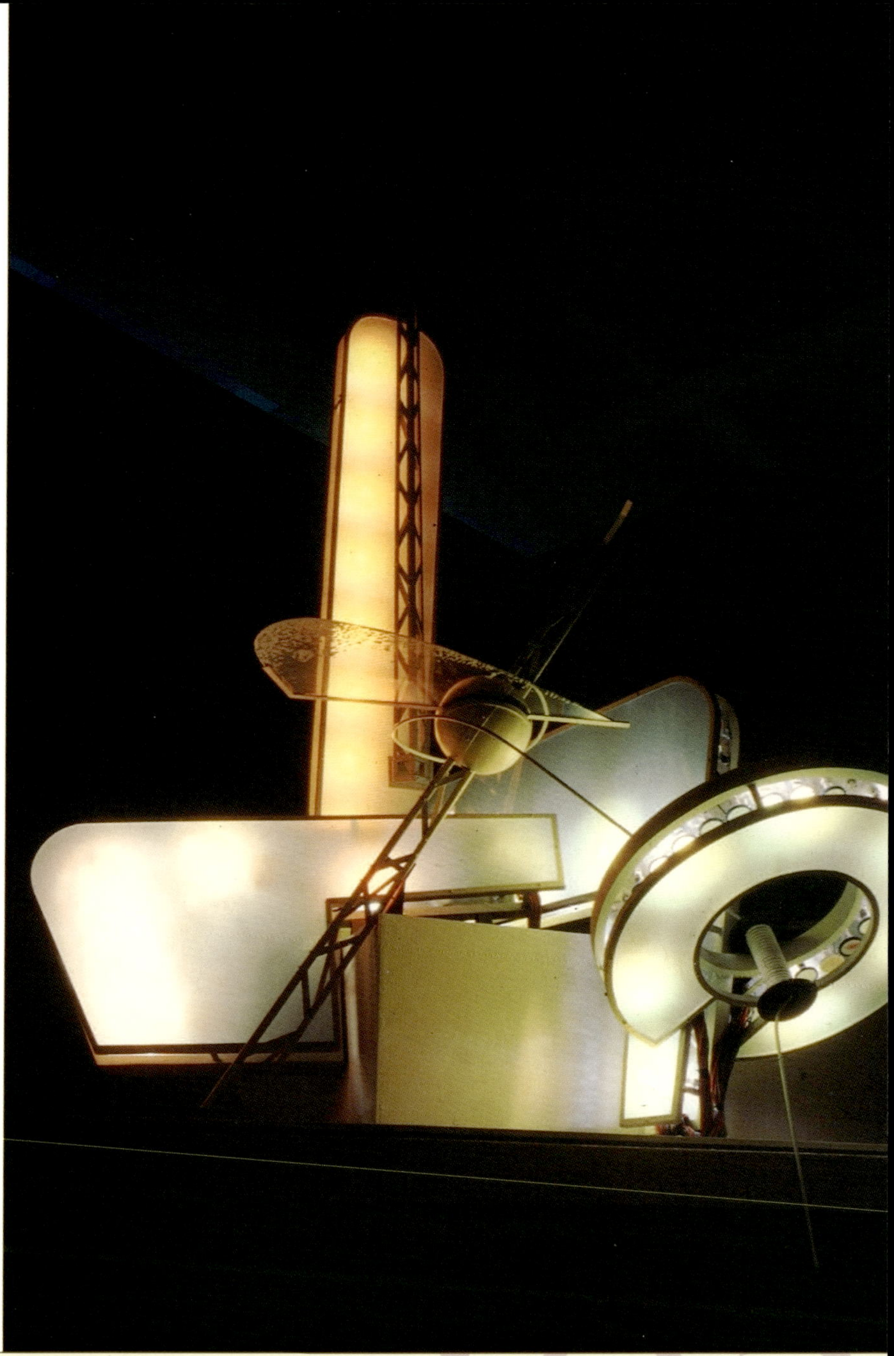

FIGURE 3

Zdenék Pešánek
Kinetic-Light Sculpture for the Edison Transformer Station, Prague. 1929-30. Metal, glass, light bulbs, electric circuits. Destroyed. Pictured in a reconstruction fabricated in 1995-1996.
Photograph National Gallery, Prague. Archives.

1931

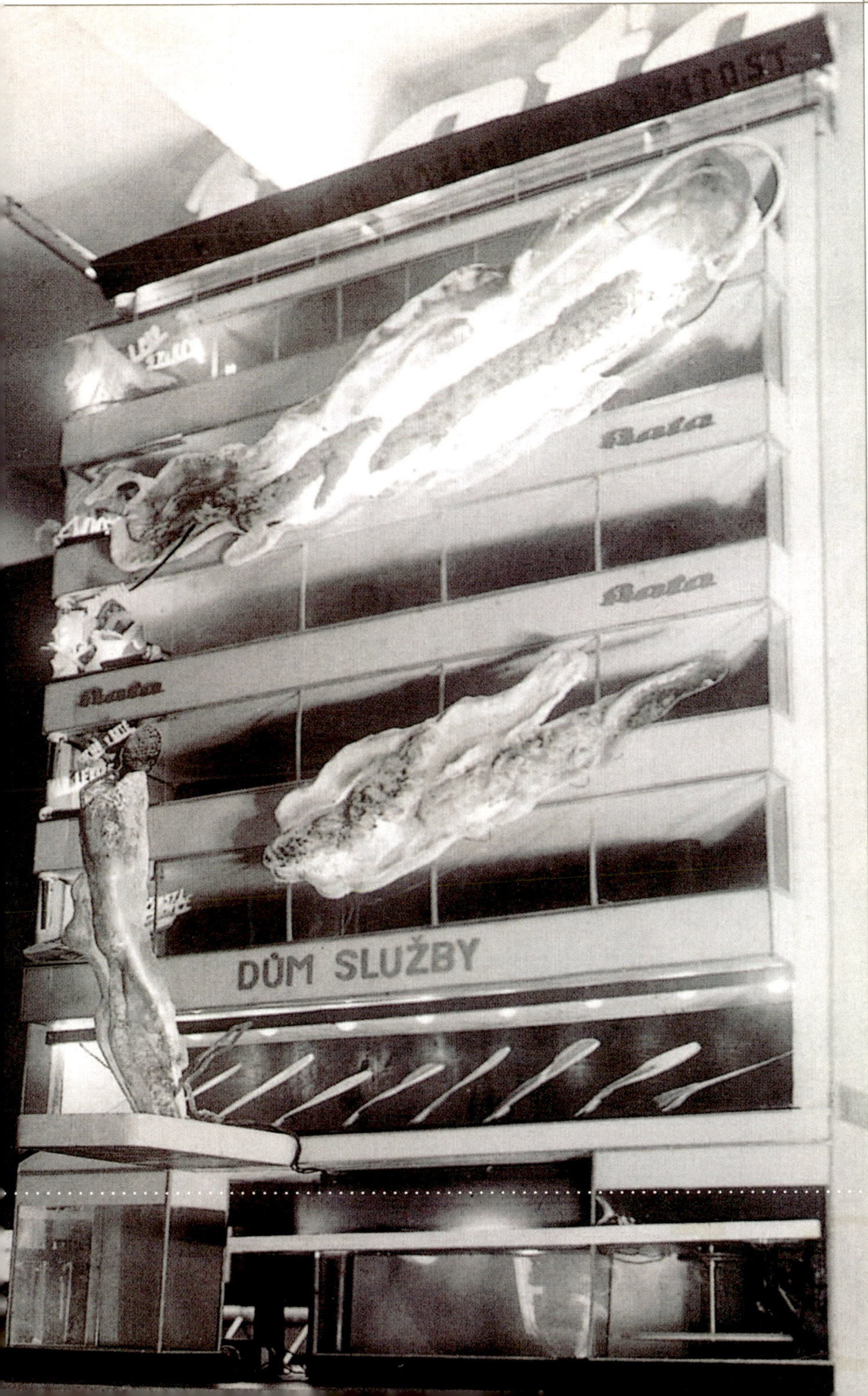

Islands. Jan Zach would experience his own version of this type of Edenic sojourn in Brazil in the 1940s. Both Kysela and Nejedlý are significant figures in the history of Czech modernist design and painting, and studying with them assured Zach a certain pedigree in Czech modern art.

Zdeněk Pešánek

While his studies with Jan Angelo Zeyer, František Kysela, and Otakar Nejedlý were crucial to Zach's training, a more significant influence on his long-term development as a sculptor was the work of Zdeněk Pešánek (1896-1965), with whom Zach never studied directly. Zach later wrote that he was inspired by the work of the Czechoslovak sculptor-architect whose electric piano/fountain at the Czech pavilion for the International Exposition in Paris in 1937 "considerably influenced my way of thinking"[11] – especially regarding light and motion in sculpture. Pešánek was a sign designer for the Electricity Corporation of the City of Prague, which "carried out a sustained campaign to increase the utilization of electricity both for interior and exterior illumination and for advertising displays."[12] Zach learned of Pešánek and his work through Jaromír Fiala, Pešánek's assistant and a sculptor with whom Zach shared a studio and a life-long friendship.

A pioneer of kinetic art, Pešánek is best known for the remarkable illuminated kinetic sculptures that he designed as architecturally scaled outdoor advertising apparati for electric substations and commercial buildings in Prague. His works have been described as "part of a project of civilised utopia, aiming at a link between art and technology"[13] and in this way relate to the otherwise more traditional work of Kysela. During the 1920s Pešánek created three-dimensional constructions of metal, plastic, and painted wood as studies for the kinetic sculptures he would make beginning in 1929. Now known only in photographs and through copies made in the 1980s and 1990s by contemporary Czech artists, the studies related to the Russian Constructivist sculptures by Naum Gabo and Antoine Pevsner but were more specifically cultural in their references. Pešánek's *Film* (1928), for instance, with its spiral of plastic suggesting the unfurling of cinematic film, addresses a specific technological phenomenon more

FIGURE 4

Zdenék Pešánek
Design for Bat'a Department Store Signage. 1935.
Photograph National Technical Museum, Prague.
Architecture Archives.

concretely than Russian Constructivism, which was thought to be universal and "pure" in its forms. Different from Constructivism, too, was Pešánek's interest in the merger of art, advertising, industry and, by extension, economic growth and modernization. Installed in 1930, his kinetic light sculpture for the Edison Transformer Station on Jerusalem Street in Prague (Figure 3; later destroyed, it was reconstructed in 1995-1996) was a construction of metal, glass, "artificial material," light bulbs, and electric circuits. Pešánek juxtaposed a circle with horizontal and vertical planes, outlining these forms with rods of metal to give the sculpture a graphic clarity in its urban setting. Illuminated from within, the sculpture must have been an astonishing beacon of modernity, glowing on the roof of the transformer that helped generate power for a new Prague.

In 1935, Pešánek proposed a light-kinetic advertising installation for the façade of the Bat'a Department Store (Figure 4) on Wenceslas Square. Never realized, the installation would have resulted in the collision of Ludvík Kysela's International Style building made of glass, steel, and stucco with Pešánek's over-scaled, neon-outlined plaster cloud forms, diagonally placed as if in upward drift on the façade, the portico over the entrance featuring a vertical biomorph suggesting a human figure. The combination, as seen in the model, was startling, idiosyncratic, dramatic, and thoroughly original. The neon tubing would have further electrified, in every sense of the term, the overall effect. The concept for the Bat'a façade is oddly Baroque, and indeed Prague Baroque sculpture was a probable influence on Pešánek. Jan Zach later noted that both Pešánek's wildly original kinetic sculptures and Prague Baroque sculpture of the seventeenth and early eighteenth century were inspirations for his own eventual work as a sculptor.

During his student years Zach worked as a successful artist, and several of his paintings had been acquired by Prague museums by the time he left Czechoslovakia in 1938. His painting *Stefanik Bridge* (1936; see Figure 5) was purchased by the Municipal Gallery of Prague (later transferred to the City of Prague, it has hung in an office in the parks department since 1997).[14] The bridge, with masonry arches and diagonal cables, anchors the composition at the left, while to the right a tug plies the waters of the River Vltava and buildings of old and modern Prague line the far bank. As an urban landscape, *Stefanik Bridge* is in the tradition of André Derain's paintings of London Bridge or Oscar Kokoschka's panoramic views of cities (such as his *View of the Thames*, 1925-1926, in the Albright-Knox Art Gallery in Buffalo, New York). But Zach's scene, with its dark blue palette and bridge structures silhouetted against a smoke-filled sky, speaks of the coal-based industrialization of Prague in the 1920s and 1930s, when Czechoslovakia was considered to be the tenth most industrialized nation in the world. Zach recalled that the Municipal Gallery purchased a second of his paintings in 1938; another one, entitled *Country Road* or *Alej* ("Lane"), was purchased that year by the Modern Gallery of

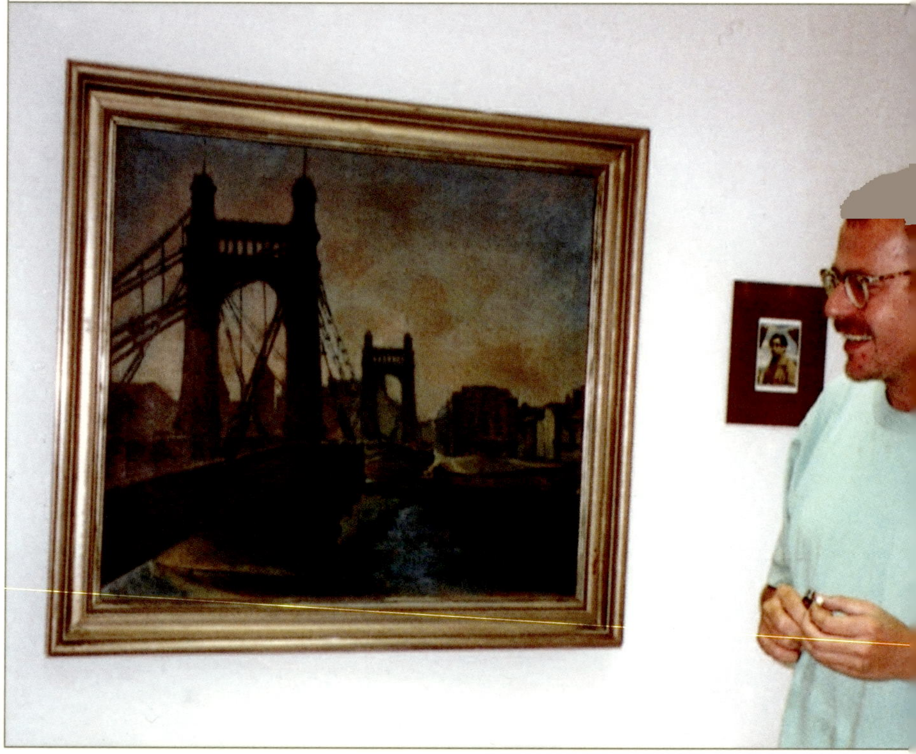

FIGURE 5

Vladimír Student in his office at the City Parks Department, Prague, July 2002, with Jan Zach's painting *Stefanik Bridge* (1936; oil on canvas; 33 1/2 x 39 3/8"; City of Prague Collection). Photograph by JoAnn Elizabeth Seibert, who located this and other works by Zach in Prague collections.

1936

Czechoslovakia (records show this painting was also transferred to the City of Prague). The acquisition of paintings by Prague museums confirms that Zach was recognized as a promising talent while still in his mid-twenties.

In the tradition of the Czech modernist interest in the merger of art, craft, design, and economic life that he had learned in his studies, Zach was not solely a painter. In 1937, he was awarded first prize for glass vase design at the Czech pavilion at the Paris International Exposition. As a commercial designer, he helped create the exhibits for a number of large expositions in Czechoslovakia: he worked on the Exposition of Gas, Water and Health Technology in Prague in 1937 and on the Municipal Exposition in Pilsen and the Exposition of Oriental Czechoslovakia in Košice, both in 1938.

The practice of staging big industrial fairs in Prague and elsewhere in the country began soon after the formation of Czechoslovakia, with Prague as its capital, in 1918. Nineteenth-century international expositions in London, Paris, major cities of the United States, and elsewhere had demonstrated the effectiveness of such fairs in celebrating progress, anticipating the future in positive terms, paying homage to past and present art, and promoting new concepts in architecture, display, and design. The exposition movement had a big impact on the development of modern architecture in Prague–the Trade-Fair Palace of 1924-1928, designed by Oldřich Tyl and Josef Fuchs, was the largest Functionalist style building of its time in Europe. During its two decades as an independent nation, Czechoslovakia presented exhibits in the world's fairs in Rio de Janeiro (1922-1923), Paris (1925 and 1937), Chicago (1933-1934), and Brussels (1935). The phenomenon of the twentieth-century international fair provided Czechoslovakia with cultural connections and exposure, and the nation's pavilion at the New York World's Fair of 1939-1940 became a widely recognized symbol of Czech resistance to Germany's occupation of Czechoslovakia.

Experienced in the design of trade fairs, Zach was one of three young artists selected to paint murals at the Czech pavilion at the New York World's Fair. In what turned out to be the last days of Czech autonomy, Zach sailed for New York in December 1938, never to return. The Prague chapter of his life and career was at an end but remained of crucial importance to the directions his life and work would take in the New World. He later wrote: "Czech Gothic Art and Prague Baroque in the country of my birth were the initial influences which guided my growth. I was also strongly impressed by the [Russian] Constructivist philosophy of Naum Gabo and the [Dutch] Group *de Stijl*. But the light concepts of the Czech sculptor/architect Zdeněk Pešánek acted as a catalyst to my way of thinking, especially his electric clavier and the electric piano/fountain made for the 1937 Universal Exposition in Paris."[15]

Clearly, Prague's schools and academies, famous artists and art teachers, historical and contemporary collections, concern for art's place in life and culture, heady response to modern art Europe-wide, and pride and respect for historical arts and crafts were of enormous inspiration to Jan Zach, who responded to these influences in rich and complex ways in the years to come. The young artist from Slaný would always remember Prague as an enchanted place. "The city itself was like a museum," he said. "When I was going down to school, it was like walking through a museum. I believe that I learned my basic knowledge of design, composition, planning, and integration of design from Prague itself."[16] Before his departure from Prague he would have seen the now legendary exhibition "The Prague Baroque" at the Wallenstein Palace and gardens in 1938 (ironically, it was in celebration of Czechoslovakia's twentieth anniversary as a nation).

SOJOURN IN NEW YORK 1938

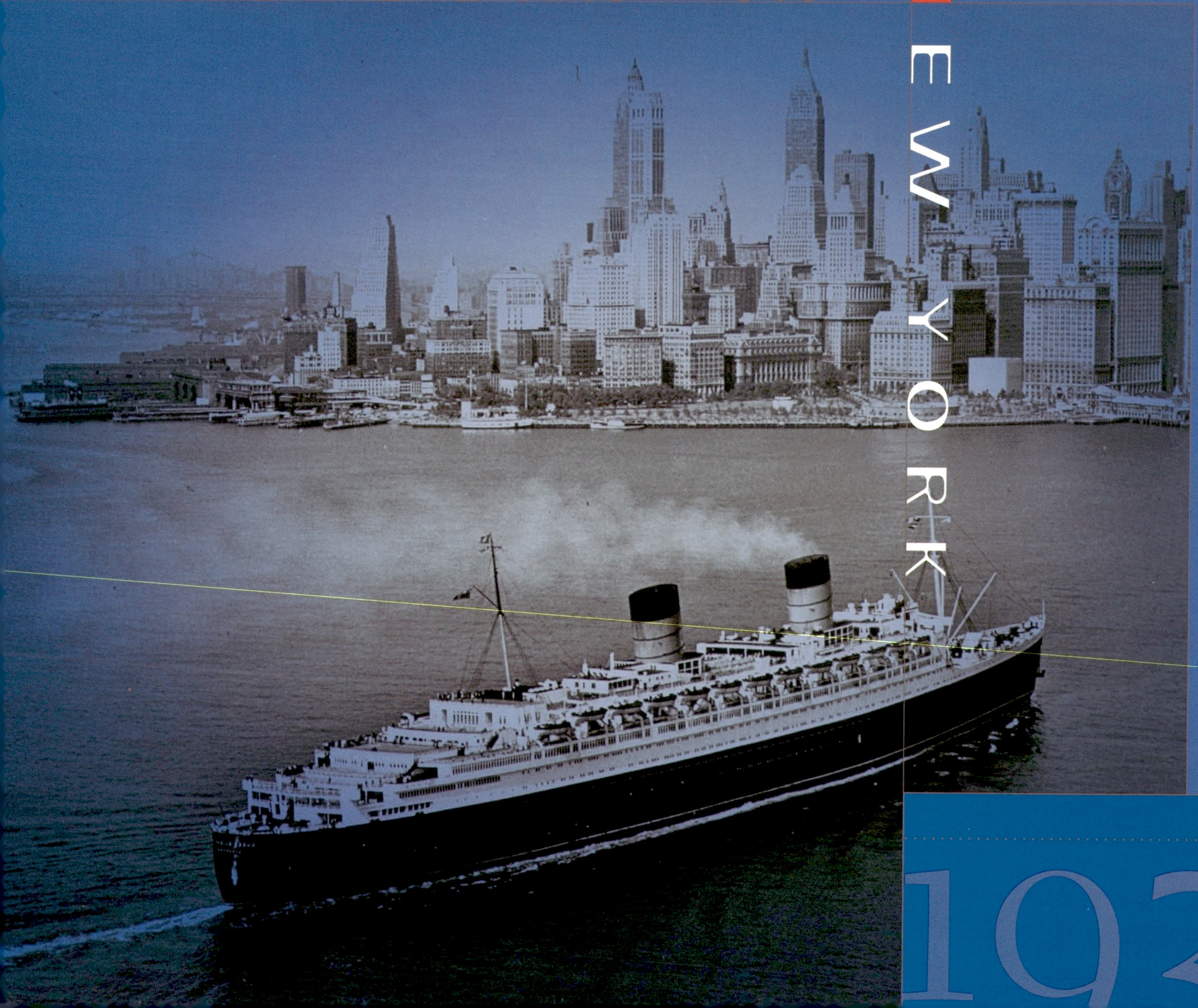

The First Republic was nearing its end as Jan Zach planned his trip to New York. On September 29, 1938, Hitler, Chamberlain, Mussolini, and the French premier Édouard Daladier met in Munich (Eduard Beneš, president of Czechoslovakia, was not invited) and signed the Munich Pact, which dictated that Czechoslovakia cede its border areas (the Sudetenland), largely occupied by Germans and German-speaking Czechs, to Germany in exchange for peace between Germany and Czechoslovakia. On October 1, Germany occupied the Sudetenland. On December 2, 1938, Jan Zach was issued a document by the chancellor's office of the Academy of Fine Arts confirming that he was the student of Nejedlý and that "in the interest of art, is obliged to depart on a foreign study trip to the United States." The chancellor's office recommended that "within the framework of the regulations, his wishes and needs be obliged."[17] Zach was allowed to depart and arrived in New York at the end of December.

Two of his sisters lived in or near New York City. One of them, Marie Zachová (1901-1952), had sent their mother Rosalie a ticket and papers to travel to the United States because of the unstable political situation. According to Judith Zach, Jan's widow, the family felt no real pressure for the mother to leave, and the papers lay on the hall table for weeks.[18] The aging Rosalie did not want to uproot and, fearing that Jan would be conscripted into the military[19] if he remained, gave him the papers and ticket when he was selected to go to New York on his "foreign study trip." Apparently because he had the travel documents in hand, he was the only one of the three designated artists actually to travel to New York. Within a few months, events in Europe made Zach an exile from Czechoslovakia. On March 15, 1939, after threatening to bomb Prague, Germany invaded Czechoslovakia and occupied the entire country, ignoring the terms of the Munich Pact.

For about a year, Zach lived with his other sister, Jaroslava ("Slávka"), her husband Frank Toensmann, and their young daughters Ruth and Frances in a two-bedroom apartment on Forty-ninth Street in Union City, New Jersey.[20] Jaroslava Zachová (1900-1977) had immigrated to New York in about 1918 to work as the live-in cook for Artur Bodanzky, the Viennese orchestra conductor of German scores at the Metropolitan Opera. In 1920, she married Frank Toensmann, an American born to German immigrants. Frank was an upholsterer and decorator. Ruth, who was ten years old when her uncle Jan came to live with the family, remembers that he was given the front room as his studio and bedroom. The dining room in the center of the apartment, with the table, a couple of easy chairs, and a radio, became the living area. Conditions were crowded but comfortable enough, according to Ruth. At first, the status of the Czechoslovak pavilion was uncertain, but by the early spring of 1939 Zach commuted almost daily to Flushing Meadow in Queens, the site of the World's Fair, working long hours helping to prepare for the opening of the pavilion, which the Nazi regime refused to support.

The pamphlet *The Czechoslovak Pavilion* published on the occasion of the World's Fair describes the reduced scope of the pavilion in the wake of the Munich Pact and the Nazi invasion and suggests the urgency surrounding the preparation of an "unfinished yet completed Pavilion." "Only six weeks before the opening of the World's Fair, the occupation of Czechoslovakia . . . cut off the possibility of shipping a large proportion of the exhibits out of the country. Full credit must be given to those intrepid Czechoslovaks who have since worked in exile, not yielding to an order from abroad to liquidate their activities."[21] A committee organized by Mayor Fiorello H. LaGuardia helped raise funds, and the Czechoslovak Government-in-Exile, headed by President Beneš, the Friends of Czechsolvakia, and Americans of Czech descent completed the pavilion in modified form.

Located between the pavilions for the U.S.S.R. and Japan in the section of the fair reserved for foreign exhibits (to the northwest of Rainbow Avenue and surrounding the Lagoon of Nations and the Court of Peace), the Czech Pavilion contained three exhibition areas on two levels. The Entrance Hall was decorated with murals, including Kamil Roškot's glass mosaic of old Prague, and the Czech-American sculptor Mario Korbel's reclining female figure entitled *Sleeping Republic*. An inscription on the wall above the sculpture stated that "it had been originally planned that this pavilion was . . . to prove what may be achieved within two decades if industry, labor, art and creative patriotism work in harmony. By an unfriendly stroke of fate the young republic became the victim of a ruthless invasion which strangled

[OPPOSITE PAGE]

New York City, 1938.
Photograph Archive
Holdings, Inc./Getty Images

the liberty of her people." The Main Hall contained an exhibit designed by Antonín Strnadel and Joseph Novak of the School of Applied Arts (referred to in the pamphlet as the School of Industrial Art) of Prague, Zach's former school. The exhibit was of Czech industrial machinery (including a Kaplan turbine and a coil spring that "whirls down from the ceiling in a length of over 200 feet"), optical instruments, tiles, textiles (accompanied by a print by Kysela depicting the Czech linen industry), and Bohemian glass. The centerpiece of the glass exhibit was a cut crystal cup, three feet high, with the Statue of Liberty and New York skyline on one side, a view of Prague on the other.

Zach's documented contribution to the pavilion related to the glass exhibit. On the balcony wall of the Main Hall, he painted a mural designed by another artist about the origins of the glass and ceramic industries. "The original of the mural was designed by A. Wiesner in Czechoslovakia, and was painted upon the wall by Jan Zach in his own individual color conception," according to the pavilion brochure. Zach's niece Ruth Gilombardo recalls that the mural depicted workers as "large people with large legs and arms." Zach's other responsibilities in decorating the pavilion are unknown, but certainly his experience in exhibit design was put to use as pavilion organizers worked against the clock to get the displays ready for the opening of the World's Fair on April 30, 1939. Zach worked late the night before finishing up details at the pavilion and slept for a few hours on the floor. He had just made himself presentable for the opening when Eleanore Roosevelt arrived and, he recalled, shook his hand.[22] According to David Gelernter, "on opening day the still-unfinished pavilion was thronged. (The Nazi press made the best of the situation by pointing to the incomplete building as evidence of democracy's intrinsic incompetence.) Edvard [Eduard] Beneš, the dead country's last president, came to the pavilion to announce that 'Czechoslovakia is still alive. It will continue to live. And here is the evidence of that fact.'"[23]

New York in 1940-1941 was emerging as the world center of avant-garde artistic activity, with artists so diverse as Piet Mondrian, Max Ernst, Yves Tanguy, and André Breton fleeing Europe for New York under circumstances quite parallel to those of Jan Zach.

The New York World's Fair bracketed the brief period between the end of the Depression and the outbreak of World War II. Zach was not alone among internationals who came to work on the fair and could not go home; the Poland pavilion's staff had no homeland to return to and opened a restaurant in New York.[24] Zach struggled to learn English and painted in his improvised studio at the Toensmanns' apartment in New Jersey. Cut off from his homeland but sustained by his two sisters, he was forced to make a new life for himself. Frank Toensmann, who commuted by ferry to New York to work each day, noted that Jan kept the schedule of an artist–painting late into the night, sleeping late into the morning. He painted portraits (including one of his niece Ruth; whereabouts unknown), still life (a study survives of a vase of red tulips and a lemon; Figure 6), and views of New York from the New Jersey side and of Central Park, including a scene with the towers of the Waldorf Astoria in the background.[25]

After living with the Toensmanns for approximately a year, Zach moved to New York City. His sister Marie apparently helped him locate an apartment and may have helped support him. The Czech community provided Jan Zach with studio space (a meeting room on an upper floor of a building on the upper west side, around Seventy-fifth Street). Zach designed a doll of which Czech women in New York made replicas to sell to raise funds for the Czech pavilion.[26] He exhibited a group of sketches and prints at International House in New York in 1939. He apparently also taught courses in painting and ceramics at the YWCA and painted murals in New York and Connecticut depicting the lives of famous North Americans.[27] At age twenty-five, he was putting together a professional artist's life in the New World, but the steps he should take and the nature of his goals remained unclear.

New York in 1940-1941 was emerging as the world center of *avant-garde* artistic activity, with artists so diverse as Piet Mondrian, Max Ernst, Yves Tanguy, and André Breton fleeing Europe for New York under circumstances quite parallel to those of Jan Zach. The influx of European artists helped ignite the radical artistic creativity of a whole generation of young Americans epitomized by Jackson Pollock. But Zach left New York shortly before these developments, and it's not known if he visited the Julien Levy Gallery, for example, which in the 1930s already featured European Surrealist and American Magic Realist painting that at times resonated with Zach's work. He left New York in April 1940, just before many of the European artist exiles arrived (Tanguy, one of the earliest, came in 1939), and headed for Rio de Janeiro. Zach had been thinking about Rio since before he left Prague, and a chance visit to Radio City Music Hall rekindled his desire to go to Brazil.

In the Prague cinemas Zach had seen the 1933 film *Flying Down to Rio* starring Dolores del Rio, Ginger Rogers, and Fred Astaire. "It was fantastic film," Zach recalled, speaking the elliptical, accented English for which he was known. "Then, one day, I am in Music Hall in Rockefeller Center, and I see a fabulous travelogue on Brazil. I scream in Czech, 'I have to go there!' I go back to my studio. I open my studio door. There was a telegram. I open the telegram. There was, 'If you are interested for two weeks in Rio de Janeiro, phone us.'"[28] The telegram was from the Bat'a Shoe Company offering him the job of compiling and illustrating a report on the industrial development of Brazil and Bat'a's efforts in this industrialization. He seized the moment and headed off on a two-week freelance assignment. As it turned out, he remained in Brazil for eleven years. The international crossroads of Rio was to be his New York.

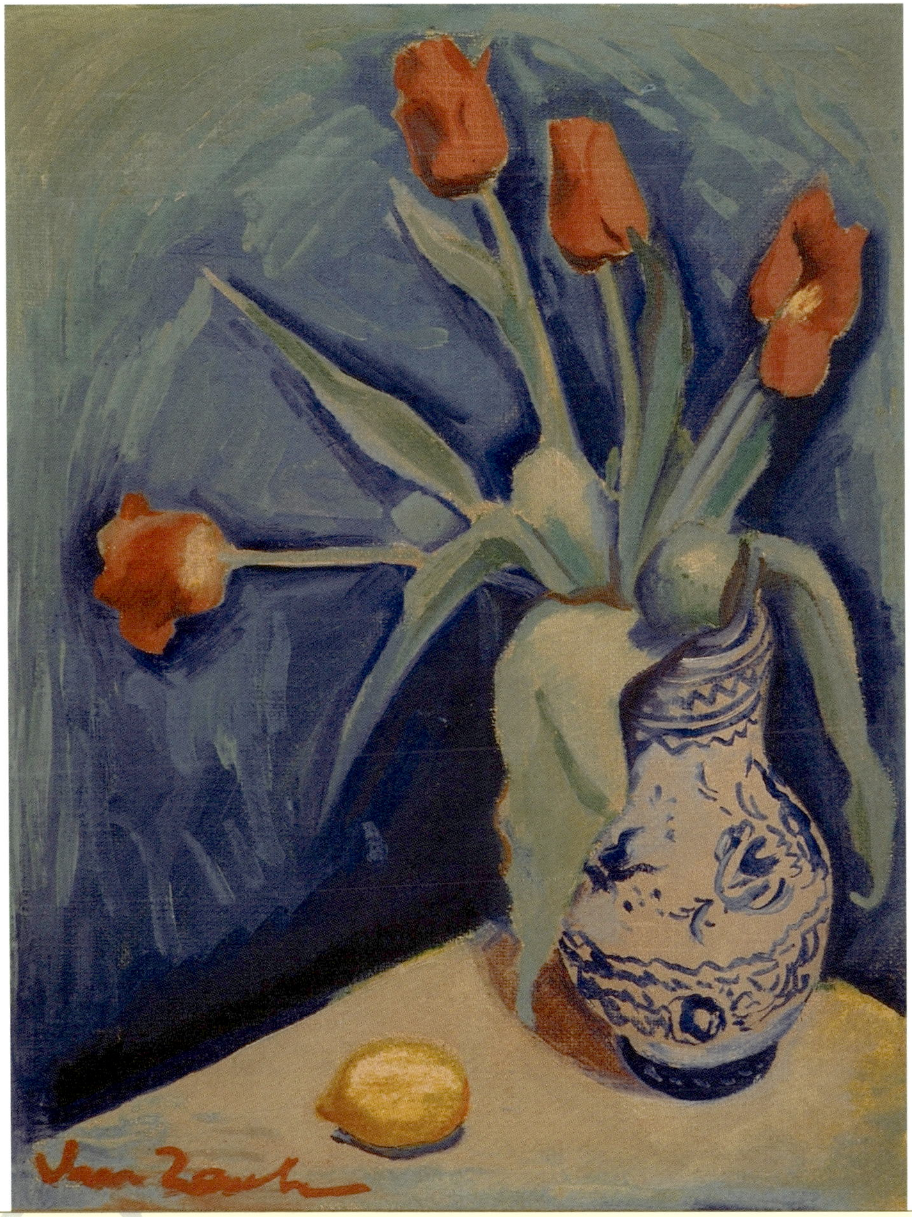

FIGURE 6

Jan Zach. Untitled Still Life with Vase of Tulips. 1939-40. Oil on canvas. 20 x 16".
Collection of Ruth Gilombardo, Belmont, California.
Photograph by Dale Peterson, 2002.

BRAZIL

THE RIO YEARS

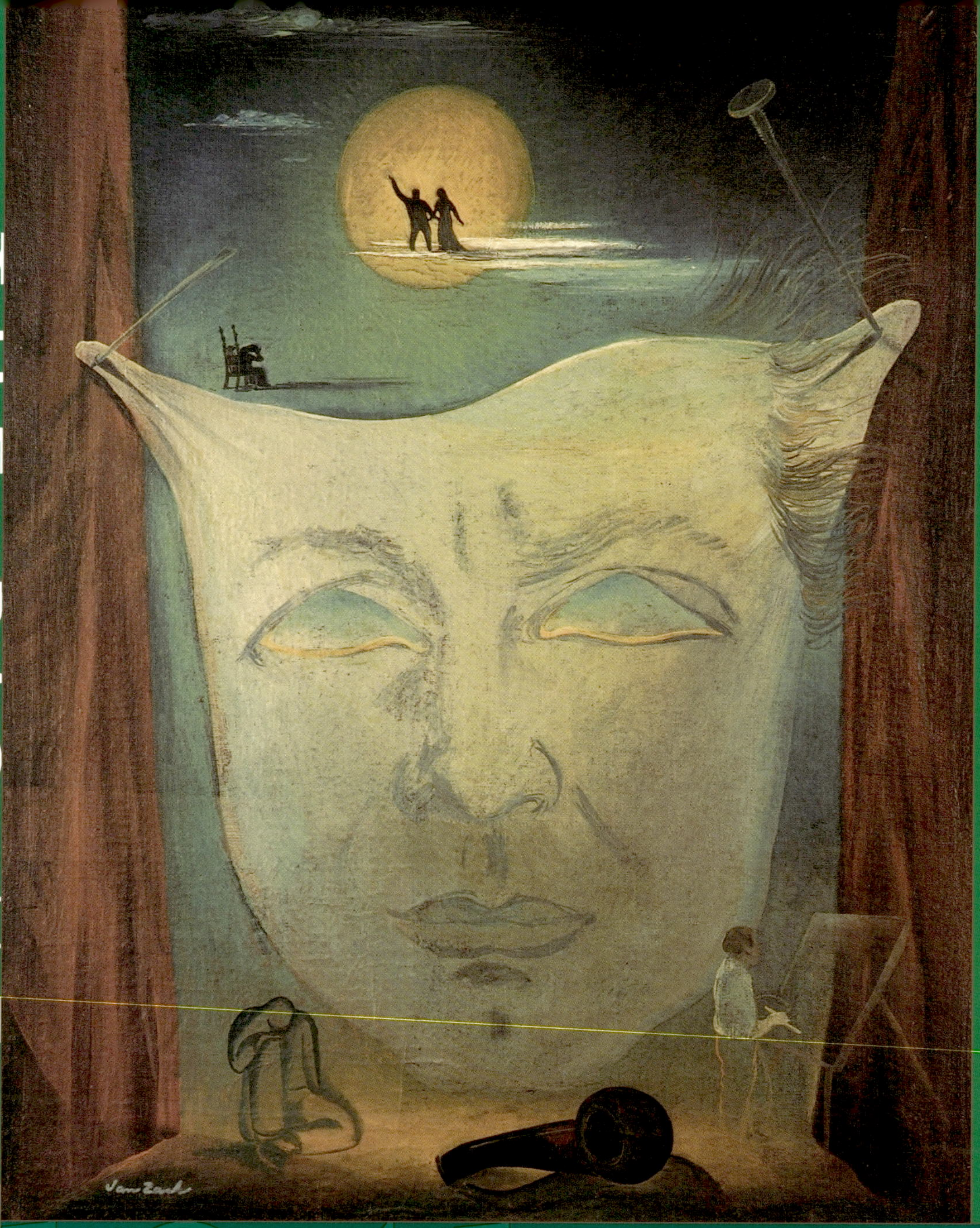

1941

In Rio, Zach completed the work for Bat'a, and the report was presented by the company to the president of Brazil, Getúlio Vargas. Whether by choice or legal necessity (his impetuous departure from New York without following official procedures cost his sister Marie the $500.00 bond she had posted when he entered the country, and he was not permitted to re-enter the United States from Brazil,[29])he decided to remain in Rio. There he met Francisco Fisher, the former Paraguayan consul in Prague who was living in exile a wealthy man. Fisher acted as a mentor for Zach,[30] arranging his first exhibition in Rio, which may have been the show at the Palace Hotel mentioned in a review in the newspaper *A Noite* on May 7, 1941. The exhibition included *Self-portrait (Remembering Europe)* (Figure 7), showing the artist facing the viewer in the lower left with a sweep of Brazilian beach in the distance. On the sand is an oversized telephone receiver at the base of a temporary power pole. The communication system is makeshift, displaced, and ineffectual: Europe is seemingly as far by wire as it is by sea. Zach's image against the beach and the blue Brazilian sky speak of isolation, separation, and the futility of attempting communication with home. With its scale discrepancies and stage-like sweep of space and isolated objects rendered in the manner of Giorgio de Chirico's *Pittura Metafisica*, the painting is Surrealist in nature, one of numerous Surreal portraits of himself and others that he would paint during his Brazilian years (Figure 8, for example).

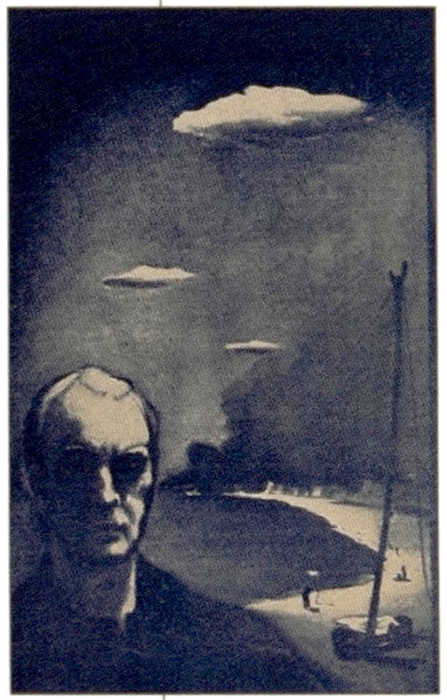

Through Fisher's influence and the resulting opportunities that Zach fully and engagingly exploited, his years in Brazil were astonishingly successful professionally. He worked as a commercial illustrator and also a painter and printmaker with exhibitions that were enthusiastically reviewed in the Brazilian press. The Brazil years were also a time of personal happiness as Zach emerged as a dashing young figure in Rio's cultural circles, made lasting friendships, and eventually met and married the beautiful Judith Ella Monk of Canada. It was while living in the Brazilian countryside in 1948 that he began to work seriously as a sculptor.

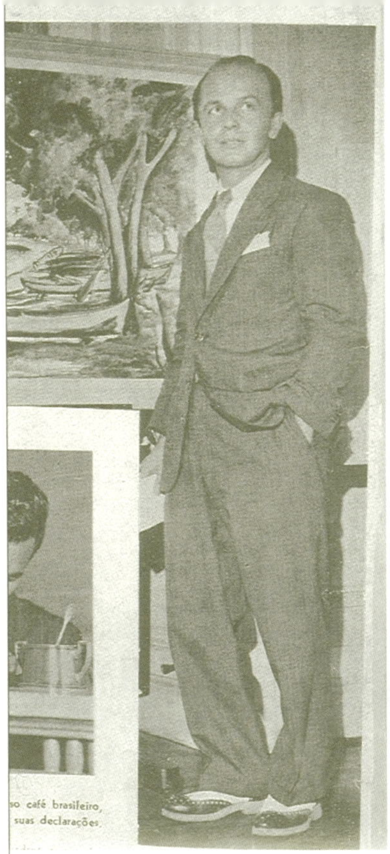

The dapper figure Zach cut in Rio is indicated as early as 1941. On the occasion of the Palace Hotel exhibition, his photograph appeared in the issue of *Revista da Semana* for May 31 (Figure 9) showing the 26-year-old Zach standing beside one of his paintings. He looks up and away from the painting with his wide set eyes, lips parted, his thinning dark hair combed back to emphasize a wide forehead. Dressed in a tropical weight suit, a red tie, and white and brown leather spectators, he stands with his hand in his pocket, a small, well- contoured man, gentlemanly and sexy. Rio and Zach, it appeared, were a good match.

Zach's first major exhibition in Brazil came in November 1943 at the National Museum of Fine Arts in Rio de Janeiro. Presented under the patronage of the Ministry of Education, the exhibition included sixty-six oils, watercolors, tempera paintings, and pastels. The exhibition catalogue illustrated five of them, reflecting Zach's wide range of subject matter in his paintings of that period: cityscapes, portraits, still life, figure studies, and expressionistic anti-war paintings in the spirit of contemporary work by the German Expressionist George Grosz. *A Ultima Paz* (location unknown), for example, was a haunting rendition of a field of cross-marked graves addressed by a giant tree-stump figure, propped on crutches, waving a white flag of surrender. Clearly, Zach believed that the "ultimate peace" would be a hollow one based on the death of millions.

Figure 7 [above]

Jan Zach. *Self-portrait (Remembering Europe)*. 1941. 39 x 23 5/8". Oil on canvas. National Gallery, Prague. Copy photograph of a newspaper illustration. Hallie Ford Museum of Art, Willamette University, Salem, Oregon. Judith and Jan Zach Archives.

Figure 8 [opposite page]

Jan Zach. *Self-portrait*. c. 1945. Oil on canvas. 23 1/4 x 19". Hallie Ford Museum of Art, Willamette University, Salem, Oregon. Judith and Jan Zach Collection. Photograph by Dale Peterson,2002.

Figure 9

Jan Zach at his exhibition at the Palace Hotel, Rio de Janiero. Photograph published in *Revista da Semana*, Rio de Janiero, 31 May 1941.

The surreal and expressionist tendencies of some of Zach's paintings during the early Brazil years are reflected in the jacket illustrations he made for books published by Casa Editôra Vecchi and two other publishers, Editôra Prometeu and Edições Mundo Latino. For Editôra Vecchi he produced more than thirty cover illustrations for novels, many of them by European or North American authors including Anatole France, André Gide, Émile Zola, Maxim Gorky, John Steinbeck, and Sinclair Lewis. His cover illustration for a collection of stories by Aldous Huxley (Figure 10) depicts a man and woman cropped to shoulder level in the foreground, empty space behind them. The composition and mood are similar to Zach's *Self-portrait (Remembering Europe)* of 1941. A coiled spring, evoking the one that "whirls . . . in a length of over 200 feet" that had been displayed at the Czech pavilion in New York, spirals around a secondary figure that casts a stark shadow toward the couple. *Pittura Metafisica*, Surrealism, and the resulting uneasy moods of hallucinations and dreams recur in Zach's book jacket illustrations as they do in many of his paintings in this period. The jacket illustrations were almost always signed "Jan Zach" in his distinctive signature script, bringing imagery identified as his before a far wider audience in Brazil than attended his exhibitions of fine art.

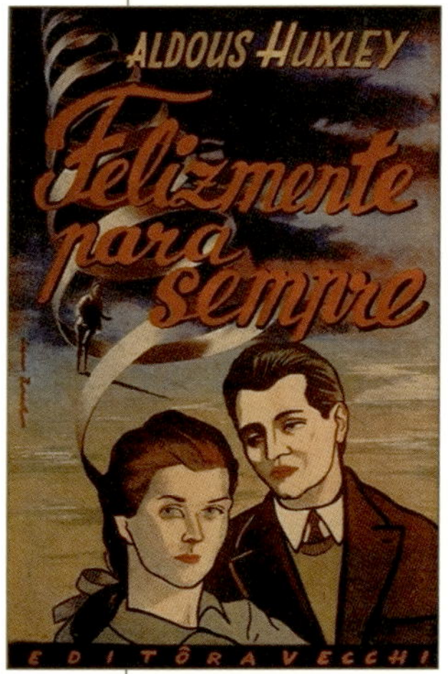

Another commercial art enterprise that exposed him to audiences beyond the gallery was his role as art director of the magazine *Cocktail*, published in Rio. He designed the covers, front and back, for this stylish, large-format magazine. The fronts and backs are generally entirely different from each other–one issue, for instance, illustrating on the front cover a garden of calla lilies and roses with a sidebar of books by Einstein, Freud, Bergson, and Newton floating out of a martini glass (Figure 11), while on the back is a drawing of a barbed wire barricade on the frontier. Zach signed the front and back illustrations and seemed to be making a point about the stark contrasts between the fashionable comforts of such a place as Rio and the battlefields of Europe.

Exhibiting frequently, illustrating widely, and working steadily in his studio (see Figure 12) in the Santa Therese district with a sweeping view of Guanabara Bay, Zach produced a large body of work: still life paintings (Figure 13, for example), landscapes, city views, and portraits. He was acquainted with a wide circle of musicians, writers, and artists, and one of his major Brazilian exhibitions, in Belo Horizonte in the state of Minas Gerais in December 1944, included portraits of the pianists Tomas Terán (Figure 14) and Arnold Estrêla, the conductor Arthur Bosmans, the sculptor Martin Barral, and the Hungarian painter Arpad Szenes. On the occasion of the exhibition, Zach was made honorary professor of fine arts at the Institute of Architecture and Fine Arts in Belo Horizonte. He was also involved with the world of theater and dance and in 1946 designed the sets and costumes for the ballet inspired by Sibelius's *Valse Triste*, presented by the Original Ballet Russe in a world premier in July at the Municipal Theater in São Paulo. Always concerned with Czech issues, he organized for the Free Czech Government an exhibition of photographs of Czech industry at the Brazilian Press Association in Rio in 1945, the year the Nazi occupation of Czechoslovakia was ended; in 1946, he organized an exhibition of the works of the seventeenth-century Czech artist Václav Hollar; and also in 1946 Zach organized traveling exhibitions of the work of contemporary Brazilian and Czechoslovak artists. In this busy period, he continued to find opportunities for one-person shows of his own work. In 1945 and again in 1948, he exhibited his work under the patronage of the Brazil-United States Institute and the Institute of Architects of Brazil. It was in this period, too, that he met his future wife and was married.

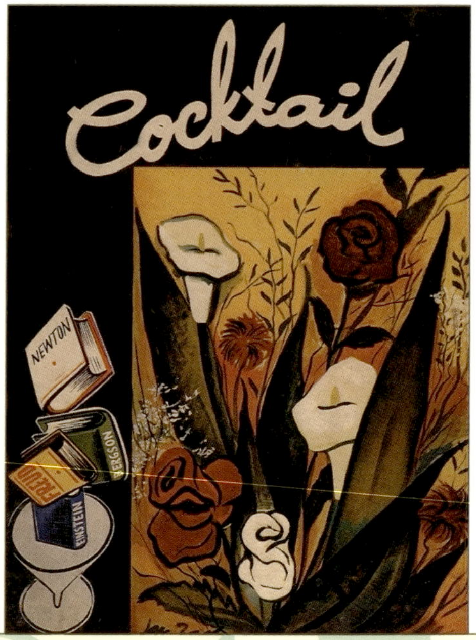

1944

FIGURE 10

Jan Zach. Jacket illustration for a book of short stories, including "Felizmente para sempre" ("Happily Ever After"), by Aldous Huxley, published by Editôria Vecchi, Rio de Janeiro. 1940s. Hallie Ford Museum of Art, Willamette University, Salem, Oregon. Judith and Jan Zach Archives.

1945

FIGURE 11

Jan Zach. Cover illustration for the magazine *Cocktail*, published in Rio de Janiero, 1940s. Hallie Ford Museum of Art, Willamette University, Salem, Oregon. Judith and Jan Zach Archives.

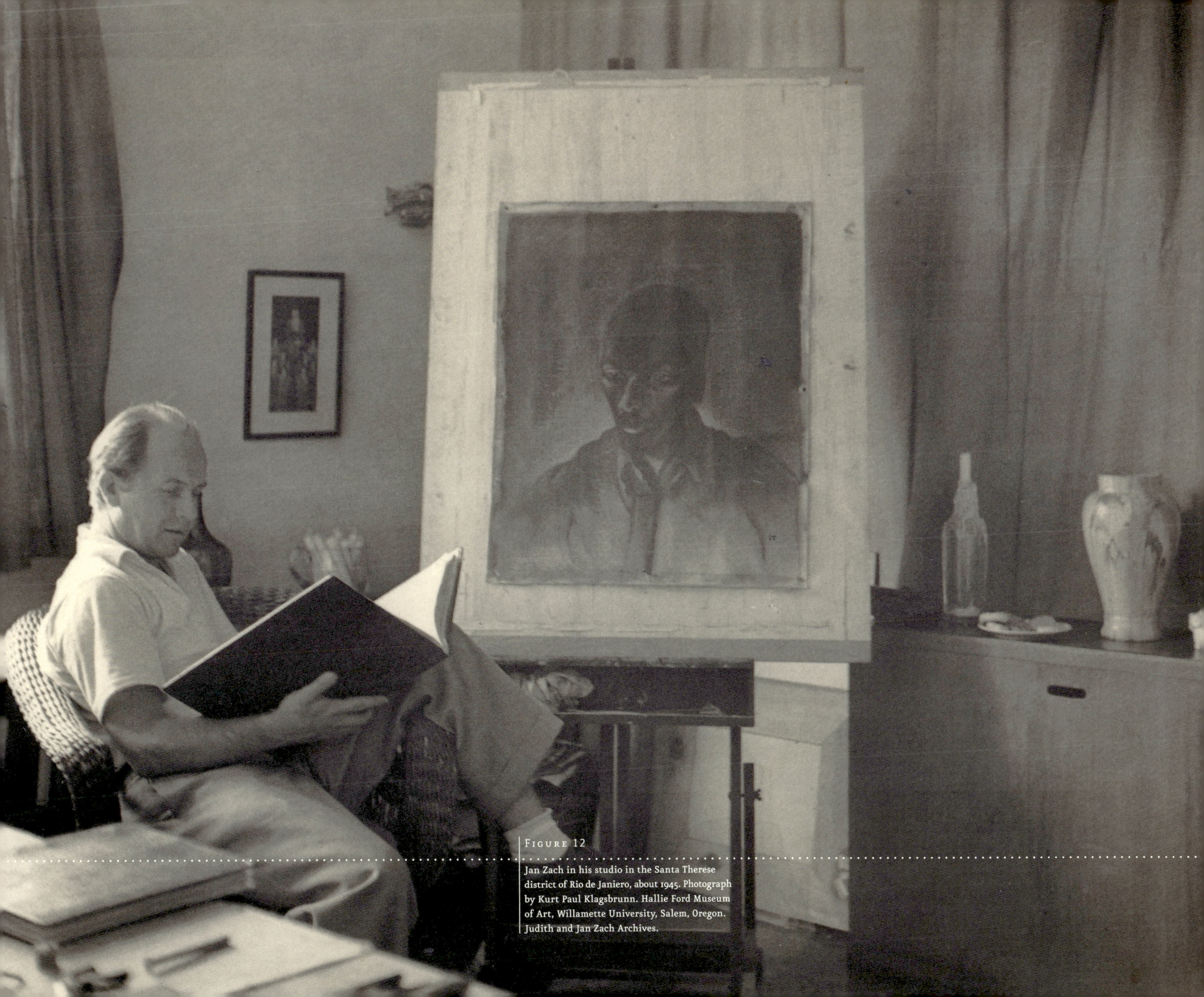

FIGURE 12

Jan Zach in his studio in the Santa Therese district of Rio de Janiero, about 1945. Photograph by Kurt Paul Klagsbrunn. Hallie Ford Museum of Art, Willamette University, Salem, Oregon. Judith and Jan Zach Archives.

Intrigued by Rio, probably for the same generally romantic reasons that had drawn Jan Zach in 1940, the Canadian Judith Monk arrived in August 1945 on board a freighter. She had been born in Victoria, the daughter of Theodore and Juliana Monk, and raised with her sister and two brothers in a house across the street from Beacon Hill Park. As a girl, Judith took riding lessons, and horses and animals generally remained of great interest to her all her life. She attended a Catholic high school, where her courses included four years of Latin, and then Victoria College, but the Depression interrupted her education after a year. She taught herself to type, learned stenography, and during World War II worked as a stenographer for the Combined (later Joint) Chiefs of Staff in Washington, D.C.

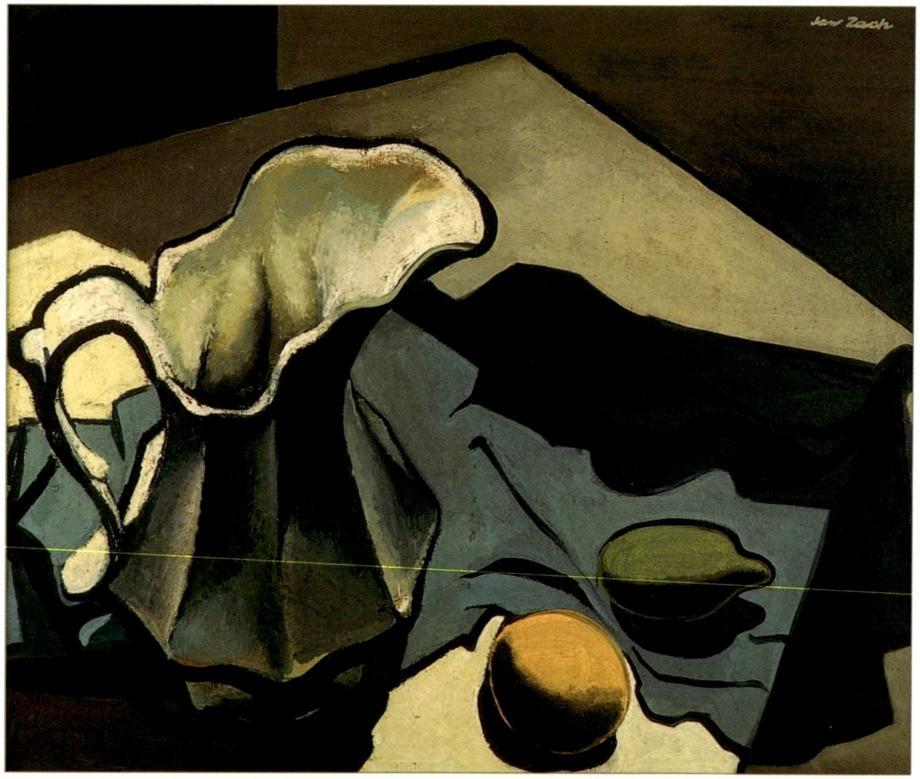

In Rio, she obtained a stenographic job with the United Nations Relief and Rehabilitation Administration, associated with the Marshall Plan (rubber, rope, and other Brazilian products were being shipped to Europe). She lived with Regina Arruda (with whom she had studied Portuguese in a Berlitz course) and in 1947 met Jan Zach at an exhibition of paintings by the Brazilian artist Candido Portinari. Years later, Judith recalled that to reach Jan's studio they climbed 122 steps. He spoke little English so at first they communicated in Portuguese (and continued to do so, alternating with English, throughout their lives together). Judith Ella Monk of Canada, age thirty-two, and Jan Zach of Czechoslovakia, age thirty-three, both of the Roman Catholic faith, were married on November 12, 1947, in the church of the Abbey of Saint Benedict in Santa Rita Parish.

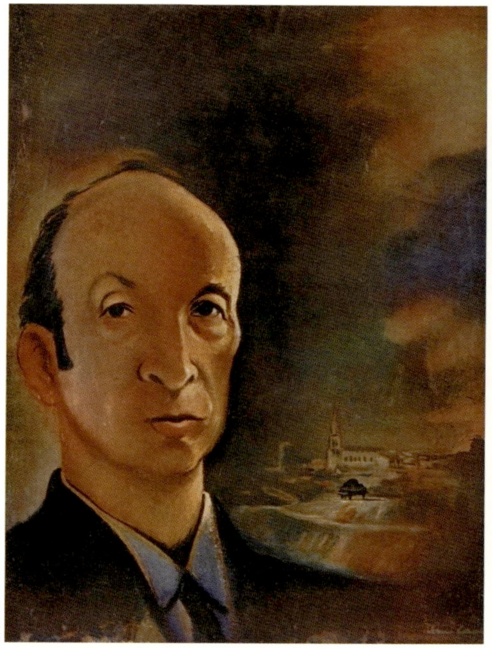

Rio in the 1940s was an international cultural crossroads, and Judith and Jan Zach were part of a lively group of artists, writers, musicians, business people, and embassy personnel. A 1947 photograph (Figure 15) shows artists, journalists, and others gathered at the residence of the Americans Polly and John McDonnell on the occasion of Polly's home exhibition of her paintings. McDonnell was director of General Electric, and the house stood on the GE grounds in Rio. Jan and Judith (not yet married), the McDonnells, and their friends are posed on the leafy patio dappled with sunlight. They make an engaging group–youthful (most of them are in their thirties), confident, stylish, relaxed and healthy, involved in the arts, successfully embarked on life in an exotic city. More than fifty years later, Judith Zach could identify nearly everyone in this photograph of internationals who had made Rio their home.

FIGURE 13

Jan Zach. Untitled Still Life with Pitcher. 1946. Oil on canvas. 19 1/2 x 23 1/4". Hallie Ford Museum of Art, Willamette University, Salem, Oregon. Judith and Jan Zach Collection. Photograph by Dale Peterson, 2002.

1946

FIGURE 14

Jan Zach. *Portrait of Tomas Terán*. c. 1944. Oil on canvas. Location unknown. Copy photograph of a color reproduction. Hallie Ford Museum of Art, Willamette University, Salem, Oregon. Judith and Jan Zach Archives.

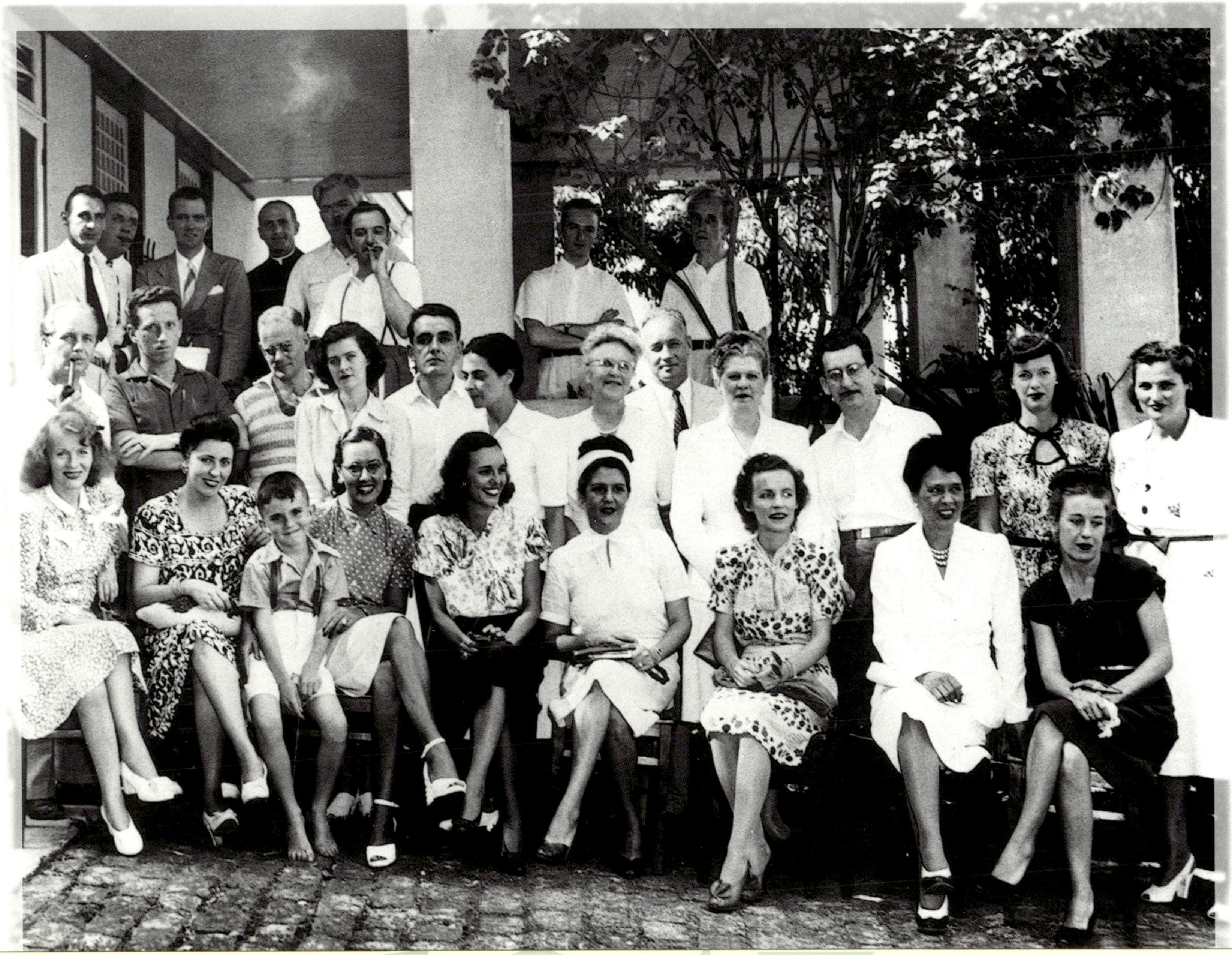

1947

Figure 15

Guests at Polly McDonnell's painting exhibition at the McDonnell home on the grounds of the General electric plant in Rio de Janiero, 1947. Polly McDonnell is in the front row, fourth from left, with the McDonnells' son; John McDonnell, director of General Electric in Rio, stands in the back row, fifth from left. Guests include Jan Zach (middle row, far left, with pipe), Judith Monk (middle row, fourth from left), the art critic Marc Berkowitz (next to Zach), the painter Maria Therese Szenes (middle row, sixth from left), the cartoonist and painter Augusto Rodriguez (back row, sixth from left, in front of John McDonnell), and the Hungarian painter Arpod Szenes (back row, far right).

Hallie Ford Museum of Art, Willamette University, Salem, Oregon. Judith and Jan Zach Archives (identifications by Judith Zach, 19 July 2000, Elmira, Oregon).

The *Fazenda Penedo*, Resende, and Cataguases

In 1948, the Zachs moved inland to the foot of Itatiaia, a peak in the Mantiqueira mountain range, to live in a *fazenda*, or hacienda. The move from the city was inspired by a number of factors, including Jan's profound disagreement with many in Rio who were sympathetic to the *coup d'etat* by the Czechoslovak Communist Party in February 1948. Another reason was Judith's love of animals and horseback riding, and yet another was probably Jan's interest in seeking inspiration in Eden, as his teacher Otakar Nejedlý had done in Ceylon and India early in the century.

The Zachs lived at the *Fazenda Penedo* (Penedo being the name of the family that once owned it; during the Zachs' time there it was owned by the Swiss drug company Geigy). Here, Jan not only continued his painting but also focused more and more on sculpture, working with native materials such as terra cotta and wood, as well as concrete. He limited himself to these because of "a lack of other materials, a lack of technology (there was only one art foundry in Rio), and the difficulty in transporting heavy materials into the interior."[31] The sculptures Zach made at *Fazenda Panedo* were figural abstractions (compare Figure 19), some of them similar to the more figurative work of the English sculptor Henry Moore. At this point, his potential as a sculptor was greater than his accomplishment, but already such diverse influences as the plant forms and light-shadow effects of tropical Brazil, Czech kinetic modernism, ballet, and the flowing forms of Prague Baroque sculpture were intersecting in Zach's creative imagination. Zach recalled that "I was drawn into close contact with verdant, tropical nature. I became very conscious of the tremendous impact of sunlight and of shadows. I observed that the shadows projected by a group of trees created a fourth-dimensional visual experience. This experience came to dominate my outlook as a sculptor."[32] A photograph of banana plants (Figure 16), presented to Zach in 1951, suggests the drama of tropical plants seen in brilliant sunlight and the impact they had on Zach's mature sculpture, such as his fifty-foot high stainless steel construction, *Can-Can* (Figures 57-59), erected in Eugene, Oregon, in 1968-1969.

Living in exotic countryside, with inspiring, fantastic vegetation, away from the city, paralleled the experience of the European artist exiles who gravitated to New York in the War years but found true inspiration in rural Connecticut. The French Surrealist André Masson was inspired by the luxuriant natural growth of New England to produce his vigorous new paintings such as *Meditation on an Oak Leaf* (1942; Museum of Modern Art, New York), while the Armenian Arshile Gorky, who like Zach came to the New World to stay with a sister and remained permanently, was influenced by the lush growth around Sherman, Connecticut. A fact that seemed to link Zach to other European moderns displaced in the Americas was an increased interest in nature as a central element in creativity. Zach's lush painting of

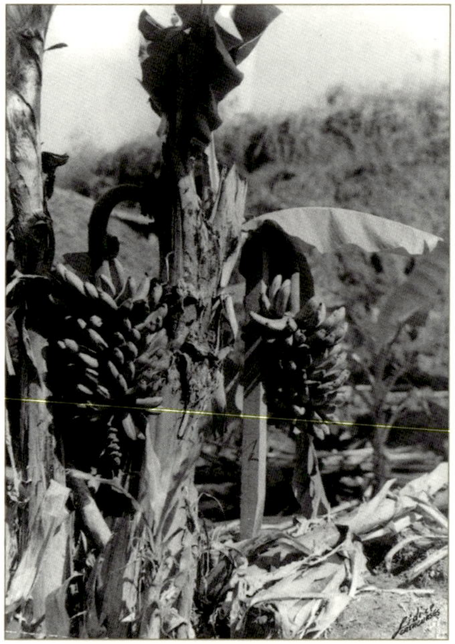

FIGURE 16

Banana plants, sunlight, and shadows. Photograph by Lidice. Cataguases, Brazil, inscribed to Jan Zach, 1951. Hallie Ford Museum of Art, Willamette University, Salem, Oregon. Judith and Jan Zach Archives.

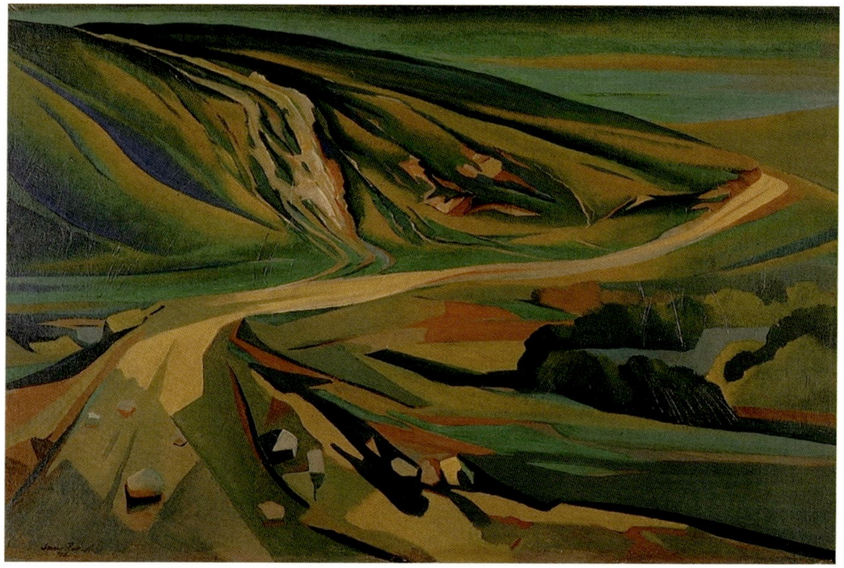

FIGURE 17

Jan Zach. *Fazenda Penedo, Brazil.* 1948. Oil on canvas. 27 3/4 x 42 1/4". Hallie Ford Museum of Art, Willamette University, Salem, Oregon. Judith and Jan Zach Collection. Photograph by Dale Peterson, 2002.

1948

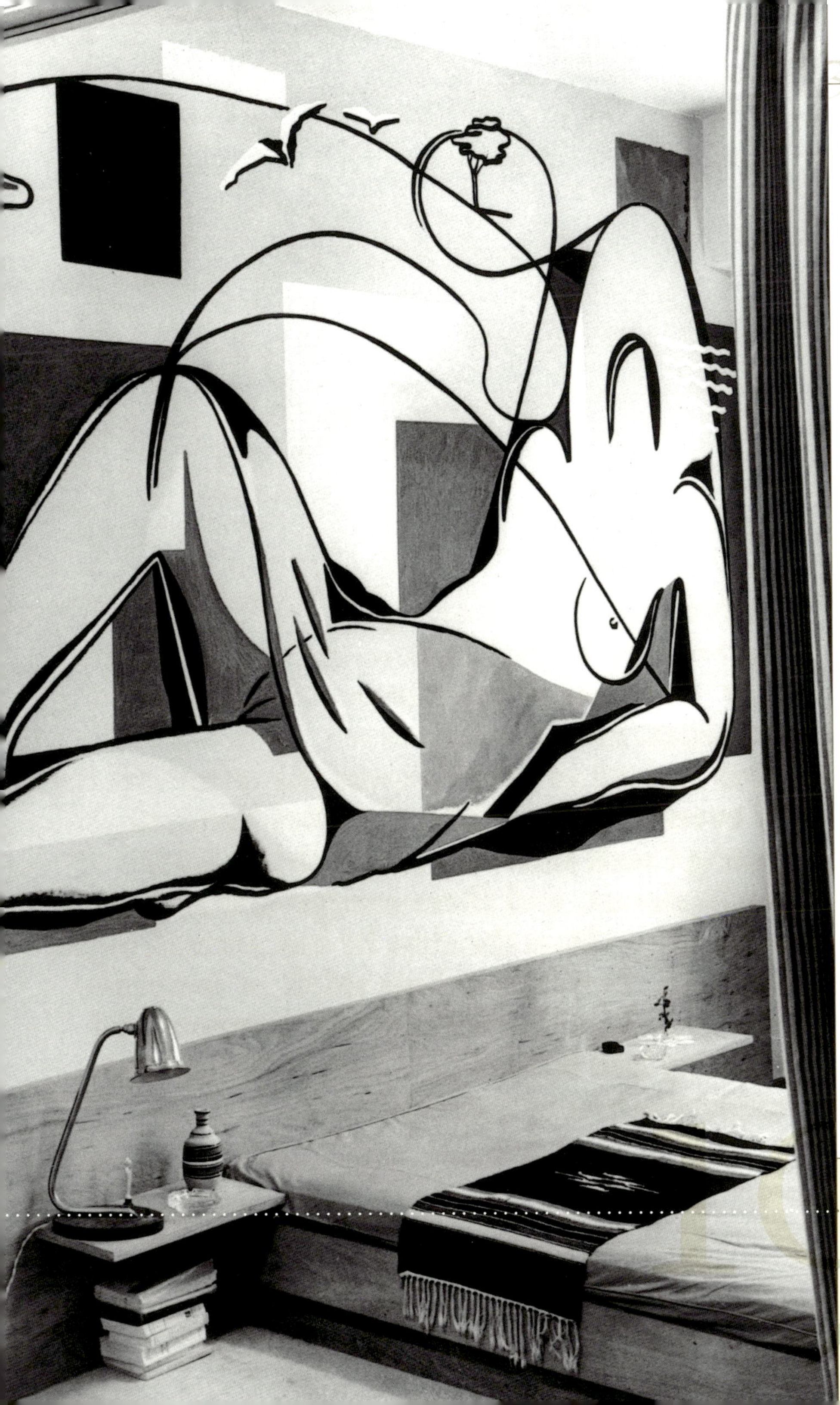

the countryside around the *fazenda* (Figure 17), saturated with red, yellow, green, and blue, indicates the extent of his intoxication with the luxuriant natural beauty of Brazil.

Life at *Fazenda Penedo*, though lasting only a couple of years, was paradise for Judith and Jan Zach. While Jan for the first time in years had time to contemplate his next steps as an artist, Judith savored the open spaces of the countryside and resumed horseback riding, a sport she had enjoyed since her girlhood days in Victoria. The nearest town to the *fazenda* was Resende, a small place with a large military school. Judith owned a retired racehorse called Fellow that she sometimes rode into Resende on errands. All in all, "the Zachs live a rustic and delightful life amidst the beauty of their fazenda," Walter Harris wrote.[33] He reported that they lived "in the midst of a Finnish colony, founded thirty years ago, near Resende. The Finnish influence in the life of the Zachs is portrayed in a very unusual woven rug, whose pattern was taken from one of Jan Zach's paintings and reproduced through the medium of the loom, by a Finnish lady." Zach's paintings, Harris noted, embodied "a modern European style carried out in the beauty of a Brazilian rustic environment." From the Finnish community, Judith purchased a puppy as a birthday gift for Jan. They named the dog Šeryk, the Czech word for "close companion" (see Figure 21).

But "even in paradise," Zach said later, "there was the snake."[34] In the late summer of 1948, Zach contracted osteomyelitis, a bone infection caused by an insect bite. The infection developed in the bone of his leg, which he nearly lost. Returning to Rio for several weeks, the Zachs stayed with their friend Alison Hardy, an officer at the Canadian Embassy, in her apartment on Avenida Copacabana. She helped Jan contact a bone specialist, who put his leg in a cast and deputized Judith as a nurse. She recalls that she had to give Jan four penicillin shots every eight hours. She practiced her injection technique on an orange. Zach recovered completely except for a slight deformation of the bone in his upper leg, but the experience was drastic and set the stage for re-thinking long-term life in Brazil.[35]

While Zach was laid up, his exhibition of paintings (reviewed by Walter Harris and numerous other critics) opened at the gallery of the Institute of Brazilian Architects in Rio (October 27-November 30,

FIGURE 18

Jan Zach. Mural and interior design for the residence of the writer Marques Rebelo, 1949-50, Rio de Janiero. Photograph by Kurt Paul Klagsbrunn. Hallie Ford Museum of Art, Willamette University, Salem, Oregon. Judith and Jan Zach Archives.

1948). He could not attend the opening, but Alexander Calder, who was in Rio for an exhibition of his own, opened the show. A photograph taken at the reception shows Calder and Judith Zach seated at a table surrounded by a group of Brazilian, American, Canadian, Czechoslovak, and German guests–the international cultural community that the Zachs were part of in Rio. Guests included the American painter Polly McDonnell, the German sculptor Hans Etz and his wife, the critic Marc Berkowitz, the conductor of the Brazilian Symphony, the Czechoslovak and Canadian ambassadors to Brazil, and various aides to the embassies, including the Zachs' friend Alison Hardy of the Canadian Embassy. The guest book contains the signatures of "A. Calder," all the others, and, a few pages down the list, "G. Vidal."[36] Apparently not present that day was the writer Marques Rebelo, a friend and mentor who was catalytic to Jan Zach's accomplishments during his last years in Brazil.

Marques Rebelo (1907-1973), born Edi Dias da Cruz in Rio de Janeiro, was a noted Brazilian journalist and novelist. The author of numerous publications in the course of a forty-year career, he is best known for his romantic depictions of life in Rio in the first half of the twentieth century. In the 1940s, Rebelo was establishing museums of modern art in each of the Brazilian states and began to exhibit, and sometimes sell, Zach's works in them. "Each month, Rebelo sent Jan a check for the works he sold."[37] Rebelo wrote the foreword to the portfolio *Álbum de Pintura: Jan Zach*, published by Editôra Vecchi in 1949. The unbound portfolio contained tipped-in photographs of a tapestry, a screen, and paintings, as well as original prints and an original watercolor. Thirty portfolios were prepared. Two of the photographed paintings, including *Stefanik Bridge*, had been painted in his student days in Prague. Most were Brazilian works, including portraits of European and Latin American musicians and artists.

Zach's association with Marques Rebelo continued in additional important ways: in 1949-1950, he decorated Rebelo's residence in Rio with murals, sculpture, and furniture (see Figure 18), and in the course of 1949 Rebelo supported and helped realize Zach's idea that a museum of modern art and art school be founded in Resende. Rebelo organized the inaugural exhibition of the Museum of Modern Art of Resende, a show in March 1950 of work by international artists including Alfred Kubin, Marie Laurencin, Victor Vasarely, Gino Severini, and others, as well as Jan Zach and the Zachs' American friend Polly McDonnell. Zach had a one-person exhibition of twenty-eight paintings and prints beginning April 29, 1950, at the new museum; included was a portrait of Judith sitting on a straight backed chair wearing an elegant dress and heels. Zach's pupils were featured in a show that opened on May 27.

According to the museum's later director, "The Museum of Modern Art of Resende was founded in 1950, by suggestion of Jan Zach and full support of Marques Rebelo and Macedo Mirando. The Museum of Modern Art of Resende was inaugurated in 1950 and closed in 1952, remaining so for 22 years. In 1974 it was reopened as a community museum, developing temporary exhibitions, courses, art movies, etc. Jan Zach was indeed very important for the Museum during its first stage, having contributed to the Museum's collection and with a course of painting in 1950. His work as a professor did not leave any influences here, but the foundation of the Museum was very important–and it still is–for the cultural life of the Region."[38]

In June 1950, the municipal prefecture of Resende presented Zach with the "key to the city" in honor of his role in establishing the museum. Presented some ten years after he first arrived in Brazil, it was the latest in a list of events and accolades that had honored the young Czech artist for his talents, ideas, enthusiasms, and sheer energetic momentum – his brio – from the time he had arrived in the country. Zach's vivacious spirit in combination with Brazil's own cultural diversity and vivacity had buoyed Jan Zach to remarkable accomplishment and celebrity.

1950

Marques Rebelo introduced Zach to Dr. Francisco Inacio Peixoto, a businessman (in cotton production), writer, and art patron, whose house was being designed by the Brazilian architect Oscar Niemeyer in Cataguases in southeastern Brazil. Niemeyer was also designing a hotel and a college in Cataguases, and Zach was commissioned for several projects in conjunction with Niemeyer's buildings. He and Judith lived in Cataguases for about six months in 1950-1951. Zach's cast concrete *Woman* of 1950 remains in the entry to Peixoto's residence, and another concrete *Woman* (1951) by Zach still overlooks a pool at the Hotel Cataguases, for which Zach also painted murals and designed the lighting and decor. He was also commissioned to create a sculptural monument (see Figure 19) in memory of the founder of the College of Cataguases (designed by Niemeyer). Niemeyer, who had been part of a team with Le Corbusier in building the Ministry of Education and Health in Rio beginning in 1937, was one of a number of Latin American architects who created radically modern, streamlined structures, often involving curved surfaces and colorful materials. The Cataguases projects for Niemeyer were the grand finale to Zach's artistic life in Brazil.

In 1979, Zach returned to Cataguases and visited Inacio Peixoto and his children and grandchildren; snapshots record their visit in the garden of the house designed by Niemeyer, with a carved wood sculpture by Zach in the background. Another Brazilian friend was Lauro Salazar (Regueira), a banker/financier who bought work by Jan and later visited the Zachs in Elmira, Oregon. The visits confirm the long-term friendships that the Zachs established in Brazil. But in 1951, despite all the successes and friendships and Judith's interest in remaining, the Zachs were preparing to leave. Jan's experience with osteomyelitis had heightened his awareness of the health concerns that faced them in Brazil, and he seemed to be looking ahead to new horizons. When the Cataguases commissions were completed, he had two offers: to be the director of the School of Fine Arts at the University of Cuyo in Mendoza, Argentina, or to teach at the Banff School of Fine Arts in Alberta, Canada. "The dictator Juan Peron was in power in Argentina, so in the spring of 1951, Jan chose Canada."[39] His marriage to Judith eased the way for his immigrating to Canada, and he may also have wished to relocate as a means of establishing Canadian citizenship. Since the Communist takeover of Czechoslovakia in 1948, he increasingly thought of himself as a man without a country.

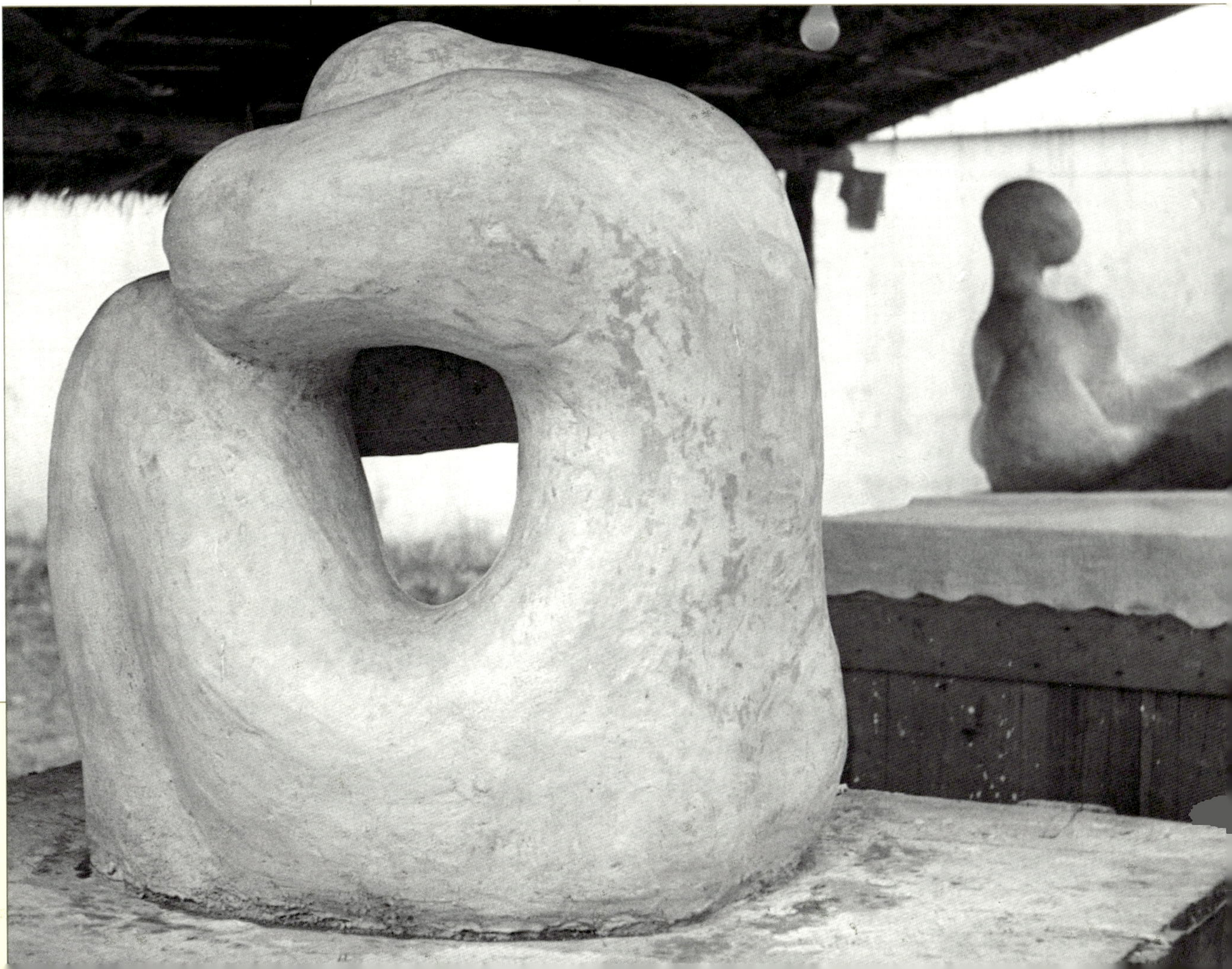

FIGURE 19

Scultpures by Jan Zach in his studio in Cataguases, Brazil, c. 1950. The figures were incorporated in the monument to the founder of the College of Cataguases, designed by Oscar Niemeyer. Photograph by Kurt Paul Klagsbrunn. Hallie Ford Museum of Art, Willamette University, Salem, Oregon. Judith and Jan Zach Archives.

SETTLING IN CANADA

1951

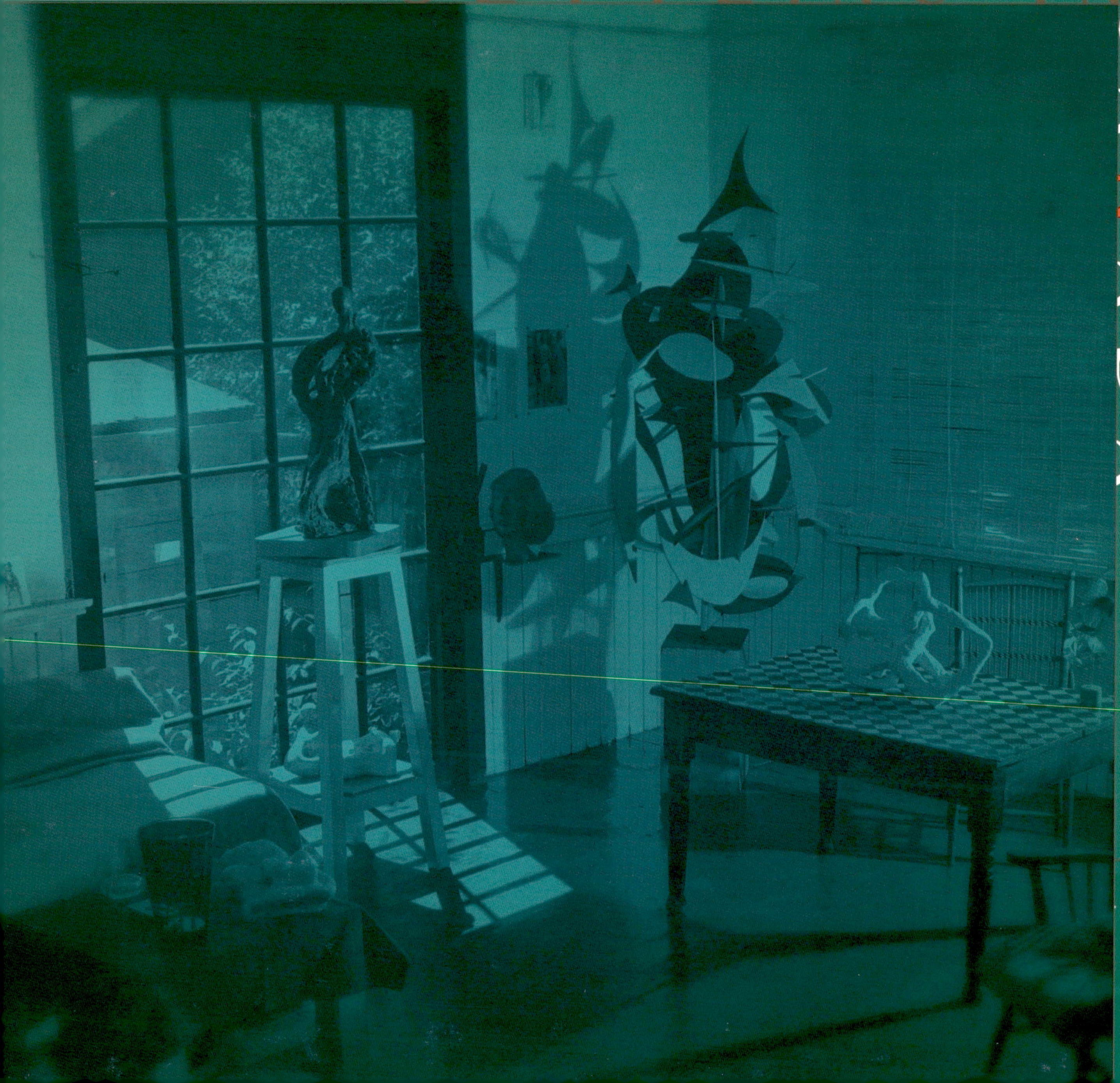

The Zachs, accompanied by Šeryk and a black cat named Chu-Chu, traveled by ship to Jamaica, and Jan flew from there to Toronto and from Toronto to Banff. He arrived in June 1951 and was so cold that he bought gloves. Judith completed the trip on the ship with Jan's artwork, mostly paintings. Jan had considered taking three terra cotta sculptural figures to Canada but decided against this. (Judith said later that they never completely moved from anywhere, always leaving something behind.) Her trip, by way of the Panama Canal, took thirty-eight days. The art was unloaded in Vancouver, B.C., and left in the warehouse overnight–on carts, luckily; during the night the floor of the warehouse flooded. The art was not damaged and was transported to Victoria to be stored at Judith's parents' house. Judith, perhaps somewhat reluctantly but willingly enough, was home again after nine years. Jan was about to meet his wife's family for the first time.[40]

During the summer of 1951, Zach taught design and painting at the Banff School of Fine Arts, a summer program established in 1933 by the University of Alberta at Banff. The 1951 session included courses in drawing, painting, design, composition, and art history (sculpture was not offered). Zach taught a section of design and composition and also a painting technique course for teachers and advanced students. The catalogue noted that "Mr. Zach's specialities are fresco secco, mural, mosaic, graphito, stain glass windows, decoration of glass (First Prize in Universal Exposition in Paris, 1937, for vase)." The profile emphasized him as a designer/decorator rather than a painter and emerging sculptor.

Like many Canadian and American art schools of the era, the Banff program featured outdoor teaching sessions, and a 1951 photograph shows Zach instructing a class overlooking a spectacular view of Canadian forests, lakes, rivers, and mountains. A more complete contrast to the terrain and vegetation of the Brazilian tropics cannot be imagined, but Zach appears robust and at ease in his new environment as he stands in bright sunlight, conferring with a girl in a plaid shirt who works on a painting on a portable easel. Teaching was to be central to Zach's life as an artist for the next quarter century and more.

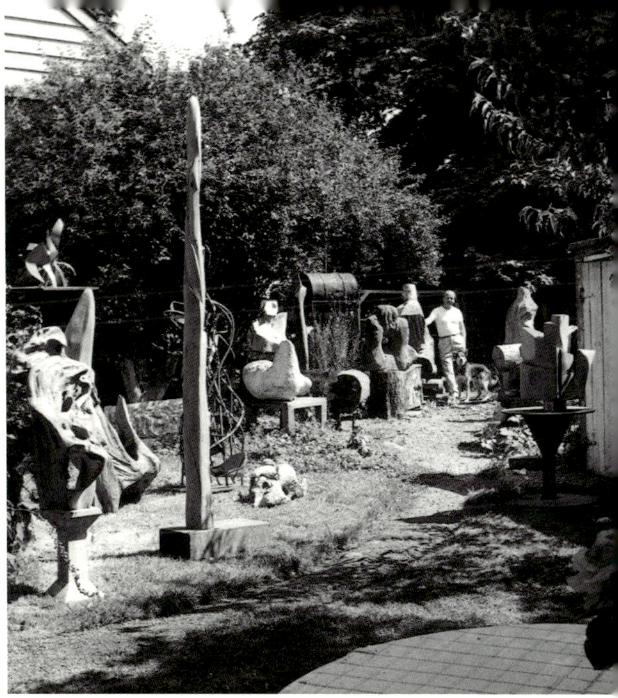

The Zachs spent the summer session in Banff but by the end of August 1951 were in Victoria "for an indefinite stay" with Judith's parents at 1557 Yale Street. The *Victoria Daily Times* for August 31 printed a photograph of the couple posed on the Monks' lawn. "Brazil is terribly interesting but has a very different way of life to ours in Canada–fundamentally different,"[41] Judith told the reporter. She and Jan appear fresh, vital, and eager to make the most of their new life in Canada, where just as in Brazil they were to be recognized as a dashing, vital couple. Anne Mayhew recalled that as a teenager in Victoria she was "stunned by Judith's turquoise-blue eyes and the stylishness of the broad shiny silver 'collar' she wore which was so gorgeous on her, and her sharp mind."[42]

Zach taught at Banff for one more summer, but essentially he and Judith were settling in Victoria and would live there for some seven years. Although Theodore Monk cleared space in the basement of the family house for Jan to work, the Zachs soon rented one-half of a wood frame house at 218 St. Andrews Street from Alice M. Carr, sister of the famed Canadian painter Emily Carr, who had used half of the dwelling as her home and studio for several years before her death in 1945[43] (her sister lived separately in the other half). The location in James Bay within walking distance of the Empress Hotel and the Parliament Buildings was convenient for Judith, who went to work at the Provincial Archives. The portion of the house they rented provided both a residence and a studio (Figure 20), and a long side yard served as a sculpture garden for Zach's work and work in progress (Figure 21). The Zachs lived at 218 St. Andrews Street until they left Victoria in 1958.

Figure 20 [opposite page]

Jan Zach's studio at 218 St. Andrews Street in Victoria, British Columbia. Scultpures include *Creation* (1954; concrete, cast in bronze 1979) on pedestal near window; *Totem* (1952; lumino-kinetic sculpture made of painted plywood) in corner; and model for *Wrestlers* (c. 1952; plaster) on table. Photograph by A. David Rogers. Hallie Ford Museum of Art, Willamette University, Salem, Oregon. Judith and Jan Zach Archives.

Figure 21

Jan Zach with Šeryk in the sculpture garden beside the house at 218 St. Andrews Street, Victoria. The sculptures reflect his interest is driftwood found on Victoria's beaches, totem forms, meshes of branches, wire, or rods, cast concrete biomorphic shapes, and stone carved in both expressionistic and cubist vocabularies – all elements central to his sculptural language emerging in the 1950s. Hallie Ford Museum of Art, Willamette University, Salem, Oregon. Judith and Jan Zach Archives.

Jan Zach and the Development of Modern Art in Victoria

Jan Zach arrived at an auspicious time in the history of the arts in Canada and was one of a handful of newcomers to the city in the early 1950s who essentially introduced modern art to Victoria. Arriving almost simultaneously in the fall of 1951 was Colin Graham, hired as the first and long-time director of the Victoria Art Gallery, which in 1955 became the Art Gallery of Greater Victoria. Graham and Zach immediately became collaborators in the project of challenging conservative assumptions about art and introducing and encouraging modernism.

The two men were near contemporaries and both were artists, but their backgrounds were radically different. Graham had been born in Vancouver, B.C., in 1915, the year following Zach's birth in Slaný. The son of a Vancouver doctor, Graham attended the private Shawnigan Lake School near Victoria in the 1920s, later earning a degree in history at Cambridge University and, in 1948, a master of arts degree at the University of California, Berkeley. He lectured in art history at the California College of Arts and Crafts in Oakland and was director of education at the California Palace of the Legion of Honor in San Francisco. He was also a painter. He had spent time with his parents in Victoria, so he knew the city and its art scene when he relocated from San Francisco to become the director of the Victoria Art Gallery, which was being established in a mansion at 1040 Moss Street donated by Miss Sara Spencer.

Speaking in 2002 with David Roberts, a researcher at the Hallie Ford Museum of Art, Colin Graham described "the cultural background into which poor Jan, quite unknowingly, came" when he arrived in Victoria. "There had been in Victoria since 1911 an art group called the Vancouver Island Arts and Crafts Society, which consisted of mostly well-to-do people from England familiar with the Royal Academy in London. They came out with what you could call Edwardian values, and they hadn't changed very much. Their annual exhibitions dealt with extremely conservative watercolors and so on." This conservatism had been challenged in the World War II period by Mark Kearley, an Englishman "stuck in Victoria during the war and surprised to find that Victoria didn't have a public art gallery or art museum." He and others formed a group in 1944 that established an art center in various short-term locations, predecessors of the Victoria Art Gallery that opened in 1951 under Graham's directorship. Kearley had been particularly interested in Emily Carr (1871-1945), who now is recognized as the major modern painter of her era in Western Canada. Kearley "lectured on her and began promoting her interests," according to Graham. "And also he began bringing in reproductions of Post-Impressionists, people like Van Gogh and Renoir. Mark Kearley told me he was walking one day with his two sons in Beacon Hill Park when, [from] behind a bush, came a mustachioed colonel who was president of the Vancouver Island Arts and Crafts Society. He had a riding crop with him and when he approached Mark Kearley, he said fiercely, 'You, sir, are the upstart Kearley, are you not? You with your Emily Carrs and your Picassos and your Renoirs. We have no need for your kind in this city.' I mention all this to give you a sense of the extremely conservative environment that Jan came into. Though I am quite sure that his wife, Judith, could have filled it in, quite a lot of it. Anyway, Jan came along, and we got to know each other immediately." Zach and Graham realized that they were both radicals in Victoria. "We worked quite closely and supported each other when we could."[44] As the columnist Tony Emery noted, "After [Emily Carr's] death the cause of art in Victoria was left to the care of a few devoted souls who saw to it that interest in painting and sculpture was not allowed to die. These few . . . were the people who gave us our art gallery. Their task was lightened by the arrival of an artist-scholar and an artist-teacher in

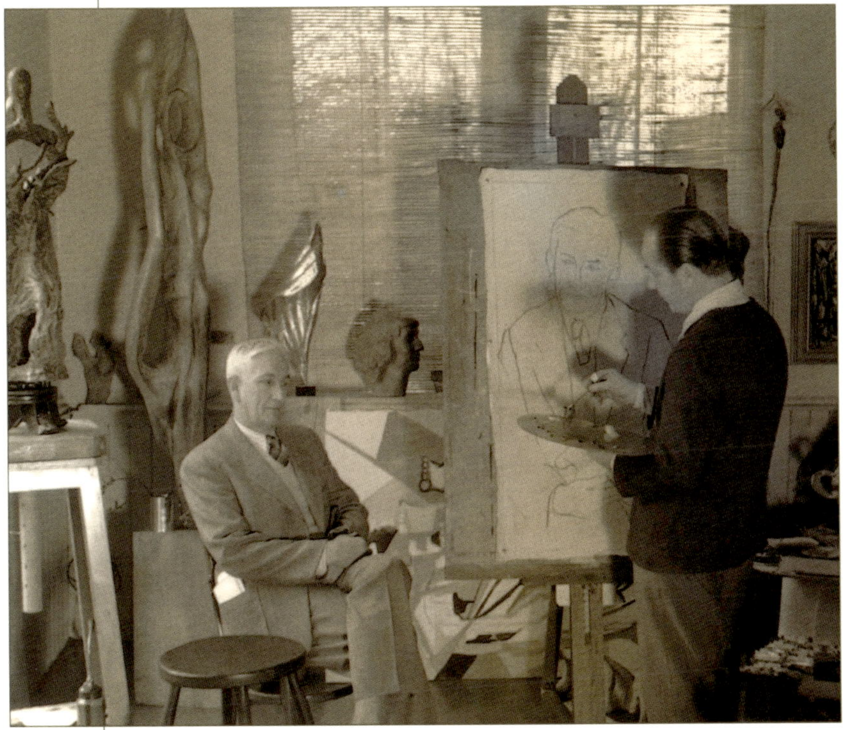

the persons of Colin Graham and Jan Zach."[45] One of the many portraits that Zach painted and sculpted in Victoria was of Graham, who posed in the Zach's studio on St. Andrews Street (see Figure 22) soon after they both arrived in Victoria.

Graham saw that his challenge as the director of the Victoria Art Gallery was to introduce twentieth-century modernism as regular fare in Victoria while not alienating the source of funds needed to operate the gallery, which was not city-owned and depended on private donations and membership fees. The Gallery's first exhibition, "Quebec Painters," opened on November 21, 1951. Audrey St. D. Johnson wrote in the *Victoria Daily Times* the next day, "It was a new experience! It was a stimulating and thrilling one for this reporter and for the dozens of people who moved through the spacious, well-lit rooms of the new premises on Tuesday."[46] Presumably the Zachs were in attendance, and in February 1952 the featured artist at the new gallery on Moss Street was Jan Zach, showing thirty-seven paintings and prints, mostly made in Brazil. Audrey Johnson praised the "deeply expressive union of exuberant color and form" in Zach's paintings and noted the "tropical luxuriousness in the rich greens and yellows which proves that, for all his preoccupation with formal values, Mr. Zach is intensely sensitive to the character of his environment."[47] Colin Graham said of the exhibition fifty years later, "It was filled with very powerful things."[48]

When Zach arrived in Victoria in August 1951, he announced that he was considering opening a "school of fine arts" in Victoria.[49] The enthusiasm of two local students who had studied with him in Banff encouraged him to think about the possibility, he said. Graham's recollection was that "Jan coming into Victoria quickly realized that he had to establish a teaching thing in order to make enough money to survive."[50] It was soon announced that "a school of fine arts, conducted by renowned painter and sculptor Jan Zach, is opening. . . in conjunction with the Greater Victoria Evening Classes under school board auspices."[51] The 1951-1952 syllabus for the evening classes listed two new art courses to be taught by Zach in the art room of the Victoria High School. By the time of his one-person exhibition at the Victoria Art Gallery in February 1952, he was teaching some forty students in night classes and private lessons.

Beginning with the 1952-1953 school year, his classes were taught "in Mr. Zach's new studio in preference to a school room, where work can be carried on in keeping with the most advanced system of artistic education," as the Victoria School Board's brochure explained. The owner of the real estate firm Pemberton Holmes, who was a collector and sympathetic to the artist, had rented the empty top floor of his building as a teaching studio for Zach. On his *curriculum vitae* in later years Zach described his evening classes beginning in 1951 as a "school of painting [opened] in cooperation with the Victoria School Board," and he is remembered in Victoria as, in effect, operating a school. "Zach taught all levels, amateur artists who were interested in learning and honing their skills, professional artists, and those who would go on to become professional artists. His students learned to see, to draw,

FIGURE 22

Colin Graham, director of the Art Gallery of Greater Victoria, posing for his portrait by Jan Zach. Graham and Zach, who both settled in Victoria in 1951, were pioneers in introducing modern art to Victoria audiences. Sculptures displayed in Zach's studio include (from left) *Creation* (1954; concrete), *Aphrodite* (1953; wood), and a hammered aluminum sculpture (1951; to the right of Graham's head. Photograph by A. David Rogers. Hallie Ford Museum of Art, Willamette University, Salem, Oregon. Judith and Jan Zach Archives.

1952

and all were encouraged in their own directions."[52] Zach's best known students in Victoria were the sculptors Robert deCastro and especially Elza Mayhew, who went on to earn her Master of Fine Arts under Zach at the University of Oregon. In 1964, Mayhew's sculpture represented Canada at the Venice Biennale.

Zach returned to Banff for the summer of 1952, his last year there. In 1953, he taught summer classes at the Victoria Art Gallery. By now it was clear that with Judith's family connections, the supportive presence of Colin Graham, the willingness of the school board to support his school of fine arts, and the opportunities to create and show new work, Victoria was the place to be despite its artistic conservatism. Further, the natural beauty of British Columbia was enormously inspiring to Zach. Moncrieff Williamson wrote that "in Brazil [Zach] was bedeviled by merciless light. In Alberta he felt cramped on the edge of great mountains; no doubt a species of claustrophobia illuminated only by lightning storms in the Rockies. Then to British Columbia. Here, at last, he found comfort and knowledge. Here, for the first time, he felt entirely at home in a land where the natural forces demand so much of the people. Rugged, unexplored, fertile country of tremendous intensity and where the natural formations, native carvings, fantastic driftwood and other natural phenomena demanded to be seen."[53] And as Colin Graham suggests, he may have been oblivious to the real handicaps facing avant-garde artists in Victoria in the 1950s. "He was so intensely involved in his own ideas, in his own dynamic, creative sort of feelings," Graham recalled, "he didn't have a great capacity to sense the surrounding [social and economic] environment. I remember sometimes Jan would phone me and say, 'Colin, I have a great project. Could you find me just $15,000.00?' Well, I would have to explain to him that the gallery's budget for the entire year was $11,000.00. You just didn't find that kind of money in Victoria."[54]

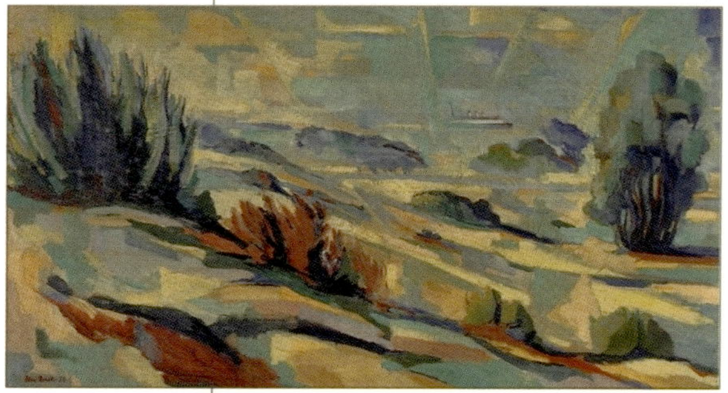

Nevertheless, with the same aggressive exuberance and optimism and the same personal charisma that he had brought to Prague, New York, and especially Brazil, Zach embraced Victoria and made opportunities for himself there. The school of fine arts was underway within little more than a month of his arrival in town. He quickly allied himself with the Victoria Art Gallery for the betterment of the Victoria art scene, including his own place within it. "The Gallery regarded Jan as a valuable ally in introducing modern art to a rather reluctant city, while he looked on the Gallery as a principal ally in his struggle to make a career in Victoria," Graham stated.[55] He recalled that a few months after the Art Gallery opened on Moss Street, the Czech pianist Rudolf Firkušný came to town. "Jan persuaded Firkušný to put on a concert to benefit the art gallery, which he did with extraordinary generosity in the Empress Hotel. About 400 or 500 people turned out and we made a lot of money. I remember the day after the concert that I dropped in to see Jan, and there was Firkušný and a Czech who turned out to be the leader of the Czech underground during the time of the Nazi occupation. I remember Firkušný and Jan and this other chap deciding to sing a few Czech folk songs, which they did very beautifully."[56]

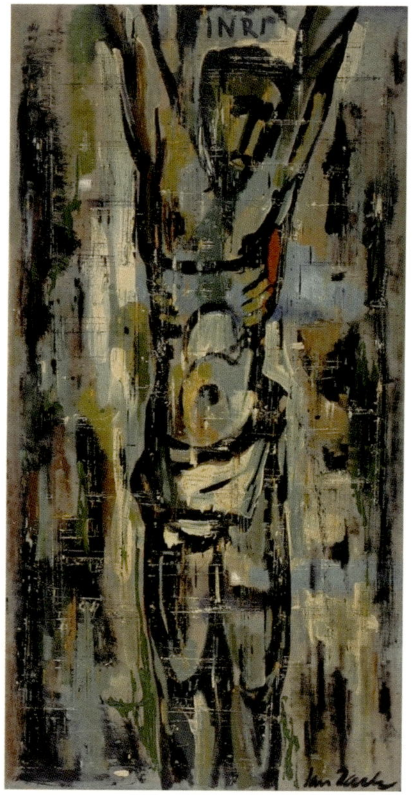

Zach also supported Graham and the Victoria Art Gallery philosophically, encouraging modernist approaches in his teaching and in an essay he published in the *Victoria Daily Times* in 1953. "Generally it is thought that modern artists do not spend enough time in mastering realistic drawing and painting," he wrote. "I would like to clear up

FIGURE 23

Jan Zach. *Seven O'Clock Boat Passing Beacon Hill.* 1953. Oil on canvas. 26 1/2 x 55 1/4". Art Gallery of Greater Victoria, Victoria, British Columbia.

FIGURE 24

Jan Zach. *The Crucifixion.* 1953. Oil on canvas. 67 x 35". Art Gallery of Greater Victoria, Victoria, British Columbia.

1953

this misunderstanding once and for all, because this impression is wrong. The artist must draw, and his technical preparation is always severe. But today's artist has been freed from the necessity of being documentary."[57] He identified Cubism as the greatest revolution in ridding art of the limitations of perspective. Readers aligned with the Vancouver Island Arts and Crafts Society were surely unconvinced, but the publisher of the *Victoria Daily Times*, Stuart Keate, was a supporter of Zach's and Graham's ideas and made certain that their ideas and activities were regularly reported and reviewed.

Keate arranged with Zach to have two of his students paint murals on the walls of the newsroom of the *Daily Times*. Lillian Rogers and Duncan De Kergommeaux, who both began studying with Zach in Banff, were selected in a competition with some forty other students in Zach's night classes. "Mr. Zach believes that in addition to being the first murals to adorn a working newsroom [in Canada], they are unique in being the only examples of this art form in Canada in whose creation the artists have been entirely free to express their own ideas."[58] Mural paintings and architectural "decoration" in general had been central to Zach's own production since his student days in Prague, and his students' *Times* project must have interested him for its merger of art and commercial enterprise–in the manner of Pešánek's sculptural projects for the Prague electrical stations and Zach's own murals and embellishments for Oscar Niemeyer's hotel in Cataguasas. In 1954, Logan Mayhew commissioned three of Zach's students to paint murals about the automobile industry for the showroom of his firm National Motors Limited of Victoria.[59] While Zach himself continued to paint throughout most of his Victoria period (see Figures 23 and 24), increasingly he turned his attention to sculpture.

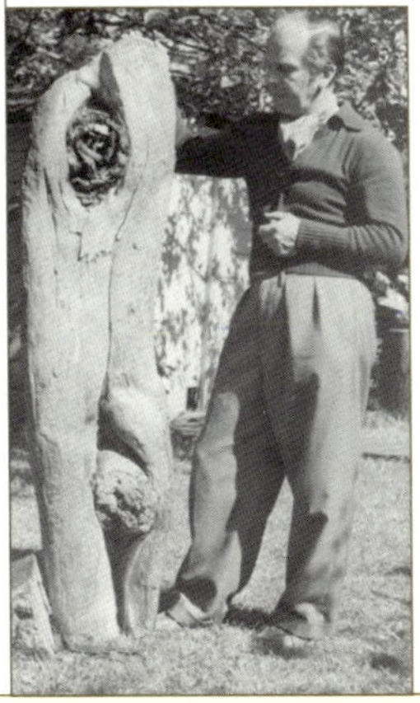

FIGURE 25

Jan Zach with the log for *Venus*, Victoria, British Columbia, 1951. Photograph by A. David Rogers. Hallie Ford Museum of Art, Willamette University, Salem, Oregon. Judith and Jan Zach Archives.

Developing as a Sculptor in Victoria

From the time he arrived in Canada, Zach's artistic focus was on sculpture. Ideas that began at the *Fazenda Penedo* expanded rapidly in British Columbia. Instead of tropical plants bathed in strong light and casting deep shadows, the new inspiration was from the astonishing logs and rocks along the ocean beaches of British Columbia. "The beaches were a revelation to me. Until that time, I had always felt like a foreigner everywhere. The magnificent beaches were something I had been looking for. The wood, the stones, the rock formations . . . all that nature was fantastic. I found my identity there."[60] As J. Škvára explained it, "The contact with the organic nature of the Pacific Northwest awakened his deep memory of Czech Gothic art andPrague Baroque, so it could be said that Zach found on the beaches of the Northwest his inner relation with his homeland."[61] A 1951 photograph (Figure 25) shows Zach standing beside the cedar log that he found on the beaches along Dallas Road and carved as *Venus* (1952; Figure 26), one of his first North American sculptures and the ancestor of a whole line of wood figures of goddesses and other more abstract expressions of human emotion and urgency. *Venus*, which stands just under five feet high, coordinates the weathered texture of the log as found on the beach with Zach's carved voids and smoothed surfaces. Holes pierce through in three places to create the head, the space between the body and the left arm, and the roughly triangular void inside the right thigh. The positive use of negative space in modern sculpture began as early as Umberto Boccioni's Futurist *Development of a Bottle in Space* (1912; Museum of Modern Art, New York) and later in the work of Henry Moore, whose massive forms inspired Zach in the sculptures he made in Brazil. But Venus is much more original than most of Zach's earlier

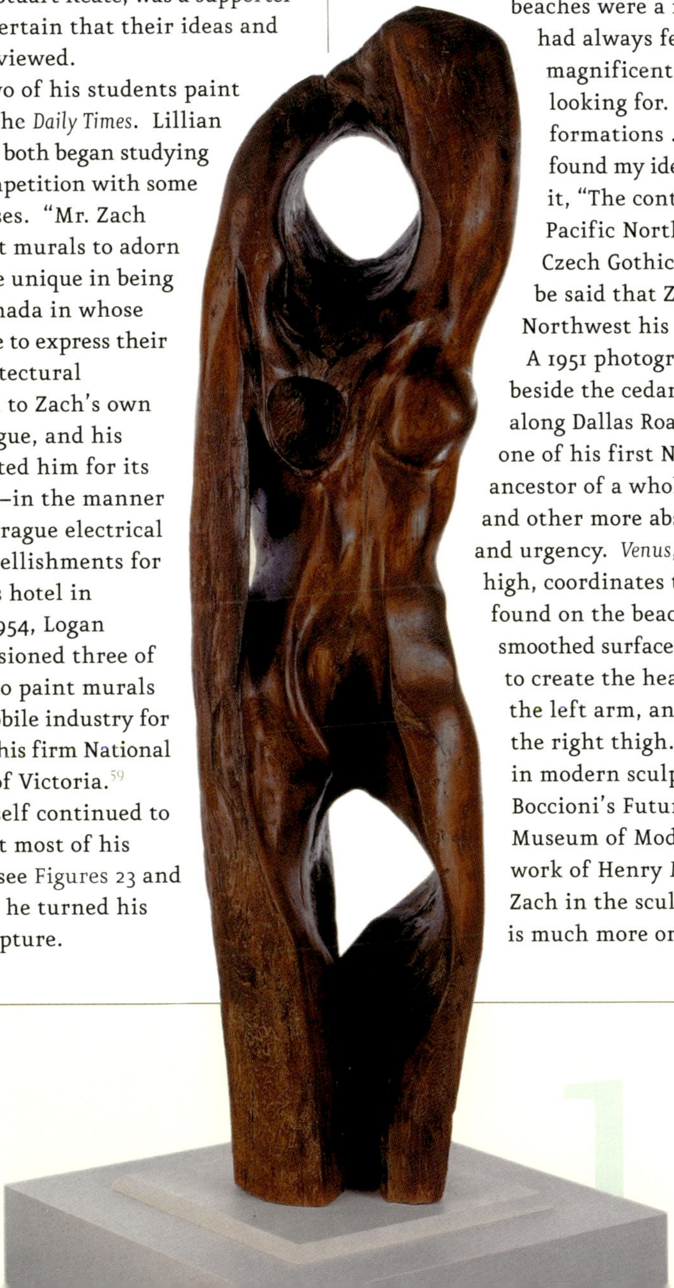

FIGURE 26

Jan Zach. *Venus*. 1952. Cedar. 4'10". Hallie Ford Museum of Art, Willamette University, Salem, Oregon. Judith and Jan Zach Collection. Photograph by Bill Enos, 1999.

sculpture: the tangibility of the cedar snag as found on the beach, the positive and negative carving (one "breast" is concave, the other convex), and the implied pan-sexuality of this Venus (which, it seems, has a penis) all testify to Zach's rush of new inspiration in Canada.

From *Venus'* mixed loins sprang progeny of quite differing personalities, ranging from works of elegant refinement to ones of harsh and rugged expressionism. *Aphrodite* (1953; see Figure 27), described by Stuart Keate as "a lean, gracefully flowing study in red cedar of a woman with her arms over her head,"[62] is a study of stylized elegance. Made of beach wood and, also like *Venus*, using voids as the figure's head and the spaces between arms and body and legs and body, it rises from a single tapered "leg," is smoothly finished, and despite its abstraction is more literal than *Venus* in suggesting muscle and flesh. It attracted the attention of the Armenian-born Ottawa photographer Yousuf Karsh and his wife Solange when they visited Victoria in 1953 while Karsh was on assignment for *Maclean's* magazine. Their purchase of *Aphrodite* was seen as a milestone in Canadian collecting. As Colin Graham noted, the purchase "was news here not only because of Mr. Zach's reputation and the international fame of the purchasers but also simply because it is so unusual for Canadians to think of buying sculpture."[63]

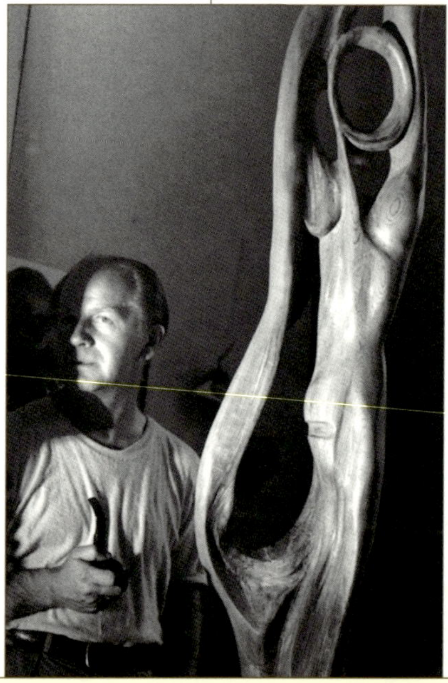

A radically different descendant of *Venus* was Zach's monumental *Resistance* (1955; Figure 28), a six-foot high chunk of alder wood that he found on the beach and then cut, carved, and incised. Unrefined and vigorous, it rejects the tapering elegance of its cousin *Aphrodite* in favor of rugged brutalism. It is anthropomorphic with a massive hip canted out in the form of the sawed-off branch at the lower right, upreaching stubs of arms, and a frightful carved void in the area of the belly – a chasm that evokes an open mouth, a stomach wound, and a birth canal. The "ribs" beside it are gouged parallel incisions that reflect Zach's interest in Native American carving. But the overall effect is European, in the spirit of the work of Jacques Lipchitz and Prague Baroque sculpture. Zach, the Central European exiled from his oppressed country, had found his idiom for expressing feelings with an intensity not apparent in his artwork before now. Zach's mighty *Persistence* (1960-1962; Figure 29), made of a black walnut log, was the culmination of his expressionistic wood sculpture.

As early as 1951 Zach made the acquaintance of the Victoria photographer Kenneth McAllister (1906-1992), a professional like Kurt Klagsbrunn in Rio hired to document Zach's work. McAllister and Zach became friends and collaborators, in 1959 holding a joint exhibition at the University of Oregon Museum of Art. When they first met in the early 1950s, McAllister took a series of photographs of a piece of weathered wood found on the beach (Figure 30) that emphasize natural forms and processes, the sculptural possibilities in natural shapes, and–this was of particular interest to Zach–the patterns of cast shadows created by different lighting and camera angles. Zach presented the photographs in a portfolio with the caption: "Example of natural wood and cast shadow forming sculptural totality." He had come to believe that sculpture was not mass alone but a totality of form, light, shadow, and by extension movement–of the light source, shadows, the viewer's point of view. He was thinking more and more about sculptures that moved, wholly or in part, to catch light, shadow, and the viewer's eye in an accelerated way.

His earliest work in this vein is *Dancer* (1948-1952; Figures 31 and 32), conceived in Brazil in response to the dancers in the Ballet Russe and completed in Victoria by carving a cedar snag found on the beach. *Dancer* was suspended by a wire from a motor on the ceiling that caused the sculpture to turn at four revolutions per minute. The moving form was lighted so that its shadow was cast on a fifteen-foot high canvas. "Because the suspension is eccentric, the shadow cast on the screen by the sculpture moves up and down, expanding and diminishing, giving the impression of a dance," Zach wrote. "Although the figure is abstract, the shadow is realistic. Light and shadow, sculpture and movement, create a unified image."[64] As the Belgian artist Henri Gabriel pointed out in his essay "The Hanging Mobile: A Historical Review,"[65] *Dancer* is one of several of Zach's works created as early as

FIGURE 27

Jan Zach with *Aphrodite (1952; cedar)*, purchased by the photographer Yousuf Karsh and his wife Solange, a newsworthy event in the history of Canadian sculpture collecting. The atmospheric photograph is by Kenneth McAllister of Victoria, who collaborated with Zach in interpreting his work and photographing natural forms in a spirit paralleling Zach's sculptural expression. Zach and McAllister held a joint exhibition at the University of Oregon Museum of Art in 1959. Photograph Hallie Ford Museum of Art, Willamette University, Salem, Oregon. Judith and Jan Zach Archives.

FIGURE 28 [OPPOSITE PAGE]

Jan Zach. *Resistance.* 1955. Alder. 6'. Hallie Ford Museum of Art, Willamette University, Salem, Oregon. Judith and Jan Zach Collection. Photograph by Dale Peterson, 2002.

1954

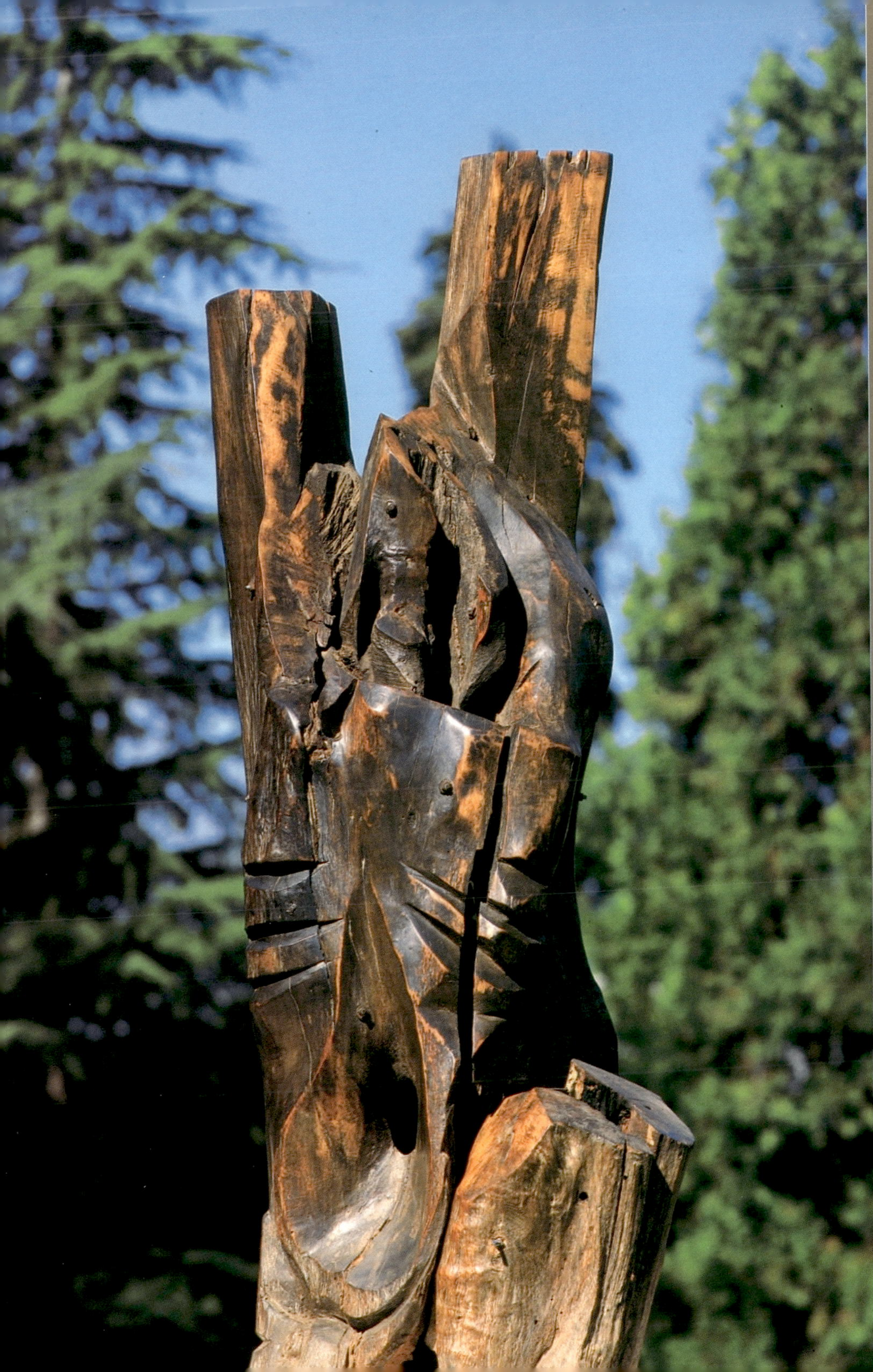

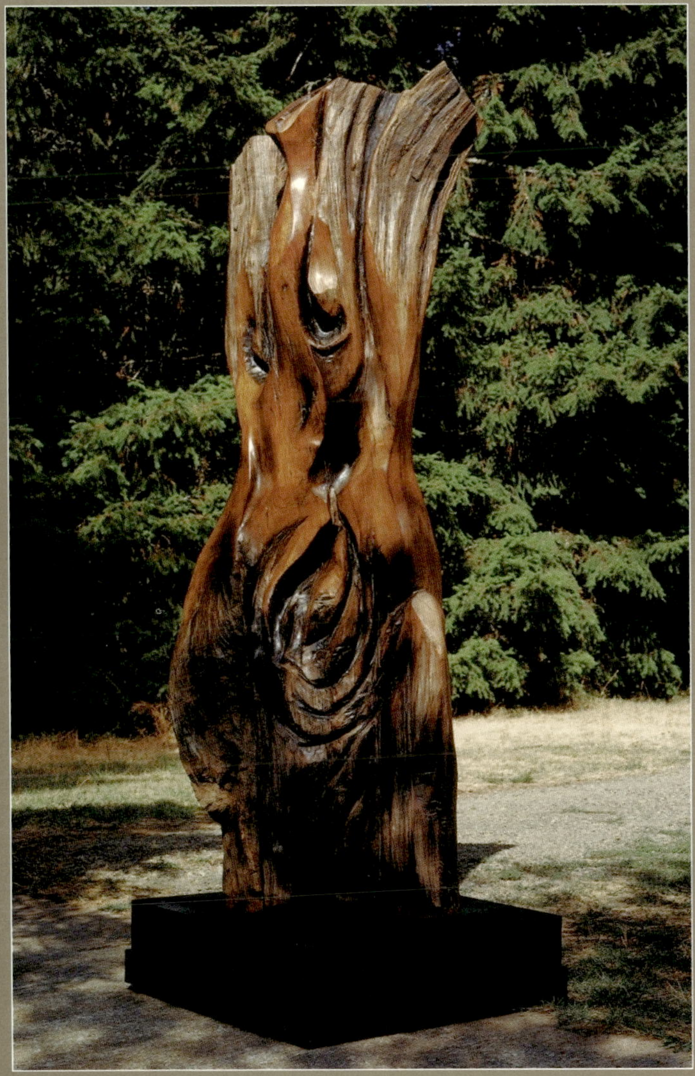

Figure 29 [above]

Jan Zach. *Persistence.* 1960-62. Black Walnut. 8'3". Collection of Judith Zach, Elmira, Oregon. Photograph by Sean Poston, 2002.

the 1950s that place him with other sculptors experimenting in notable ways with mobiles in the generation following Alexander Calder, who was born in 1898.

Dancer is the linking piece, developmentally, between Zach's stable wood carvings of the same period, such as *Venus* and *Aphrodite*, and his much more lightly constructed kinetic works made of small sheets of aluminum, wire, rods of iron, glass, painted plywood, and even neon. While Zach acknowledged Pešánek's kinetic and light sculptures of the 1920s and 1930s in Prague as important influences on these pieces, he also saw nature as he experienced it in British Columbia as crucial to his new ideas. For him, the carved wood pieces and the kinetic work were closely related (in the case of *Dancer*, synonymous). As he wrote in 1954, "the endless variety of shapes cast up by the sea–roots of trees, branch fragments, seaweed, natural rock formations–have impressed me with the immense vitality inherent in natural formations. They have clarified for me certain sculptural concepts of growth and movement through time as expressed in the twisting and thrusting trunks and roots of trees. This feeling of movement in time has prompted me to explore means of adding a fourth dimension to sculpture, of going beyond its hitherto static nature to something more closely in harmony with Einstein's new vision of nature–that of the space-time continuum. The ultimate solution of his project will involve the use of movement in sculpture itself."[66] Logs, wires, planes of sheet aluminum or glass–all were materials that excited him in his investigations of introducing into his sculpture the element of time, the fourth dimension.

Accordingly, even as he hauled home the beach logs that became *Venus* and *Dancer*, he made his aluminum and wire *Light Sculpture* (1951; see Figure 32), a piece that apparently has not survived because of its fragility. It was comprised of planes of aluminum attached to wires in the manner of Calder's mobiles but arranged more densely, like the petals of a flower or the leaves of a tree, with the planes angled in many directions to catch and reflect light as nature itself might–on

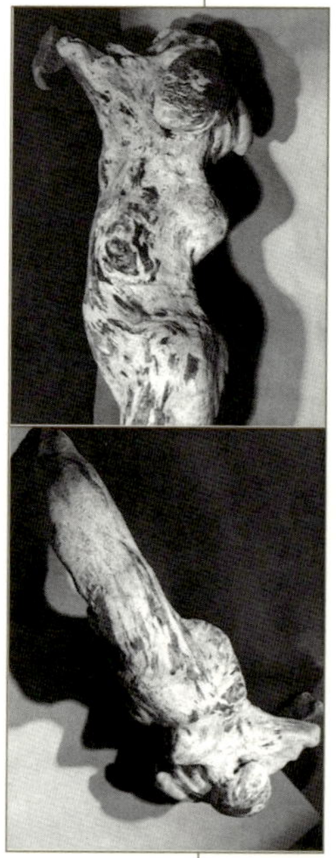

FIGURE 30

Two in a series of photographs by Kenneth McAllister of driftwood and shadows that Zach presented c. 1951 in a portfolio as an "example of natural wood and cast shadows forming sculptural totality." Hallie Ford Museum of Art, Willamette University, Salem, Oregon. Judith and Jan Zach Archives.

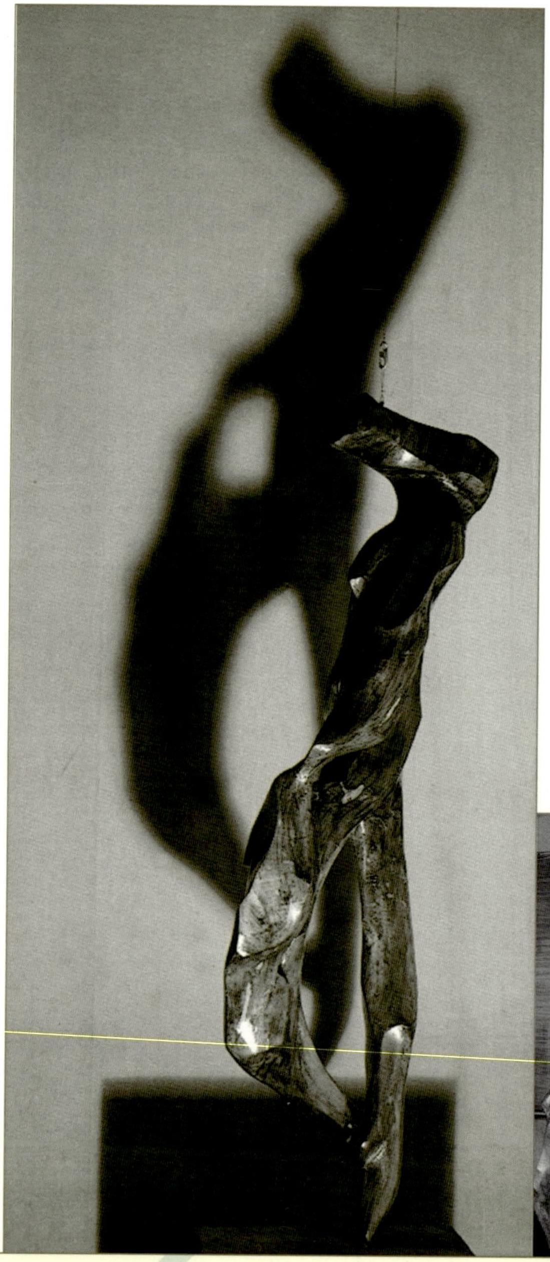

FIGURE 31

Jan Zach. *Dancer.* 1948-1952. Carved cedar snag, suspended by wire from a motor that rotated the piece, which cast kinetic shadows on a screen. 4'10". Collection of Ruth Gilombardo, Belmont, California. Photograph by Kenneth McAllister. Hallie Ford Museum of Art, Willamette University, Salem, Oregon. Judith and Jan Zach Archives.

"...the endless variety of shapes cast up by the sea–roots of trees, branch fragments, seaweed, natural rock formations– have impressed me with the immense vitality inherent in natural formations..."

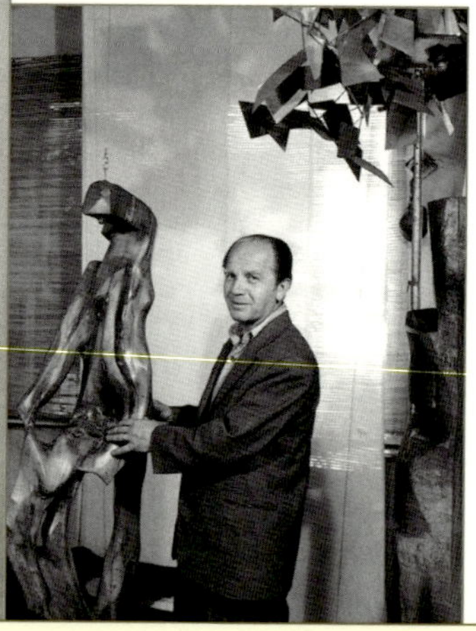

FIGURE 32

Jan Zach in his Victoria studio with *Dancer* (1948-1952; cedar) and (hanging) *Light Sculpture* (1951; aluminum and wire). c. 1953. Photograph by Selwyn Pullan. Hallie Ford Museum of Art, Willamette University, Salem, Oregon. Judith and Jan Zach Archives.

1956

a rippled surface of water or a ruffled aspen. The photograph suggests that it was aerial, cloud-like, designed to be in flux as light changed and air currents shifted. In this same period, he worked on the rod iron and glass *Neon Sculpture* (1951-1952; Figure 33), seen in McAllister's photograph as a thoroughly modern design of 1950s triangles, boomerangs, and tapered elegance. Zach's most monumental "lumino-kinetic" sculpture of the early 1950s was his eight-foot high *Totem* (1952; Figure 34), made of planes of plywood cut in curved shapes with a jigsaw, painted, and clustered around a pole, a stem for a fantastic flower or spine for another dancer *mechanique*. Arp's painted plywood reliefs, Moholy-Nagy's *Light-Space Modulator* (1930; Busch-Reisinger Museum, Harvard University), Pešánek's pioneering works, and Calder's mobiles are part of the ancestry of Zach's *Totem*, but there had been no other sculpture quite like it. In Zach's mind, it was inspired by "the tremendous vitality of the totems and masks of the Indians of the Pacific Coast with their particular rhythm of color patterns and their plastic understanding of carving."[67] (Zach's comment acknowledges his embrace of the "Pacific Northwest synthesis" of art and craft by artists of the region who have been inspired at various times by both Native American and Asian traditions.[68]) *Totem* was motorized, and David Rogers' photograph shows it in motion as a blur of diaphanous scrims– somehow transformed into luminous membranes, no longer plywood at all.

Also in 1952, Zach proposed and created a partial model for an outdoor sculpture to be called *Wrestlers* (Figure 35), designed to incorporate mirrors and solar collectors to create movement within the sculpture. Since 1951, he had been experimenting with a series of attenuated, abstracted figures of wrestlers made of stone compound. His interests in organic flow of form and the interplay of mass and void are evident in these works, which relate in type to the more massive figures he made in Brazil. For his solar proposal, he adapted the wrestler figures as positive and negative complements (see Figure 36).

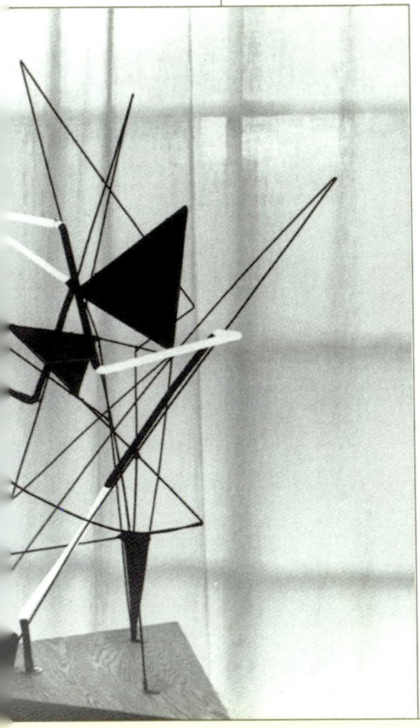

Figure 33

Jan Zach. *Neon Sculpture* (1951-1952). Rod iron, neon, and sheet metal. 4'. Destroyed. Photograph by Kenneth McAllister. Hallie Ford Museum of Art, Willamette University, Salem, Oregon. Judith and Jan Zach Archives.

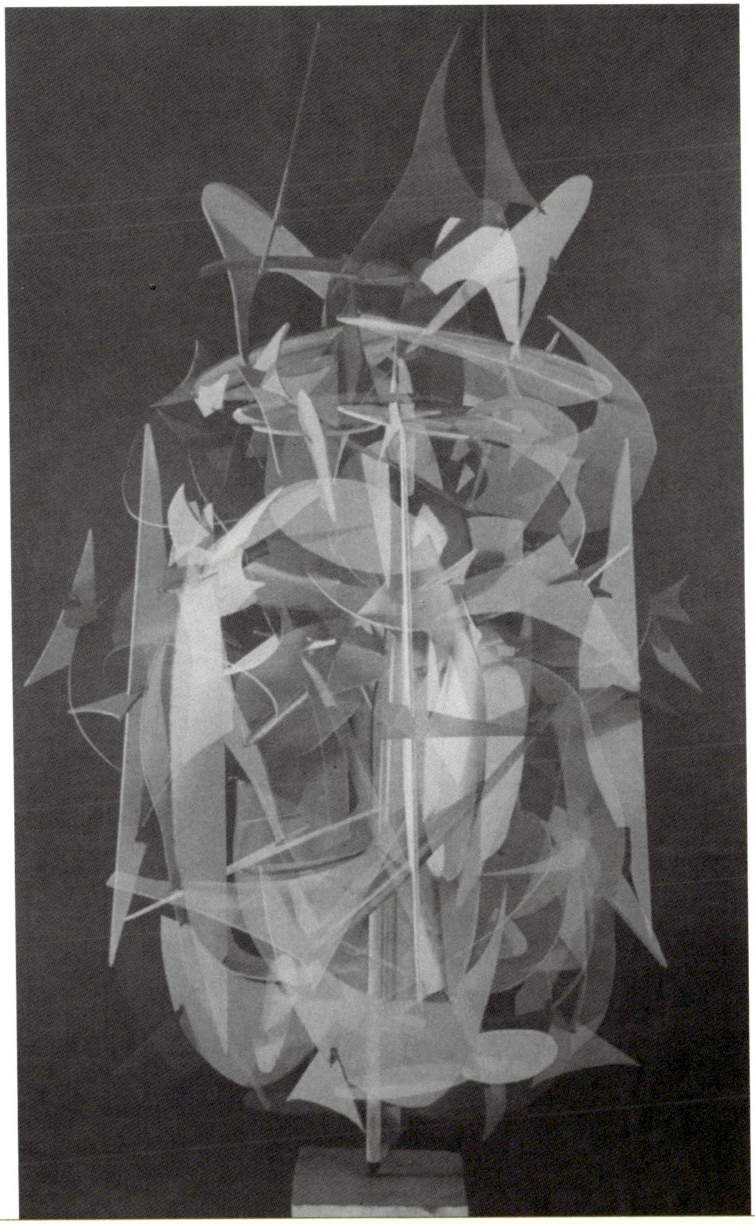

Figure 34

Jan Zach. *Totem* (lumino-kinetic sculpture). 1952. Painted plywood on a motorized central rod. 8'. Destroyed. Photograph by A. David Rogers. Hallie Ford Museum of Art, Willamette University, Salem, Oregon. Judith and Jan Zach Archives.

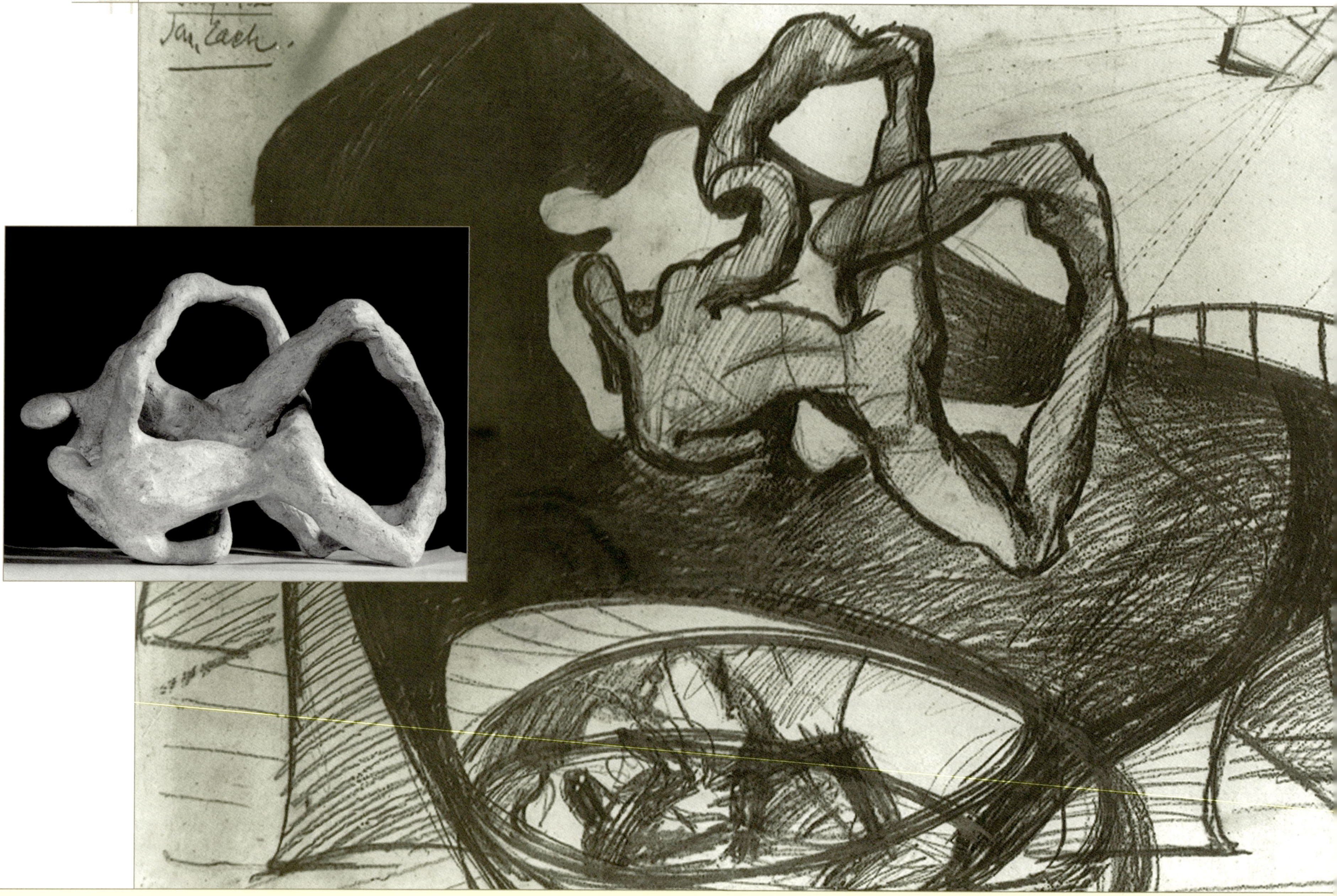

FIGURE 35

Jan Zach. *Wrestlers.* c. 1952. Plaster. 14 x 20 x 9".
Hallie Ford Museum of Art, Willamette University, Salem, Oregon. Judith and Jan Zach Collection. Photograph by A. David Rogers. Judith and Jan Zach Archives.

FIGURE 36

Jan Zach. Drawing of a proposed solar sculpture incorporating *Wrestlers.* 1952.
Photograph Hallie Ford Museum of Art, Willamette University, Salem, Oregon. Judith and Jan Zach Archives.

1957

"The solid wrestler is cast in aluminum, about 8 feet long. The negative wrestler (in the same proportion) is partly cut from a sheet of steel about 18 feet long. This steel forms the moving element, regulated by the passage of the sun. Solar illumination, reflected from mirrors upon the solid wrestler, directs his shadow into the aluminum basin below."[69]

The intention was to project into this basin the light and dark silhouettes of wrestlers engaged in a match that slowly evolves in the course of the day as the sun shifts. "This, of course, is merely an initial exploratory example and deals with only a segment of what seems to me a whole field of possibilities yet to be opened up," Zach concluded. Whether *Wrestlers* would have literally moving parts was not made clear.

In 1953, he extended these ideas in a proposal for a Guggenheim Fellowship: "I plan to use the shadows cast by the sculptural parts, when projected onto other elements of the design, as plastic units in themselves. Such shadows therefore will become design elements just as much as the solid parts of the sculpture. In other words, whereas contemporary sculpture has, in the case of artists such as Moore and [Ossip] Zadkine, employed negative volumes as integral parts of the sculptural work, I hope to add the two additional elements of shadow and time–the latter realized, of course, through moving parts."[70]

Working with materials that ranged from primeval wood and stone to modern products such as plywood and neon to solar energy and shadows, Zach was galvanized by dozens of new ideas for sculpture during the Canada years. For sheer inspiration, no period of Zach's life was more exciting and fulfilling than the years 1951-1957, and yet major collectors and patrons for sculpture were rare in Canada, as the phenomenon of Yousuf Karsh's purchase of *Aphrodite* made clear. Moving beyond concepts and proposals actually to create major experimental projects was impossible; as Colin Graham explained, grants were not readily available in Victoria or in Canada at large. The Guggenheim Fellowship did not come through, and the studio on St. Andrews Street was too small to realize big projects, as Zach lamented to the art historian Sir Herbert Read when he visited Victoria in 1956.[71] Ideas were abundant, but infrastructure and cash flow could not support them. The Zachs made ends meet by living modestly on Judith's salary as a manuscript clerk at the Provincial Archives and Jan's earnings from teaching classes and private students, sculpting or painting portraits on commission,[72] drawing illustrations for the *Victoria Daily Times* (Figure 37, for example),[73] and occasionally selling other artwork from his studio and from exhibitions. The arrival in 1954 of the German painter Herbert Siebner, who joined Zach and Graham in promoting modern art in Victoria, both enriched and complicated Zach's situation, since Siebner started teaching classes and producing his own students. "So I think eventually Jan realized he wasn't getting anywhere in Victoria," Colin Graham told David Roberts. "He was having a hard time making ends meet. He wasn't finding anyone capable of digging up $15,000.00 for this project or that project. I really couldn't see much of a future for Jan in Victoria. It was a godsend when he was invited to teach in Oregon."[74]

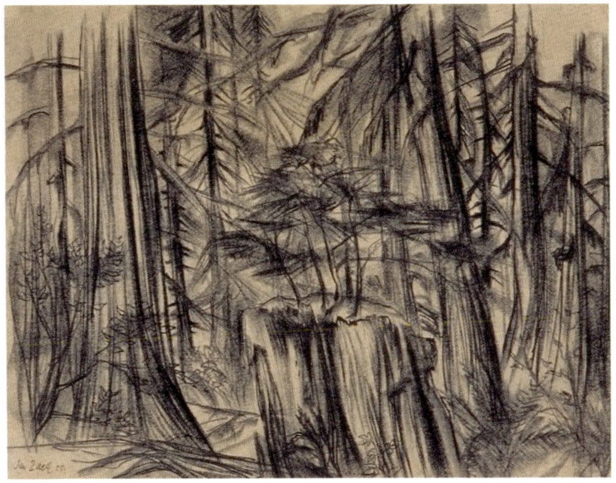

1958

FIGURE 37

Jan Zach. *Macmillan Park*. 1955. Charcoal on paper. 17 1/2 x 24".
Art Gallery of Greater Victoria, Victoria, British Columbia.
The drawing, published in the *Victoria Daily Times*, 3 September 1955, page 4, as *Rebirth*, was one of a series by Zach printed by the *Times* throughout 1955.

ON TO OREGON

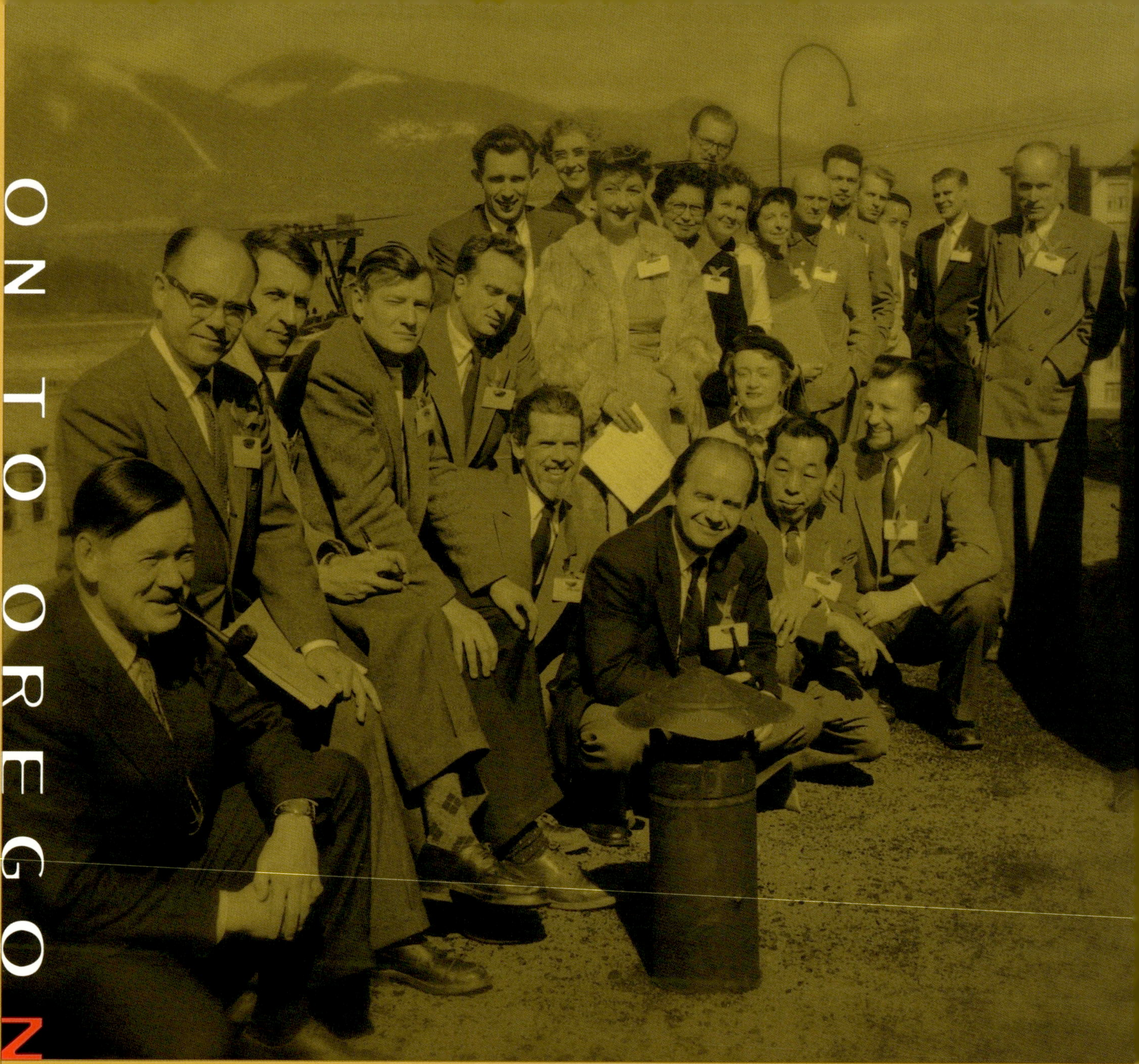

1958

Zach's temporary and then permanent appointment at the University of Oregon in Eugene was the result of a recommendation by the sculptor and art historian Mark Sponenburgh, who Zach knew through the Northwest Institute of Sculpture, an organization that drew members from Oregon, Washington, Alaska, British Columbia, and the Yukon Territory. The Institute was formed in February 1955 at the suggestion of Sponenburgh, who organized a conference of sculptors from around the region at the University of Oregon. A constitution and by-laws were adopted, and for some years the Institute organized annual exhibitions and conferences throughout the region. A photograph of the members of the Institute who convened in Vancouver in 1956 (Figure 38) shows Sponenburgh kneeling at the front left, pipe in mouth, and Zach kneeling at center, pipe in hand. Among others in the photograph are Everett DuPen of the University of Washington, George Norris of Vancouver, British Columbia, Wayne Taysom of the University of Oregon (he later taught at Oregon State University), George Laisner (Czech in origin) of Washington State University, and George Tsutakawa of the University of Washington.

Sponenburgh recalled that he was impressed with Zach's exuberance and vitality. Although they did not know each other well, Sponenburgh recommended that Zach be hired as his temporary replacement to teach sculpture in the School of Architecture and Allied Arts at the University of Oregon while he and his wife traveled to Pakistan during the winter and spring of 1958.[75] When Sponenburgh decided to resign from the University in order to head a new art school in Pakistan, Zach was hired to fill the position permanently.[76] Sponenburgh said he was asked to explain to Dean Sidney W. Little why Zach qualified for the position when he had no formal college degree (he had left Prague as a student and was not able to complete his degree at the Academy of Fine Arts). Sponenburgh's response was that Zach had been trained in the European tradition of academies and apprenticeships and brought a cultural and artistic background from Europe and North and South America that would be valuable to students in Oregon.[77]

Ironically, Zach was granted Canadian citizenship effective May 30, 1957, but by the end of the year was leaving Canada to take a position that would lead to his spending the rest of his life in the United States. When it became clear in the summer of 1958 that he would stay in Eugene indefinitely, Tony Emery wrote, "Not long ago Jan became a Canadian citizen, and now already he has been swallowed up by the United States. He is miserable at having to leave, but can you blame him? In Oregon his value to the community is assessed in terms of hard and welcome cash and – what is more important to Jan – he has rewarding work, a free hand to experiment, and a feeling that his presence is really appreciated. Oregon has gained an outstanding professor of sculpture; British Columbia has lost an artist of most uncompromising integrity; and although we shall see him back here in the summers, his friends are going to miss the stimulus that this volcanic Canadian artist could always be relied upon to provide."[78] In the same article, Emery wrote, "To many who have never met him Jan stands for all that they abhor in modern art; his work provokes the rage and fury of many of our citizens. He – the mildest and most exquisitely polite of men – is amazed that people should denounce and vilipend works which are attempts to solve formal problems. It is fitting that Jan and his wife should occupy Emily Carr's old studio in James Bay: modern painting in Victoria began with Emily Carr; sculpture begins with the arrival of Jan Zach."[79]

Early Commissions in Eugene

In Eugene as a visiting assistant professor in the winter and spring terms of 1958, Zach must have used his powers to persuade and inspire beginning the day he arrived on campus, for in June, just six months later, his monumental new sculpture *Prometheus* was unveiled and dedicated in its permanent location on the lawn near the University of Oregon Museum of Art. Commissioned by the University's chapter of the Gamma Phi Beta sorority, *Prometheus* (Figure 39) announced the arrival of a new sculptural force in Oregon. Eight and a half feet tall (with base) and made of cast iron, brass, and a concrete-like compound, it is a dramatically composed, roughly textured form, a flame-like yet anthropomorphic evocation of the Greek hero who stole fire from Zeus to give it to humankind. In its mass and monstrousness, it is at once horrific and awe-inspiring, a work of serious and sober intentions.

FIGURE 38 [OPPOSITE PAGE]

Members of the Pacific Northwest Institute of Sculpture, 1956, Vancouver, British Columbia. The group includes Mark Sponenburgh, founder of the Institute and in 1956 sculptor at the University of Oregon, Eugene (lower left), Jan Zach (front row center, holding pipe), and in the row directly behind Sponenburgh Everett DuPen (University of Washington), George Norris (British Columbia), and Wayne Taysom (University of Oregon). The bald man directly beneath the arch of the lamp post is George Laisner (Washington State College, later Washington State University, Pullman). To the right of Zach is George Tsutakawa (University of Washington). Photograph by Kenneth McAllister. Hallie Ford Museum of Art, Willamette University, Salem, Oregon. Judith and Jan Zach Archives.

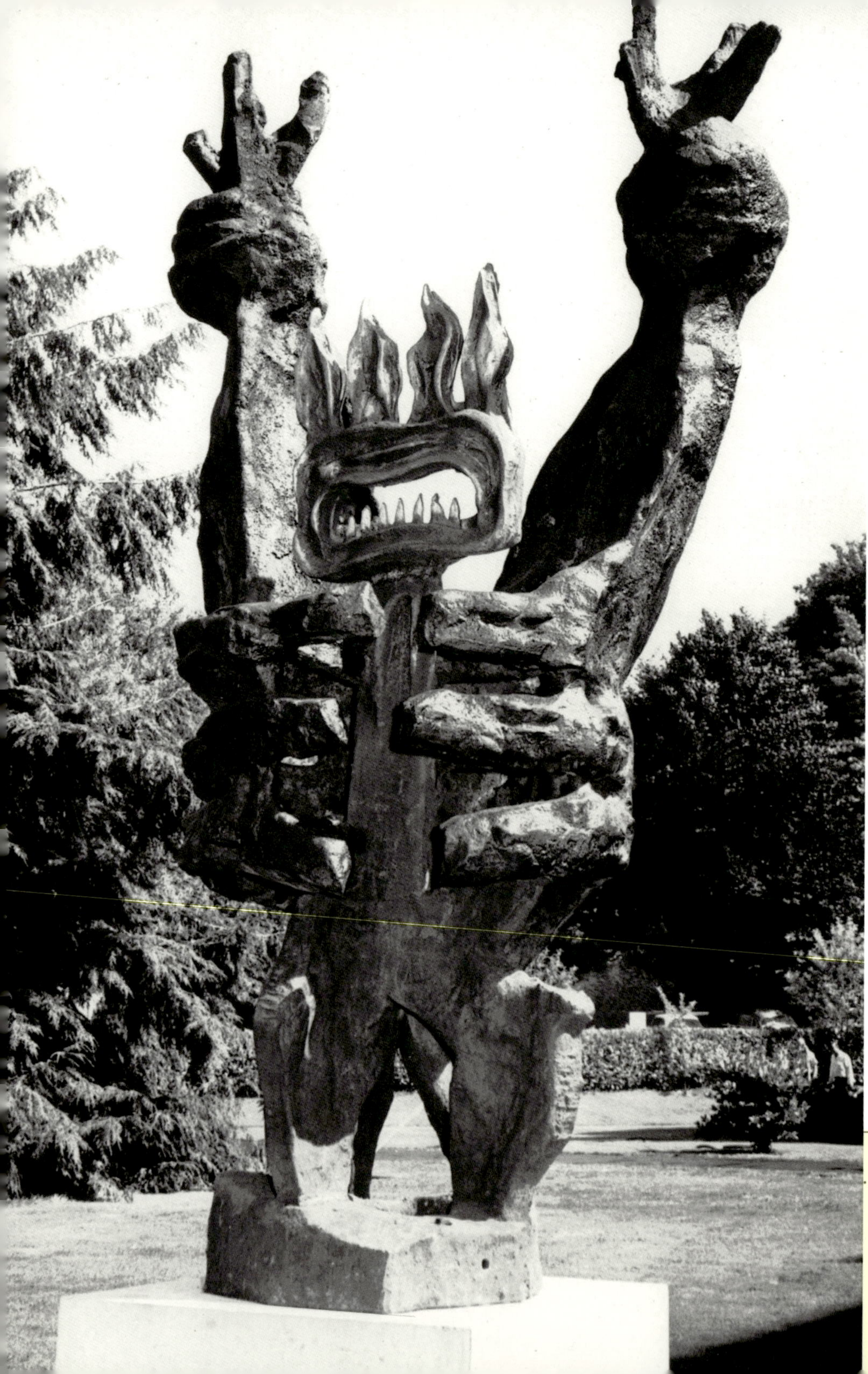

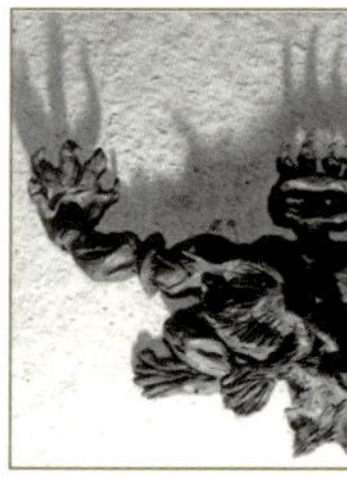

The art historian Wallace Baldinger described the work as the fusion of a fire (including a flaming grate) and a "ritualistic dancer," with massive reaching arms and enormous rib cage, the "grate" transforming into a mask. "It becomes the agonized features of a genius in the throes of creation, with hands reaching out for the unattainable," Baldinger said.[80]

Zach had envisioned a work based on the myth of Prometheus as early as 1952, when he made a clay study for a wall relief (Figure 40), photographed by David Rogers to show the flickering shadows it could cast on the wall behind and above it. The study anticipates the upper portions of the Eugene sculpture. At the same time, the study's flowing forms, turbulent energy, and reference to the vulture in the story of Prometheus correspond to Lipchitz's *Prometheus Strangling the Vulture II* (1944/1953; Walker Art Center, Minneapolis; Figure 41), a three-dimensional bronze work in which the struggling figures are balanced on a small shaft. Whether or not Zach knew of this Prometheus, he admired Lipchitz's work, later visited his studios, and shared a European expressionistic forcefulness with the Lithuanian-born sculptor who was a generation older than Zach. In the Eugene *Prometheus*, Zach adopts the anchored massiveness ofhis own *Resistance* (1955; Figure 28), the ruggedly conceived alder wood carving. Despite the different materials, the two works share massive legs, rib cages, and upward thrust arms. Both are rendered at a high emotional pitch expressing defiance and the will to survive and transform reality. Created twenty years after he left Czechoslovakia, *Prometheus* conveys Zach's on-going challenge to resist entrenched forces, whether gods or demagogues, and to forge new freedoms. Zach himself said simply, "My definition of Prometheus is an affirmation. He is the symbol of energy – a symbol of life – because fire for man is the most important element in his life."[81]

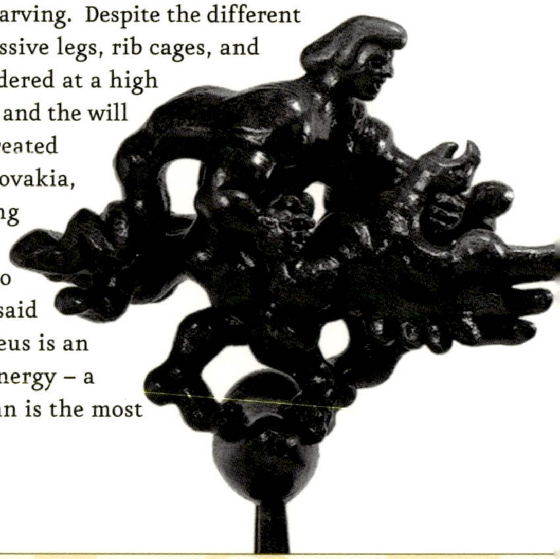

FIGURE 39 [LEFT]

Jan Zach. *Prometheus.* 1958. Cast iron, sand, and cement. 8'6". University of Oregon campus, Eugene, Oregon. Commissioned by Gamma Phi Beta Sorority. Photograph Hallie Ford Museum of Art, Willamette University, Salem, Oregon. Judith and Jan Zach Archives.

FIGURE 40 [TOP]

Jan Zach. *Prometheus.* 1952. Clay. Photograph by A. David Rogers. Hallie Ford Museum of Art, Willamette University, Salem, Oregon. Judith and Jan Zach Archives.

FIGURE 41 [BOTTOM]

Jacques Lipchitz, detail, *Prometheus Strangling the Vulture II.* 1944/1953. Bronze. 91-3/4 x 90 x 57". Collection of the Walker Art Center, Minneapolis. Gift of T.B. Walker Foundation, 1956.

1950

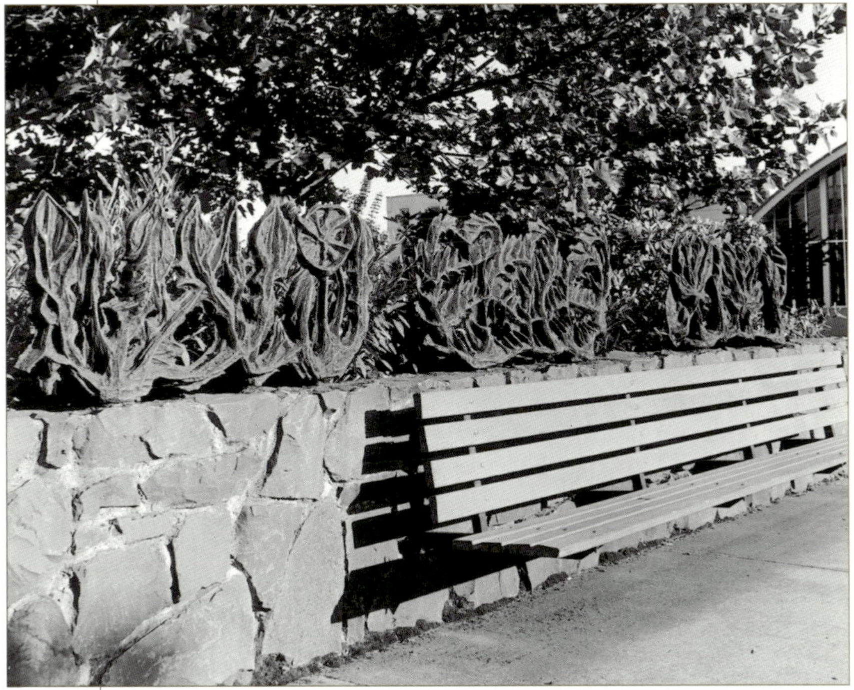

The unveiling of *Prometheus* served as a fanfare in honor of Zach's arrival in Oregon and began a new era of opportunity for him. Further, *Prometheus* was recognized by Baldinger as particularly appropriate "to the sculptor who works on metals with fire. Without Prometheus's gift, in fact, such a sculptor could do nothing." From this perspective, *Prometheus* symbolized sculptural creativity itself, and it proved to be the case that in his new and last home of Oregon Zach reached his maturity as a sculptor and created his most important work.

The major commissions that Zach had sought in vain in Canada seemed to come readily enough in Oregon. In February 1959, during his first full year of teaching at the University, he was commissioned by the Lane County Art Commission to make "two cast iron screens or walls" for the Lane County Courthouse park. *Plant Forms* (Figure 42), three twenty-six-inch high screens mounted on a rock wall, and *Three Standing Forms* (Figure 43), totem-like figures placed at the end of the stone wall at the opposite end of the two-block park, remain in place today in downtown Eugene. (At a farmers' market on a summer day in 2002, *Standing Forms* was draped with netting that enclosed a vegetable stand.)

In 1960, Zach was commissioned to make eleven enormous cast iron grills depicting "evergreen forests" with interweaving branches for the new building of the Equitable Savings and Loan Association in Roseburg, Oregon (Figure 44), designed by the firm Stafford, Morin and Longwood. Each grill is a separate one-piece cast poured at the Valley Forge and Foundry in Eugene; four of the grills are seventeen feet tall and the seven others twenty-four feet. All are about five feet wide and together weigh some 53,000 pounds, according to Zach's estimate. He claimed that it was the largest iron casting project in the western United States. With this and his other cast metal projects, he was participating in the rediscovery of casting processes by American sculptors beginning about 1960 and the resulting practice of sculptors working at commercial foundries as extensions of their own studios.[82]

Fabricating the grills at night when the foundry was closed to regular business, Zach and his assistant Warren Spady poured the molten iron into casts that Zach had carved directly into sand beds. Because of the large scale, they poured simultaneously from two foundries at opposite ends of the casts so that the pour could be completed before the iron began to harden. Half-inch steel rods were embedded in the vertical tree trunks of the design for reinforcement and to retard shrinkage of the iron as it cooled. From Eugene, the gigantic forms were transported about seventy-five miles by flatbed truck to Roseburg and put in place on the Equitable building by Jack Mathis Construction Company.[83] "All went well," Zach told fellow sculptors at a conference in 1966. "At the moment of hoisting the grills on the building, [they] waved in the air like metal sheeting but did not crack at all."[84] The dramatically over-scaled decorative screens set between the brick

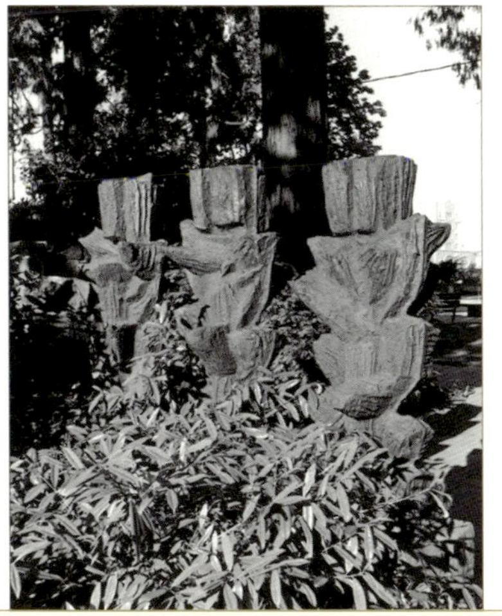

FIGURE 42

Jan Zach. *Plant Forms.* 1959. Cast iron. Heights vary from 26" to 27 1/4". Park Blocks (near Lane County Courthouse), Eugene, Oregon. Photograph Hallie Ford Museum of Art, Willamette University, Salem, Oregon. Judith and Jan Zach Archives.

FIGURE 43

Jan Zach. *Three Standing Forms.* 1959. Cast iron. Each 49" high. Park Blocks (near Lane County Courthouse), Eugene, Oregon. Photograph Hallie Ford Museum of Art, Willamette University, Salem, Oregon. Judith and Jan Zach Archives.

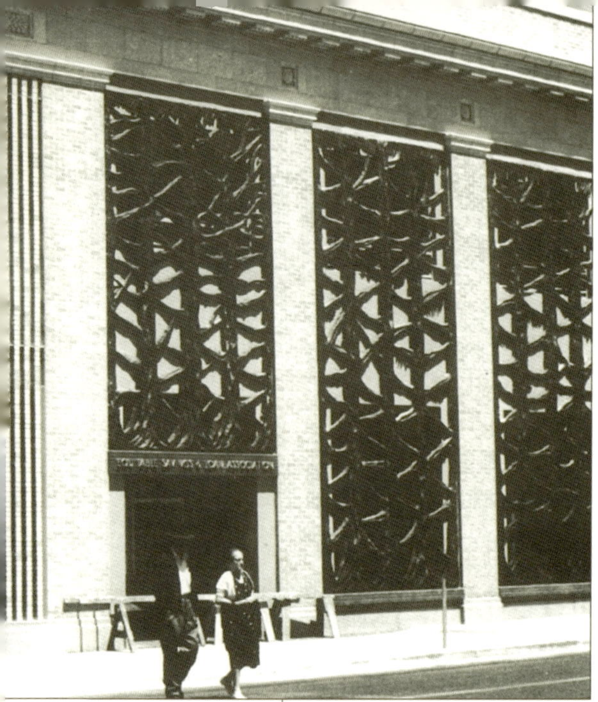

pilasters of the architecture were reminiscent of the relationship of ornament and structure in Louis Sullivan's small banks built in the Midwest earlier in the century. (The grills were removed from the building in 1993 and three of them relocated to Umpqua Community College in Roseburg.[85])

In 1961, Zach was commissioned to create sculpture for another architectural complex designed by the firm Stafford, Morin and Longwood. This was the Eugene City Hall, for which Zach made concrete reliefs, metal free-standing sculptures, and the sixteen-foot long *Reclining Forms* carved from a redwood log (see Figure 48).[86] In all, the City Hall commission involved sixteen separate works or ensembles. The project was completed in 1964. Zach's best known City Hall piece is the cast aluminum *Three Rivers (Three Graces)* (1964; Figure 45) located on the plaza. Zach identified the rivers as the Willamette, Columbia, and McKenzie. The figures, each nine feet high, were made in a process of carving and casting that had been developed in industrial circles and adapted in individual ways by numerous sculptors in this period.[87] Known as the Styrofoam displacement technique of metal casting, it involves carving polystyrene to create the model to be cast in iron, bronze, or in this case aluminum. In Victoria, Zach had discovered this process, observing that polystyrene, which is easily carved into shapes, is highly combustible and vaporizes instantaneously in contact with molten metal.[88]

To create *Three Rivers* and other works made by this process, such as *Mermaid* (1960-1961; Figure 46), Zach again worked at a commercial foundry, this time the Eugene Brass and Aluminum Foundry owned by Max Reck, who strategized with Zach on how to wrap and anchor the Styrofoam forms to prepare them for casting.[89] The visual properties of the resulting works are quite different from those of traditional casts, in which the original form is typically modeled in clay rather than carved from a semi-resistant material. Zach's cast metal works are clearly the result of both carving and casting (the "direct" and "indirect" processes of traditional sculpture): the handwork of blade incising and gouging is evident in the angularity of the planes and chiseled textures, yet the synthetic unity of the flowing molten metal used in the casting process is also apparent. A final process of grinding the cast form is often deemed necessary, since the cast transmits the nubbly texture of the Styrofoam: Zach selectively ground his surfaces to leave a combination of smooth and rough textures. Aesthetically, *Three Rivers* and *Mermaid* suggest sinuous female figures in diaphanous draperies, descendants of the graces in Botticelli's *Primavera*, for instance, as Zach suggested with his second title, *Three Graces*. Zach often remarked that for him the shimmer of light on rivers and lakes evoked the effect of flowing drapery; the graceful cast aluminum figures seem to make this connection tangible. With these carved and then cast figures, furthermore, Zach's claimed indebtedness to Prague Baroque sculpture seems as fully apparent as in such earlier wood pieces as *Resistance*, *Prometheus*, and *Persistence*. In the lime-wood figure of Saint Jude the Apostle by Matyáš Bernard Braun (1712; National Gallery Prague; Figure 47), for instance, the deeply carved draperies–turbulent, restless, and always in motion–correspond to the swirling currents in the forms of *Three Rivers*, which like Saint Jude are animate bodies with unstoppable energy.

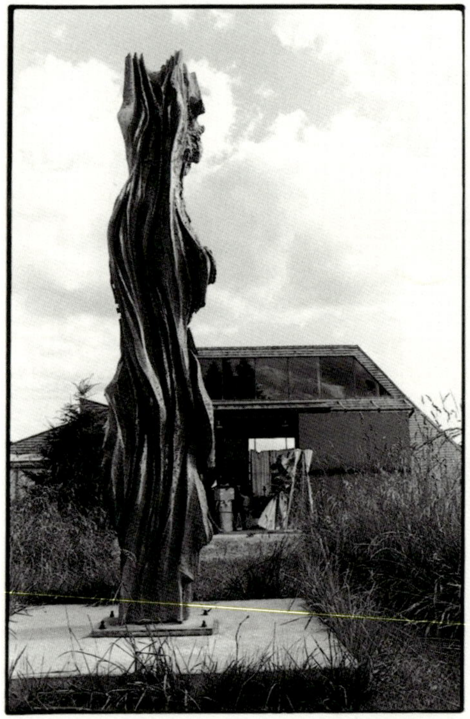

FIGURE 44

Jan Zach. Decorative grills for the Equitable Savings and Loan Association (Stafford, Morin and Longwood, architects), Roseburg, Oregon. 1960-1961. Cast iron. Four grills 17'; seven grills 24'. All 5' wide. Removed in 1993 and three grills relocated to Umpqua Community College, Roseburg. Photograph Hallie Ford Museum of Art, Willamette University, Salem, Oregon. Judith and Jan Zach Archives.

FIGURE 45 [OPPOSITE PAGE]

Jan Zach. *Three Rivers (Three Graces)*. 1964. Cast aluminum. 9'. Eugene City Hall, Eugene, Oregon. Photograph by Bernard Freemesser. Hallie Ford Museum of Art, Willamette University, Salem, Oregon. Judith and Jan Zach Archives.

FIGURE 46 [ABOVE]

Jan Zach. *Mermaid*. 1960-1961. Cast aluminum. 9'. Collection of Western Oregon University, Monmouth, Oregon. Photograph by Michael Besh. Hallie Ford Museum of Art, Willamette University, Salem, Oregon. Judith and Jan Zach Archives.

1961 1962

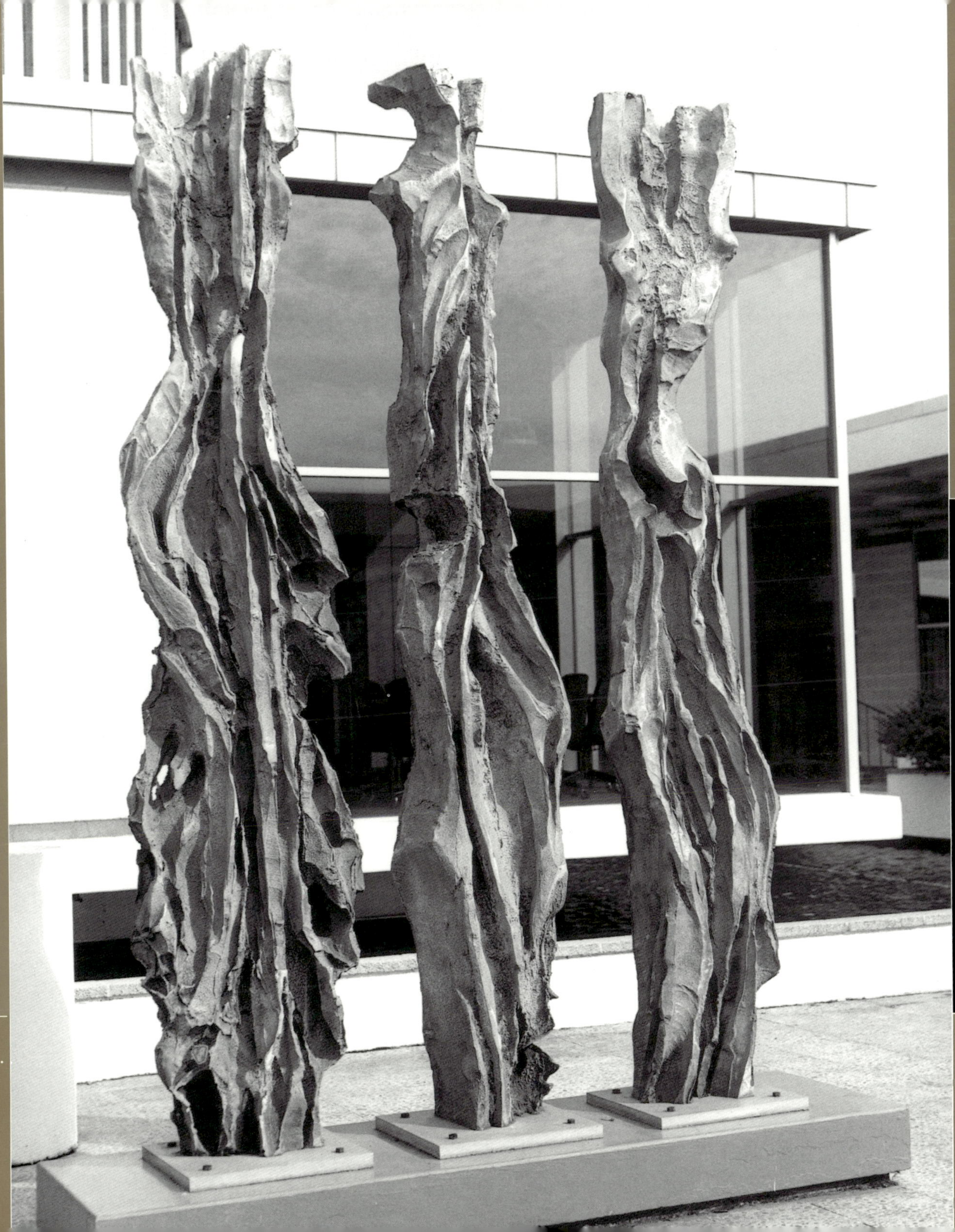

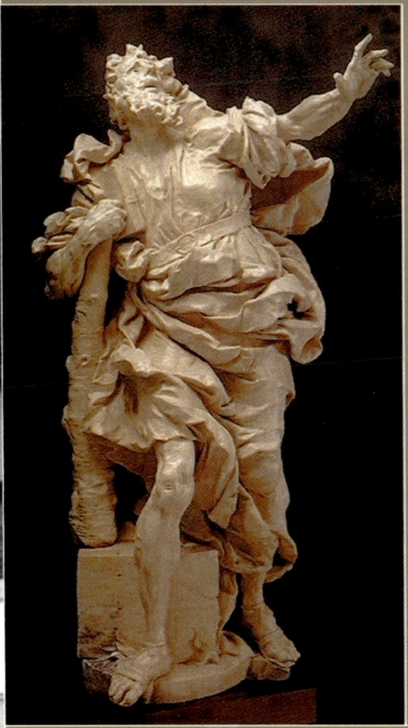

FIGURE 47 [ABOVE]

Matyáš Bernard Braun. *St. Jude the Apostle.* 1712. Limewood. 75 5/8". National Gallery of Prague.

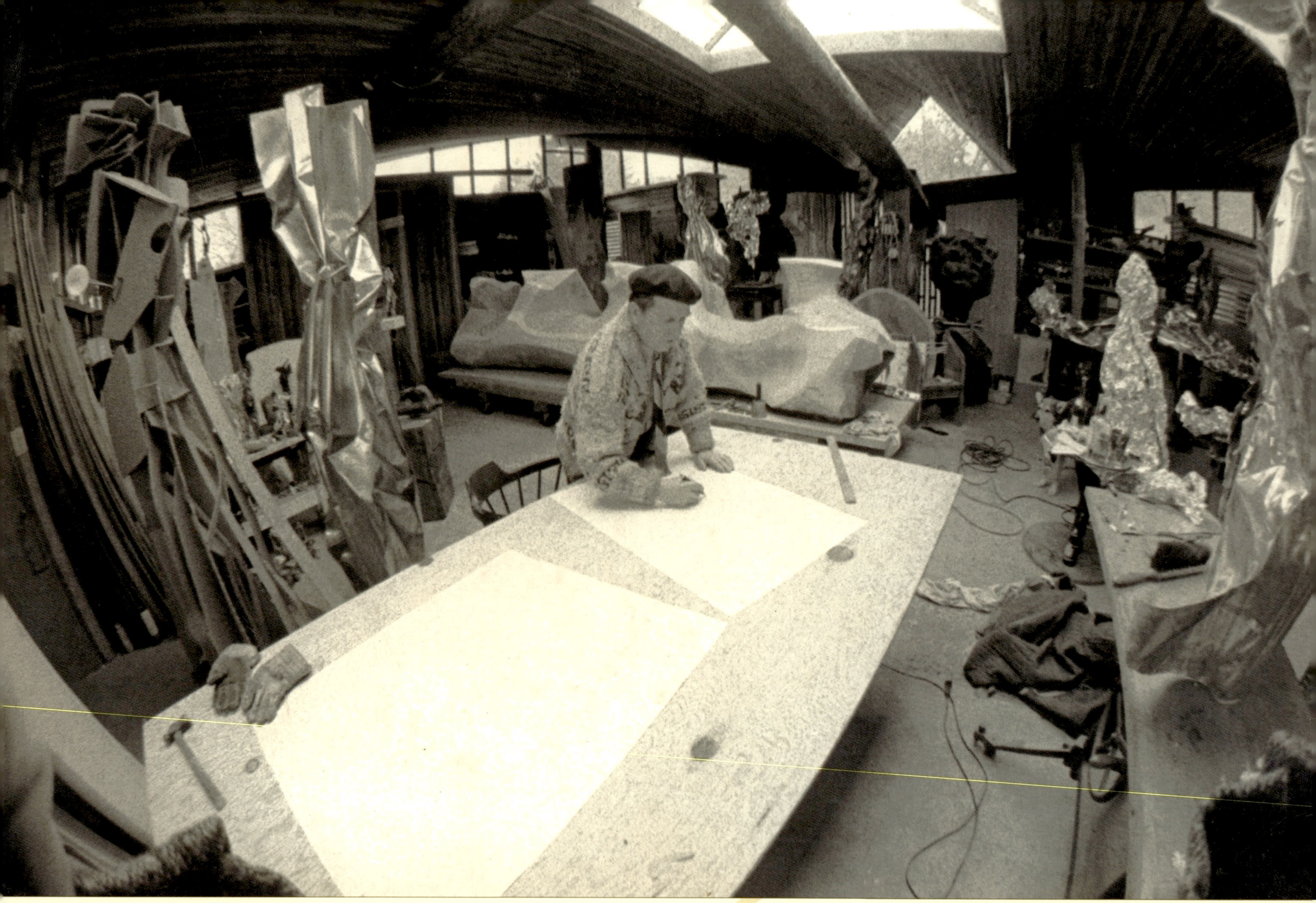

FIGURE 48

Jan Zach in his studio at 1788 East Thirtieth Street, Eugene, Oregon. 1962. Sculptures include *Reclining Forms* (1962-1964; redwood), part of the Eugene City Hall commission, and figures made of hammered sheet aluminum and crumpled aluminum foil. Photograph by Bernard Freemesser. Hallie Ford Museum of Art, Willamette University, Salem, Oregon. Judith and Jan Zach Archives.

1964

Remembering Czechoslovakia, Embracing Oregon

The Prague Baroque was but one aspect of Zach's memories of Czechoslovakia that remained in his imagination throughout his life. He missed his homeland "terribly," Judith Zach recalled, even though the landscape of western Lane County came to remind him of rural Czechoslovakia. He subscribed to a Czech language newspaper published in Chicago, clipped news items about Czechoslovakia from English language newspapers, and sometimes posted leaflets at the University calling for the liberation of Czechoslovakia from Communist rule. He corresponded with family members still living there and sometimes wrote letters in Czech for others; Zach's former pupil Kenneth Patecky, whose grandparents were immigrants from Czechoslovakia, recalled that he wrote a letter for him to send to his relatives (who reported that Zach's written Czech was elegant in its old-fashioned formality).[90] Zach was a member of the Czechoslovak Society of Arts and Sciences in America, for which he was regional secretary during 1958-1964. At the Society's conference in 1962 in Washington, D.C., he presented a paper on "The Contribution of the Czechoslovak Sculpture to the World of Art," noting that many Czech born sculptors were now dispersed in England, Paris, and the United States (he mentioned Albin Polášek of Chicago, George Laisner of Pullman, Washington, Mario Korbel, whose *Sleeping Republic* had been displayed at the Czech pavilion of the New York World's Fair, and Ludvik Durchánek of New York.[91] Zach remained in life-long correspondence with his Prague student friend Jaromír Fiala, and in 1966 Fiala invited Zach to send an exhibition of photographs of his drawings and sculptures for display at the Gallery of Plastic Arts in Litoměřice, Czechoslovakia. With funds provided by the University of Oregon, photographs of works dating from 1953 to 1965 were mounted on Masonite panels, shipped to Litoměřice, and presented in the exhibition "Jan Zach USA."

By the early 1960s, Judith and Jan Zach were renting a house at 1788 East Thirtieth Avenue in the hilly outskirts of Eugene. The owner, Wallace Hayden, architecture professor at the University of Oregon, designed a large studio on the property for Jan's use. Judith enrolled in courses at the University and completed a degree in anthropology. She and Jan campaigned to have Portuguese language taught as a regular part of the curriculum. Zach during these years was occupied with the Eugene City Hall and Roseburg savings and loan commissions and with his fulltime teaching. A photograph from that period (Figure 48) shows Zach at a large work table in the Thirtieth Avenue studio, its roof supported by log trusses and illuminated by direct and indirect lighting. Zach is surrounded by works in progress, including the carved redwood *Reclining Forms* that was part of the City Hall commission, a construction made of planes of cardboard or plywood, and hammered sheet aluminum versions of his cast river figures. These figures and the crumpled aluminum foil forms also visible in the photograph are examples of a type of work that had interested Zach as early as 1951, when he made a leaf-like hammered aluminum sculpture (see Figure 22) in Victoria. The possibility of using metal sheeting to make sculpture occurred to him again during his first years in Eugene as he experimented with the Styrofoam displacement process and encountered the problem of explosions caused by built-up gases. "I then began designing the form as if it were folded paper, so that the gases would be released vertically through the sand," he wrote in 1970. "The result of this development was that I became only interested in the designs formed by the folding, which started me using metal sheeting in my sculpture."[92]

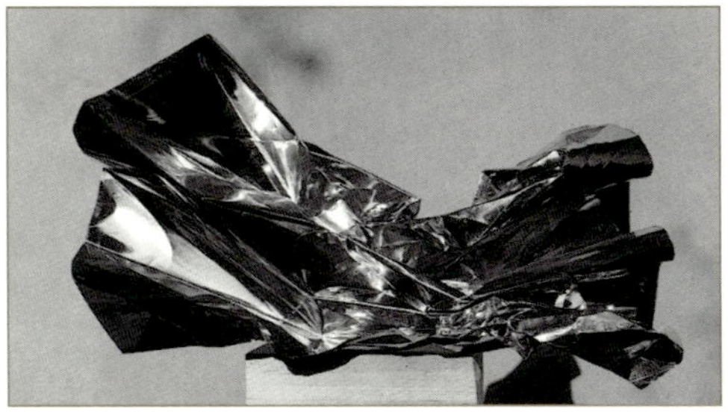

In 1965, on sabbatical leave in San Miguel de Allende in Mexico, Zach found a supply of zinc sheeting, which he crumpled into forms such as *Cloud Shape* (1964-1965; Figure 49). Zach wrote to a friend, "I had planned not to work here in Mexico–just observe and see as much as possible of historic remains. But I could not resist working. The fabulous clouds in this vicinity allow me no choice. I have limited myself to a strict discipline–sheets of metal and one tool, a hammer. I have worked a few pieces of wood with only one file and a penknife. About 20 pieces will be presented here, the result of that effort. Floating shapes!"[93] In April 1965 his exhibition of hanging metal cloud forms opened at the National Institute of Fine Arts in San Miguel de Allende.

1965

FIGURE 49

Jan Zach. *Cloud Shape.* 1964-1965. Zinc. 3' wide. Location unknown. Photograph by R. Brooks, San Miguel de Allende, Mexico. Hallie Ford Museum of Art, Willamette University, Salem, Oregon. Judith and Jan Zach Archives.

Discovering Stainless Steel

Returning to Oregon, Zach determined that the sheet metal most suitable for his purposes was stainless steel–flexible, resilient, reflective, dazzling to the eye. This material was regularly used by the American sculptor David Smith and by others as early as the 1950s, but in Smith's case he employed rigid planes of stainless that he welded to one another to form such works as those in his *Sentinel* series (1956-1961) and *Cubi* series (1963-1965). Zach first used stainless steel in his *Windflower*, No. 1 (1967; Figure 50), which employs the medium in thin, flexible sheets that Zach riveted rather than welded to create his shapes. His works in this medium thus differ significantly from Smith's, both in technique and resulting form. The earliest of a beautiful series of stainless steel flowers, draperies, clouds, and even frost that became Zach's signature pieces of his mature period, *Windflower* was shown at the Seattle Art Museum Pavilion in 1967 in a Pacific Northwest sculptors' invitational and then shipped to Toronto for "Sculpture '67," an exhibition of work by fifty-two (chosen from 250) Canadian sculptors organized to coincide with "Expo '67," the world's fair in Montreal. *Windflower* was damaged in Toronto (by children thinking it was a carousel) but repaired and exhibited again in 1968 at "Oregon Sculpture '68" at the Equitable Plaza in Portland.

The children were right, in a way. *Windflower*, the first of Zach's stainless steel sculptures, was designed to revolve like a carousel on a central pin and, with its ribbony loops of gleaming stainless steel, certainly had the festive gaiety of a carousel, albeit an extremely elegant one. A kinetic sculpture activated by the wind, it revolved and shimmered in space, reflecting and abstracting light, clouds, foliage, and everything else around it in its mirror surfaces. It carried to a new level of sophistication and potential ideas that had interested Zach since 1951, when he made his *Light Sculpture* (see Figure 32) of small segments of aluminum connected by wires.

Zach now envisioned a vast experimental sculpture of suspended stainless steel forms. Because of the high cost of materials, he wrote to the Republic Steel Corporation in Cleveland, Ohio, asking for a donation of stainless steel. In September 1967, Zach received a letter from the advertising director stating that while the "meritorious but slightly out of the ordinary" request had temporarily stymied company officials, Republic Steel was now prepared to supply the material if Zach would allow his working process with the steel to be photographed for advertising purposes.[94] With the donation of materials and a grant from the Development Fund of the University of Oregon, Zach, assisted by four graduate students,[95] proceeded to erect an astonishing project in the summer and fall of 1968.

By July 22, "the ground was cleared, four telephone poles erected, and the area covered with ample sawdust to protect very large sheets of stainless steel. Everything is in order and in progress with his massive sculpting."[96] *Sculpture in Suspension* (Figure 51) was made up

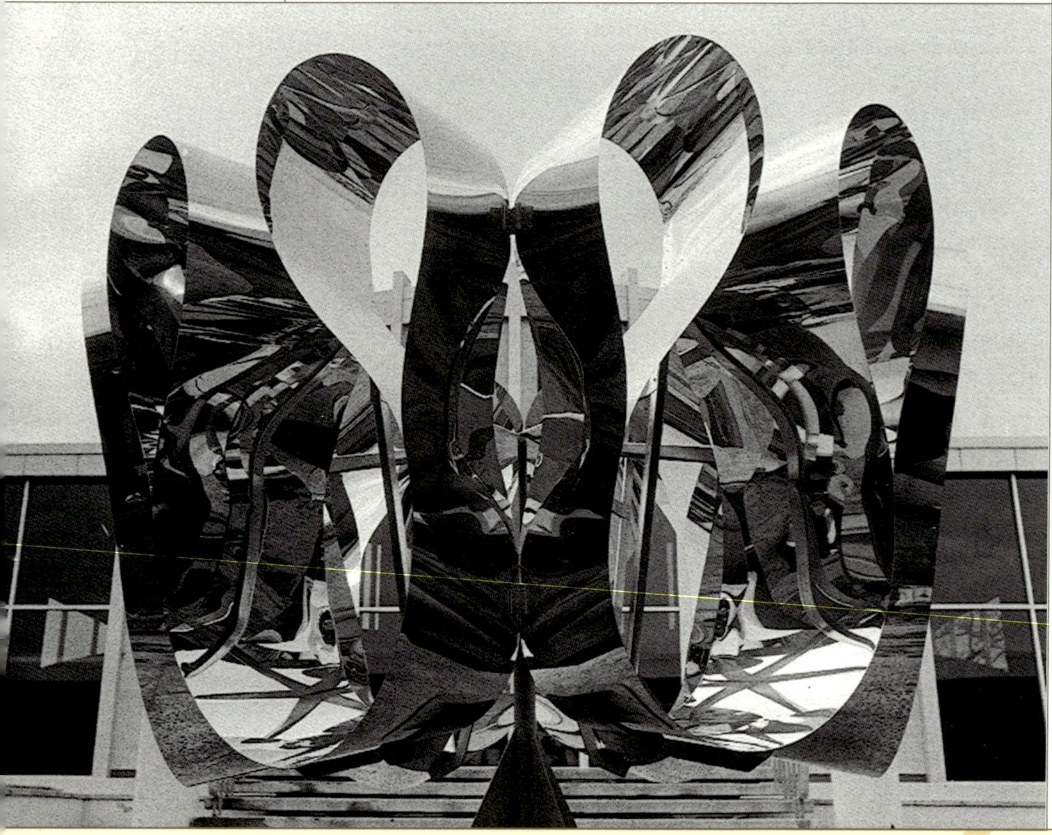

FIGURE 50

Jan Zach. *Windflower*, No.1. 1967. Stainless steel. 7 x 12' (circumfrence 27'). The work was made for the exhibition "Sculpture '67" in Toronto, sponsored by the National Gallery of Canada, Ottawa. Zach shipped the work packed in seven boxes, which together weighed over 900 pounds. Collection of Judith Zach, Elmira, Oregon. Photograph Hallie Ford Museum of Art, Willamette University, Salem, Oregon. Judith and Jan Zach Archives.

1968

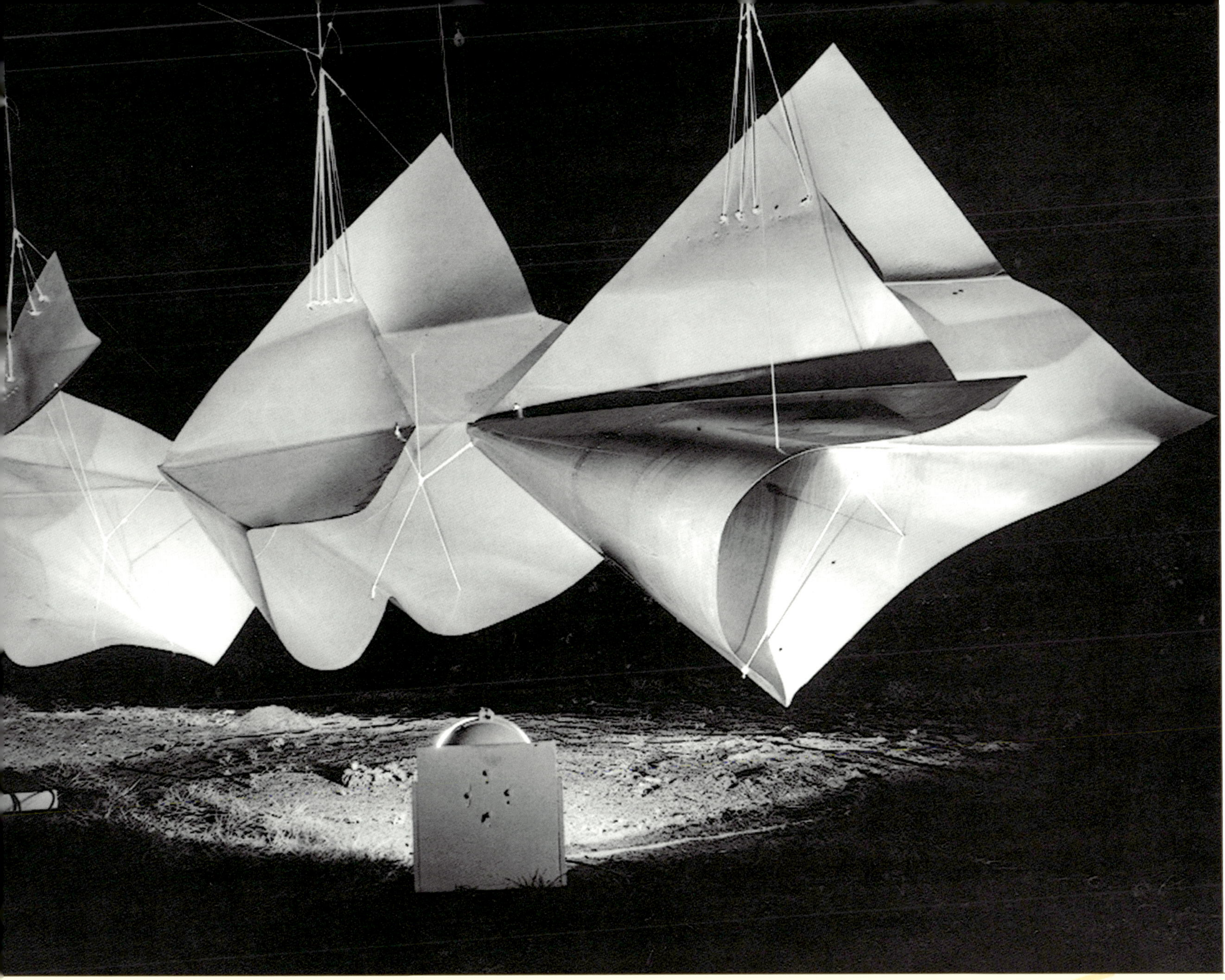

FIGURE 51

Jan Zach. *Sculpture in Suspension.* 1968. Stainless steel shapes, each 25 x 16′, suspended from four telephone poles, each 40′. The work was installed on land adjacent to Zach's studio on East Thirtieth Avenue in Eugene and dismantled when the Zachs moved to Elmira in 1970. Collection of Judith Zach, Elmira, Oregon. Photograph Hallie Ford Museum of Art, Willamette University, Salem, Oregon. Judith and Jan Zach Archives.

1967

three hanging stainless steel folded forms, each made from two strips of stainless steel twenty feet long by five feet wide. For each of the three units, the two sheets of steel were riveted together and, by means of specially devised wooden clamps, folded into shapes that resembled free-form pods or pockets, each open at one end. They were suspended by plastic cables between four telephone poles forty feet high, the whole structure stabilized by steel cables and nylon ropes. The installation occupied an area measuring one hundred by eighty feet adjacent to Zach's studio on East Thirtieth Avenue. Rather than the brilliantly polished Republic Enduro steel he had used in *Windflower, No. 1* the year before, he chose the less shiny Republic Steel Rockwell B, preferring its "silvery-frosted surface" upon which "reflections react . . . in a completely different way." The steel had been "re-softened" for Zach's use, allowing it to be folded without cracking.

The piece had the qualities of enormous wind chimes, the bent and curving stainless steel pods operating like bells colliding in the wind currents and emitting low booming sounds. "Stainless steel sculpture has acoustic qualities which I would like to explore," he wrote during the planning stages for *Sculpture in Suspension*.

"The concept of a life within the sculpture could be created by the introduction of sounds (produced, perhaps, by the stainless wires which will hold the shape together, combined with an electronic device, or by the wooden hammers of an old piano)." [97] The rumbling tones that his suspended forms did emit were oddly appropriate to their cloud-like and vaporous shapes, man-made counterparts to colliding atmospheric forces.

With their vapor-like forms, they may have resonated in Zach's mind with Pešánek's neon-rimmed clouds proposed for the façade of the Bat'a Department Store in Prague (Figure 4). The Baroque (roughly translated as "misshapen") masses of Zach's *Sculpture in Suspension*, defying the laws of gravity, also may have called to mind the vaulted interiors of Prague's Baroque churches, where in painting and sculpture massive forms seemed suspended and soaring in space.

While working on *Sculpture in Suspension* during 1968, Zach undertook a series of smaller stainless steel sculptures each entitled *Flower of Freedom*, creating seven in all "in homage to those who died for freedom and who are living for it" [98] and therefore of great symbolic importance to Zach. They were important to his development as a sculptor because they involved a new and particularly beautiful use of stainless steel. Zach referred to these works as "modular sculptures which, by articulation and reassembly, can be made to create an infinite variety of shapes." Each is a cluster of units or modules of identically contoured sheets of stainless steel. *Flower of Freedom*, No. 1 (1968; Figure 52), for instance, measuring three feet in each direction, is an assembly of concave, interchangeable parts that produce a densely petaled gleaming "flower" of remarkable beauty. The highly polished stainless steel creates exquisite effects of reflected and counter-reflected light. *Flower of Freedom*, No. 6 (1968; Figure 53), measuring seven by nine feet, is composed of modules with curving and voluptuous contours that suggest a more blossomy flower than the tightly budded Number 1. *Flower of Freedom*, No. 7 (1968; Figure 54) measures five by five feet in lateral directions but stands eight feet high. Its vertically arranged modules flare open at the center from tightly tapering points at the top and bottom. Because of its proportions, it is more anthropomorphic than some of the others and stands as an ancestress to *Lady* (Figures 71, 72), a monumental work left in planning stages at the time of Zach's death in 1986.

Six of the *Flower of Freedom* series were included in the exhibition "Jan Zach: Recent Works" at the Portland Art Museum in April 1969, the major Portland exhibition of his career. Also exhibited was *Windflower, No. 1* and *Windflower, No. 2* (1967), and other stainless steel works, including one entitled *Continuous Shape* (1968; see Figure 55), which the

Figure 52 [opposite page]

Jan Zach. *Flower of Freedom*, No.1. 1968. Stainless steel. 3 x 3 x 3'. Museum of Art, University of Oregon, Eugene, Oregon. Photograph by Nolph Studio, Eugene. Hallie Ford Museum of Art, Willamette University, Salem, Oregon. Judith and Jan Zach Archives.

1968

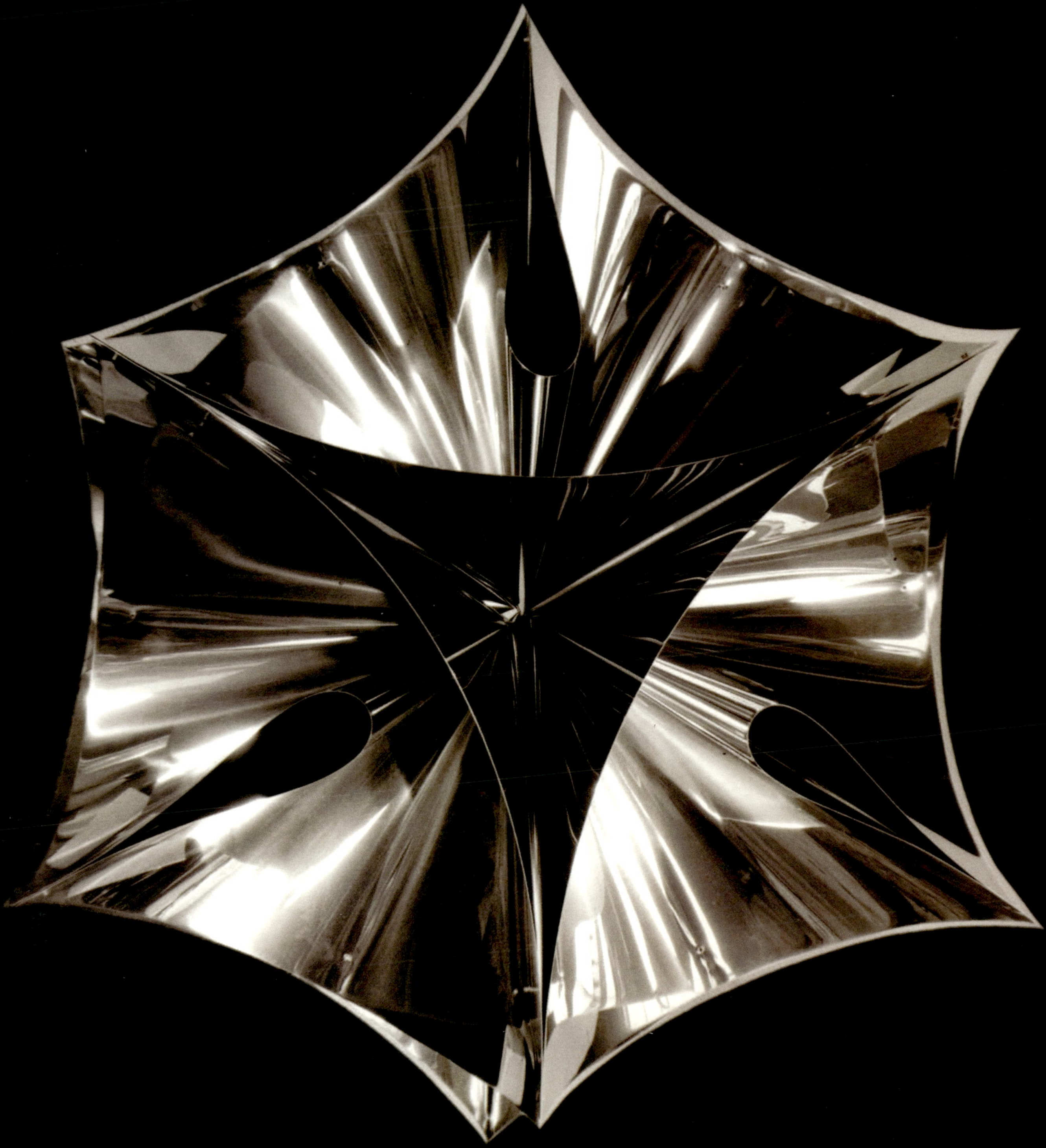

viewer could set in motion by manipulating a system of wooden levers. The show included two wooden sculptures and one aluminum cast, but the emphasis was on Zach's recent work in his new medium of stainless steel. "Though at first glance so different from his earlier works these sulptures still link insights derived directly from the material itself with an intense preoccupation with Nature," the curator Rachael Griffin wrote in the exhibition catalogue. "The broad ribbons of shining metal reflect, not the slow alteration of stone or growth of trees, but rather nature's continuous flow and movement."[99] The *Oregonian*'s staff writer Beth Fagan wrote of Zach's "forms that seem to weightlessly float – forms collecting and collating space and light with space that seems to be moving from deep within."[100]

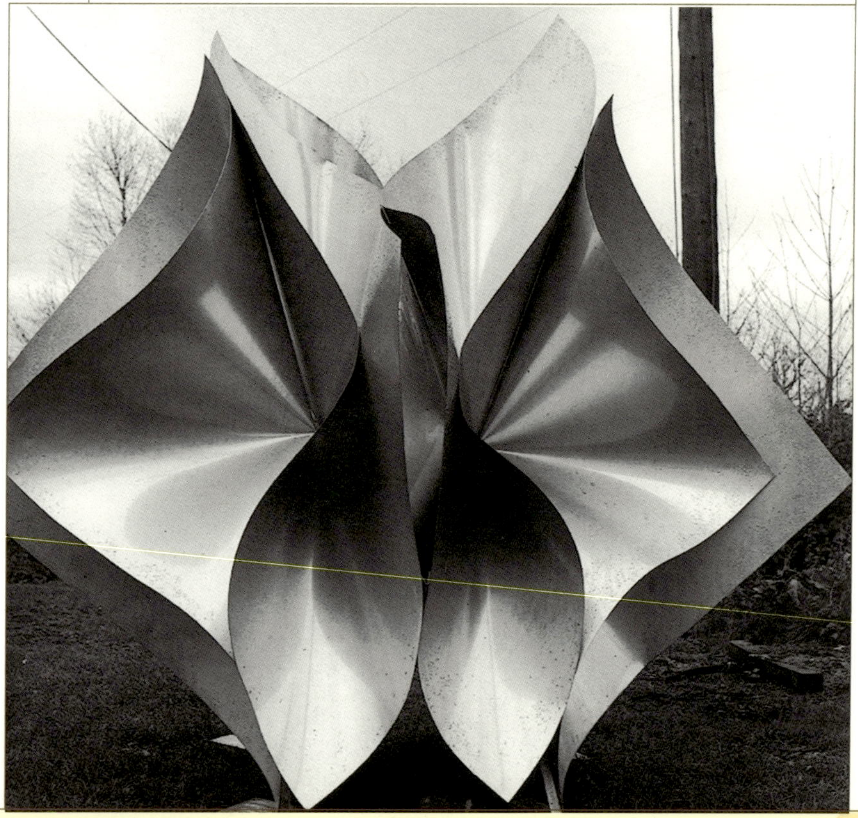

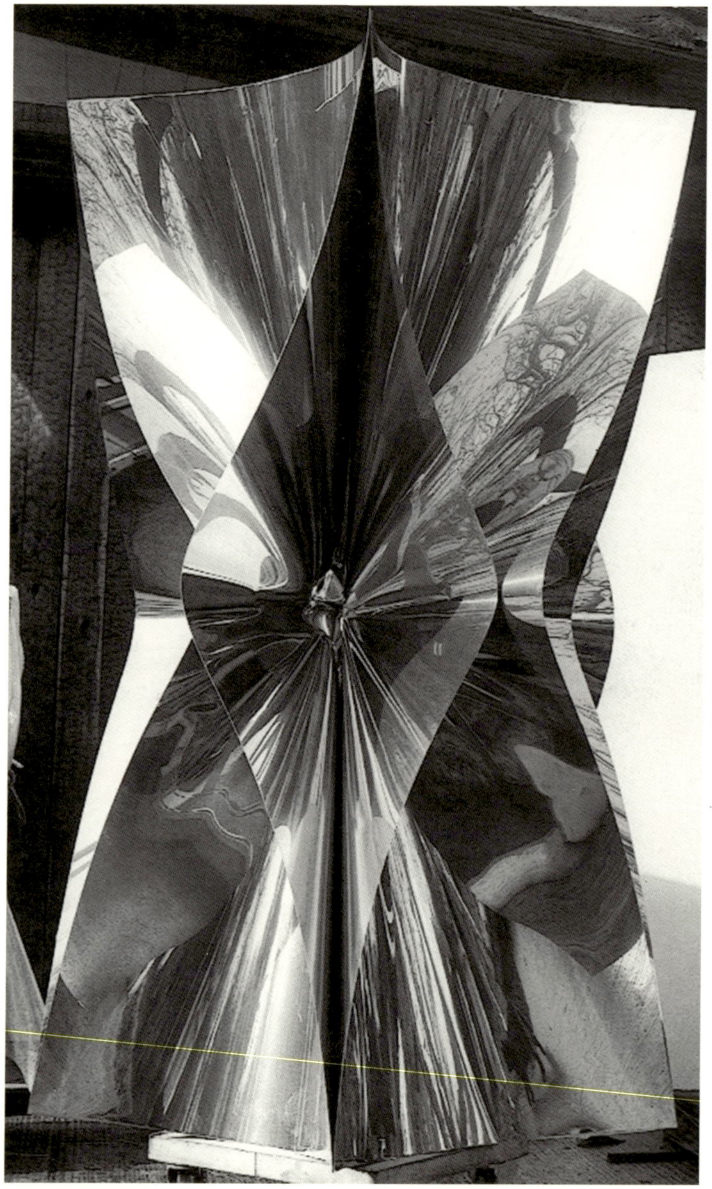

Figure 53

Jan Zach. *Flower of Freedom*, No.6. 1968. Stainless steel. 7 x 9'. Location unknown. Photograph by Judith Zach. Hallie Ford Museum of Art, Willamette University, Salem, Oregon. Judith and Jan Zach Archives.

Figure 54

Jan Zach. *Flower of Freedom*, No.7. 1968. Stainless steel. 8 x 5 x 5'. Location unknown. Photograph by Judith Zach. Hallie Ford Museum of Art, Willamette University, Salem, Oregon. Judith and Jan Zach Archives.

1968

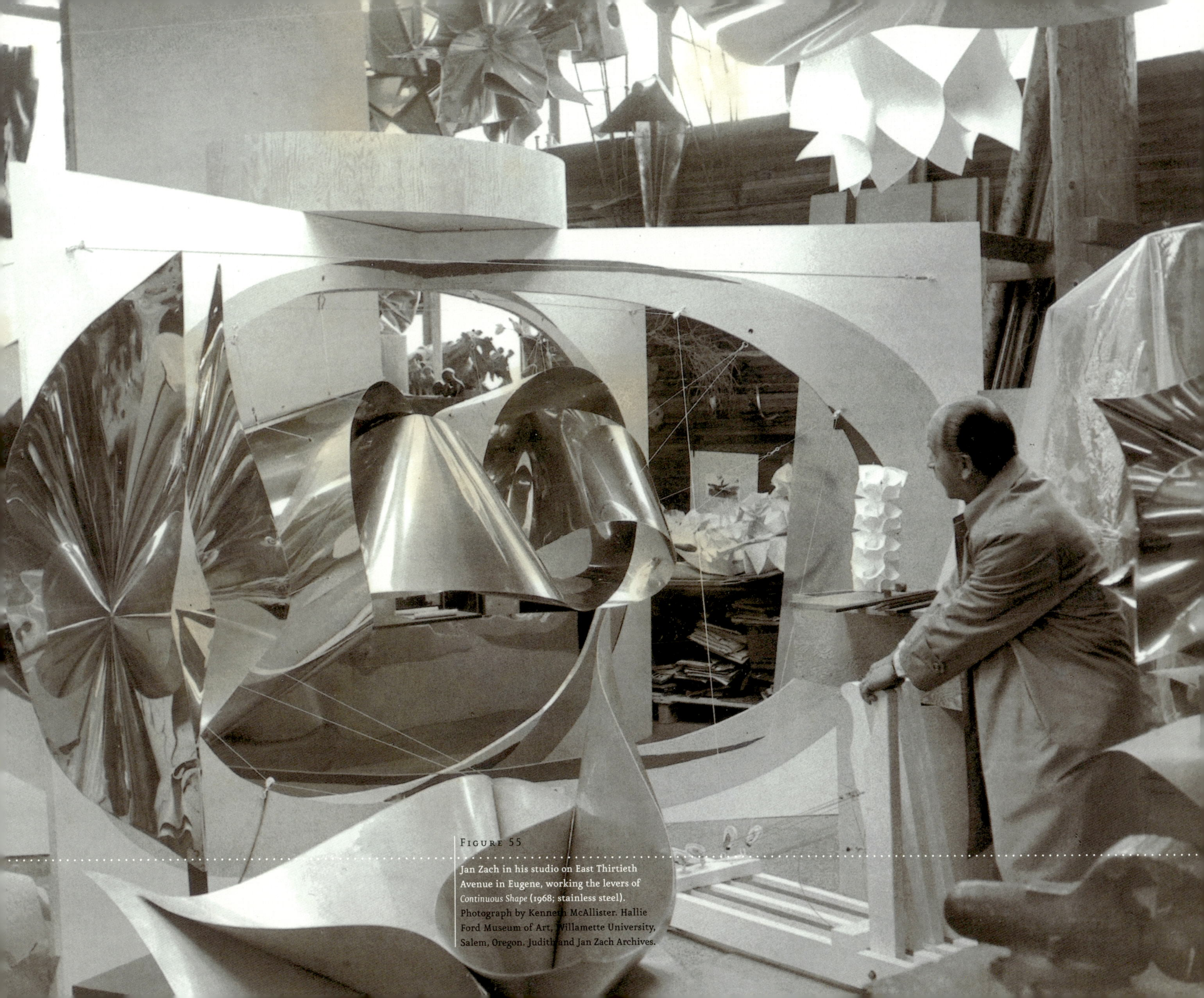

FIGURE 55

Jan Zach in his studio on East Thirtieth Avenue in Eugene, working the levers of *Continuous Shape* (1968; stainless steel). Photograph by Kenneth McAllister. Hallie Ford Museum of Art, Willamette University, Salem, Oregon. Judith and Jan Zach Archives.

Can-Can

Intrigued by the petal-like modules that he was assembling and reassembling in the *Flower of Freedom* series, Zach made sketches for a sculpture that would incorporate "several of my flower-like modular objects mounted on a central pole." The result of these drawings, thanks to a major commission, was the majestic and ill-fated *Can-Can* (see Figures 56-59). "The commission came at the right moment, for I was ready." It was from the Meier and Frank Company for its new department store at the Valley River Center in Eugene, designed by Raymond Loewy and William Snaith of New York. Envisioned was a major sculpture for the entrance rotunda sixty feet in diameter and eighty-two feet high. It was the commission of a lifetime for Zach: it asked for a major, ambitious work on a large scale; it came at a time when his ideas and concepts prepared him to create a dazzling kinetic showpiece; it involved architectural scale and collaborative work with an architectural firm; it inserted art into the marketplace, the world of commerce and daily life; above all, it was well-funded. *Can-Can* embodied Zach's fast breaking ideas and positioned them in a public, commercial space–marrying art and modern life in the way he had seen in Prague. The commission allowed Zach to create the single most important work of his career. *Can-Can* was a fifty-foot high motorized kinetic sculpture of great elegance, an exotic indoor tree with graceful stainless steel leaves (or "flowers, miniskirts or tutus of ballerinas,"[101] Zach said) or parasols or fan blades. It possessed feminine grace and technological virility. Zach considered *Can-Can* to be the culmination of thirty years of experimentation with kinetic movement in sculpture and with sheet metal as a medium.

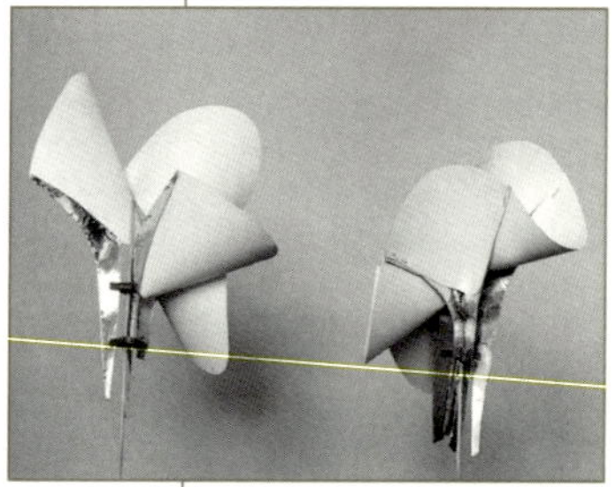

Structurally, *Can-Can* was built around a central pole, an eight-inch steel pipe that rose thirty-four feet in height and was welded to a steel plate bolted to the cement floor. Attached to the pole at the middle and top were two rotating mechanisms each made of two discs four feet in diameter mounted with ball bearings. To each of the rotating spools were bolted seven boomerang-shaped ribs that supported the curving membranes of sheet stainless steel. These flowers or leaves, which were as big as twenty-four by sixteen feet, were made of three to five triangles of steel riveted together. Overall, *Can-Can* was fifty feet high and twenty feet in diameter. Zach designed the sculpture so that the planes would turn easily on their ball bearing discs, but natural air current was insufficient and motors were installed to move the discs in opposite directions in a random program.[102]

Like its immediate predecessors, *Windflower* and the *Flower of Freedom* series, the lovely *Can-Can* reflected and re-reflected its surroundings, which included the twenty dark ribs of the rotunda. The reflected ribs became shimmering, moving stripes on the sculpture's surfaces, which also picked up and transformed the colors of the merchandise in the store. *Can-Can* was seen not only from the ground floor but also from the mezzanine at approximately the level of the lower rotating spool and "leaves." While customers shopped beneath the canopy of this great tree or beside its branches on the mezzanine, it moved in stately leisure as in a slowly choreographed dance celebrating commerce and the joy of shopping in a free economy. "As the piece did its slowly motorized pirouette in the part of the center set aside from the kachung of cash registers, its stainless steel wings caught the reflections of the surroundings and passersby, melding them into images of a revolving oneness," wrote the artist Ken Paul. "The upward lift of the work echoed one's own human form, and you could see yourself compressed into that other immaterial world."[103]

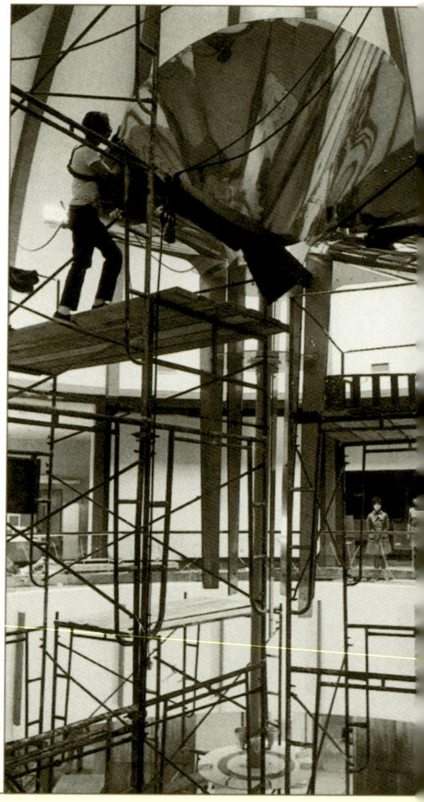

Windflower, *Sculpture in Suspension*, the *Flower of Freedom* series, and *Can-Can* made up a ground-breaking sequence of works in Jan Zach's development as a sculptor. In *Windflower*, he worked with stainless steel for the first time, introducing a medium that suffused his work with light, important to Zach from his earliest

FIGURE 56

Jan Zach. Maquettes for *Can-Can*. c. 1968. Folded paper, staples, and other materials. Hallie Ford Museum of Art, Willamette University, Salem, Oregon. Judith and Jan Zach Collection.

FIGURE 57

Jan Zach. *Can-Can* (during instllation, 1969). 1968-1969. Stainless steel with motorized components. 50 x 20'. Rotunda, Meier and Frank Company, Valley River Center, Eugene, Oregon (Raymond Loewy and William Snaith, architects). Photograph by Jacob B. Brookins Hallie Ford Museum of Art, Willamette University, Salem, Oregon. Judith and Jan Zach Archives.

1969

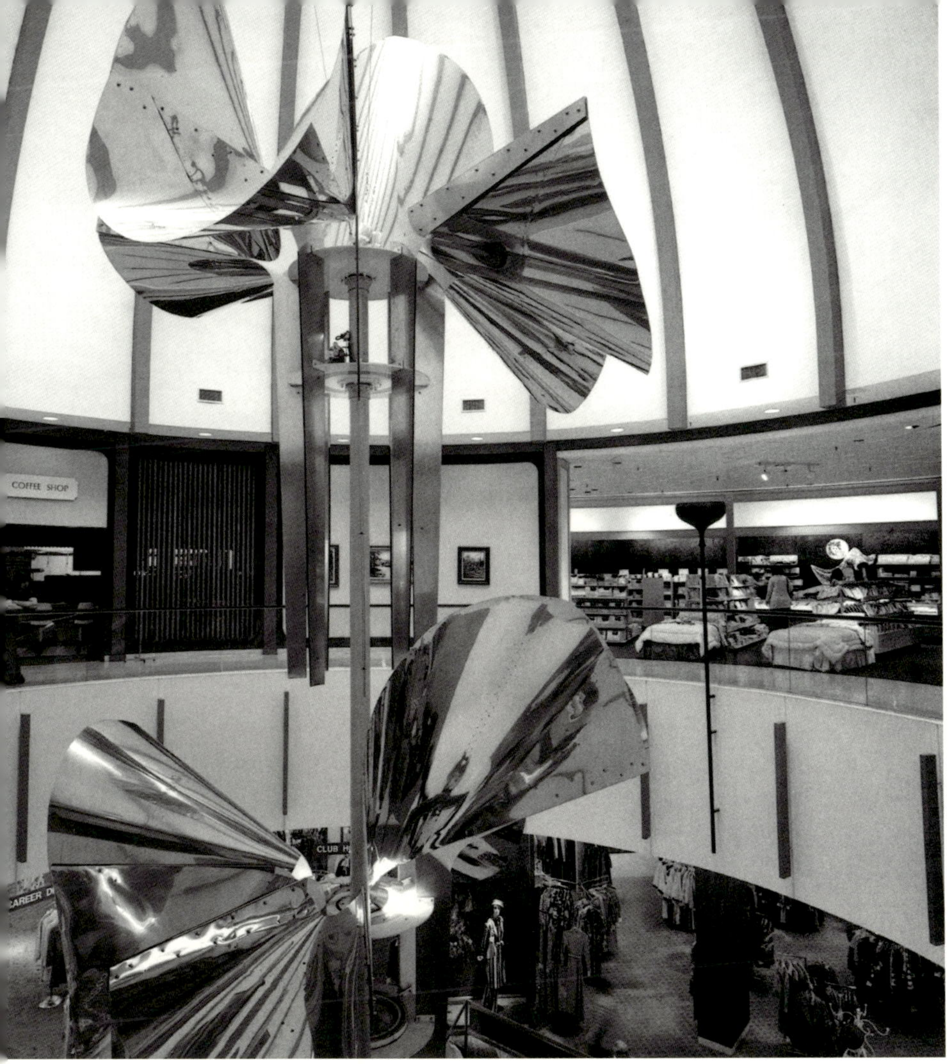

While customers shopped beneath the canopy of this great tree or beside its branches on the mezzanine, it moved in stately leisure as in a slowly choreographed dance....

days of thinking about sculpture in Prague, and that was light-weight enough to rotate in the wind, thereby assuring movement, the fourth dimension that so intrigued him. *Sculpture in Suspension*, though primarily an experiment not seen by many, allowed Zach to demonstrate the use of stainless steel on a monumental scale, to dispense entirely with a sculptural base or plinth (in this, he was concerned with one of the major issues of modern sculpture), and to consider the element of sound in sculpture. In the *Flower of Freedom* sculptures, Zach demonstrated a new level of sophistication by incorporating light into sculpture and employing stainless steel to create exquisite form. *Can-Can* combined elements of *Windflower* and *Sculpture in Suspension* with formal ideas derived from his *Flower of Freedom* series. All these works were made within the period 1967-1970–arguably the most intensely creative and productive three years of Zach's life as an artist. In 1966 he had been promoted to the rank of full professor at the University of Oregon, and his reputation as a fine teacher grew in tandem with his increasing reputation as an important sculptor.

With proceeds from *Can-Can*, said to have been $35,000.00, the Zachs were able to acquire seven and a half acres on a hill west of Eugene in Elmira and to build a house with an attached, high-ceilinged studio. They moved there in July 1970, eventually building a second studio and also a stable for Judith's horses. She owned two and for a time boarded a third. Jan said that the area around Elmira with its rolling hills, small farms, and narrow roads reminded him of Czechoslovakia. Settling in the countryside paralleled the Zachs' move from Rio to the *Fazenda Penedo*, and in some ways Elmira was a new Eden in which Jan worked productively for the last sixteen years of his life. One of the problems of moving from East Thirtieth Avenue, however, was the huge task of moving Zach's sculptures. Particularly problematic was the dismantling of *Sculpture in Suspension*, which was never reinstalled even though Zach hoped to find a permanent location for it. It lies overgrown with blackberry and other vegetation in a wooded area on the Elmira property. Also in decrepit condition is *Windflower*, entangled in blackberry vine outside Zach's studio. It was installed there in the early 1970s in repaired condition (after being damaged by the children in Toronto) but has been damaged anew by

FIGURE 58

Jan Zach. *Can-Can.* 1968-1969. Stainless steel with motorized components. 50 x 20'. Rotunda, Meier and Frank Company, Valley River Center, Eugene, Oregon. Destroyed 1989. Photograph by Jacob B. Brookins. Hallie Ford Museum of Art, Willamette University, Salem, Oregon. Judith and Jan Zach Archives.

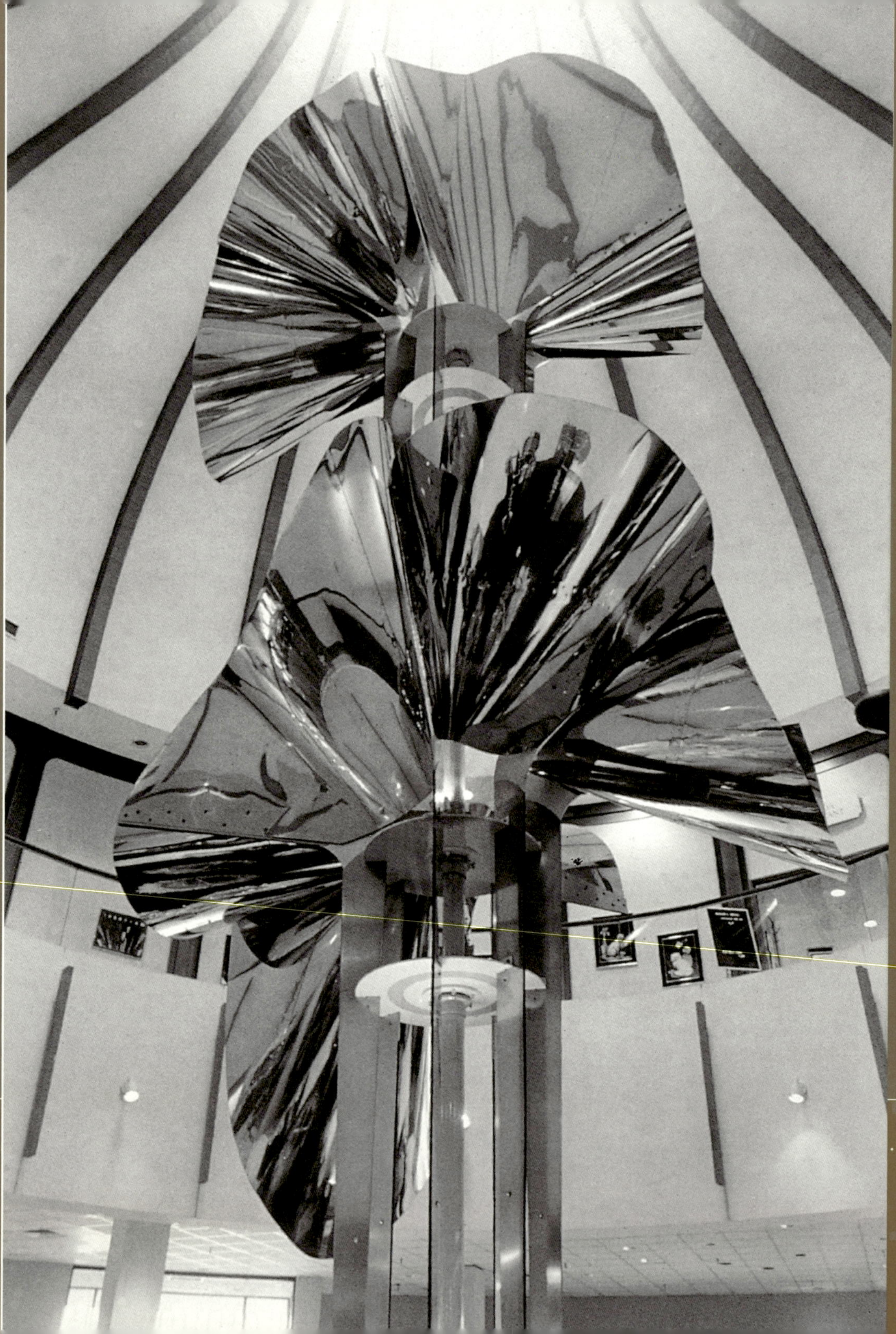

Zach considered Can-Can to be the culmination of thirty years of experimentation with kinetic movement in sculpture and with sheet metal as a medium.

1970

time, wind, weather, and the aggressive vegetation of Oregon. With the possible exception of *Sculpture in Suspension*, Zach's stainless pieces cannot withstand permanent outdoor display. Because of their thin steel sheeting, quivering forms, and shiny surfaces that are most effective when they are polished, dust free, and gleaming, like most exquisite objects they require enclosure. In this sense, *Can-Can* was well situated.

But despite Zach's fascination with Pešánek and the union between the artistic and the commercial, a commercial environment poses its own dangers for art. During a remodeling of the Meier and Frank store in 1989, three years after Zach's death, *Can-Can* was dismantled and junked. "Meier & Frank treated *Can-Can* like a window display–something to be discarded as soon as its commercial usefulness was perceived to have been exhausted," wrote Jackman Wilson. "Hippocrates observed that life is short, art long. He might have had to qualify that statement if he were alive today, when the permanence of public artworks is uncertain."[104]

Meier and Frank decided to remove the sculpture a year before actually doing so and contacted several individuals (but not Judith Zach) in Portland and Eugene asking for suggestions for relocating *Can-Can*. One of the persons queried was Tommy Griffin, the exhibition curator at the University of Oregon Museum of Art and the friend and former student of Zach. "I made several calls myself and I believed that the seeds were planted," Griffin told the *Oregonian*. "Then, I learned out of the blue that the work had been destroyed."[105] In the same article, Judith Zach was quoted as saying, "Company officials didn't even have enough imagination to save it or disassemble it. It's almost beyond belief." But like *Sculpture in Suspension*, *Can-Can* was perhaps unmovable in any practical sense. It was a site-specific work that was delicate and fragile despite its monumentality. Its survival depended on being permanently installed so that its thin membranes were suspended in the air, not bent and creased in a moving van or against the floors and walls of a storage room. The best thing for *Can-Can* and for the legacy of Jan Zach would have been to keep it in place in the store at the Valley River Center in spite of the fact that "one local power shopper described it as 'an oversize Christmas ornament'"[106] and that it probably collected dust. (As Zachary Hull has pointed out, Zach must have realized from Pešánek's experiences in Prague that a commercial environment is an unstable one, prone to "destruction and reconstruction" at almost a moment's notice.[107]) In any event, *Can-Can* was a landmark in a number of ways, certainly within the landscape of Zach's career and in the history of Oregon sculpture. It was Zach's single most important work, and with its destruction "the world has lost something very distinctive," said Judith Zach.

Establishing the National Sculpture Center

Can-Can's fate was the result of various factors, not the least of them being an undeveloped awareness in Oregon and much of the United States of the nature of sculpture and the role it might play in civic life. Zach himself had worked tirelessly to raise public consciousness about sculpture and its cultural importance. In 1966, he helped found the National Sculpture Information Center, which became known as the National Sculpture Center and later, at Zach's suggestion, the International Sculpture Center, which exists to this day and publishes the highly regarded magazine *Sculpture*. The original National Sculpture Information Center grew out of a series of conferences on bronze casting at the University of Kansas in Lawrence. Zach attended the fourth of these conferences in 1966 and took part in informal discussions about the possibility of establishing an organization for sharing information among sculptors working in all media. Elden C. Tefft, sculpture professor at the University of Kansas, invited Zach and five other sculptors from around the country to join him as members of an advisory committee to write a proposal for the National Sculpture Information Center.

The planners envisioned a center with a library of sources on historic and contemporary sculpture, a special collection of material on new technical information and theoretical ideas about sculpture, an archive of papers, tapes, books, and films, a slide collection of contemporary sculpture, a directory of sculptors, and a national conference to be held every two years. The plan was to establish an on-going forum and information center, to promote a national and even international community of sculptors, and to raise public

Figure 59 [opposite page]

Jan Zach. *Can-Can*. 1968-1969. Stainless steel with motorized components. 50 x 20'. Rotunda, Meier and Frank Company, Valley River Center, Eugene, Oregon. Destroyed 1989. Photograph by Jacob B. Brookins. Hallie Ford Museum of Art, Willamette University, Salem, Oregon. Judith and Jan Zach Archives.

1971

awareness of sculpture and its place in culture. As a member of the advisory committee in 1966 and the Center's board of directors beginning in 1968, Zach worked tirelessly to help plan the biennial conferences, held at the University of Kansas and then, beginning in 1976, in New Orleans, Toronto, and other cities. Zach gave papers and took part in round-table discussions at the conferences on such topics as casting, metals and metal fabrication, and wood as a sculptural medium.

Zach's imagination for epic sculptural projects is conveyed in the published proceedings of these conferences, as in those for 1970 when Zach, on a panel with Richard Stankiewicz, described a project requiring fourteen tons of stainless steel in sheets as big as eighty by sixty feet. "The plan was to set up four bulldozers carrying felt-covered wooden beams in diagonal position. The beams would be attached to the four sides of a large sheet of stainless steel.

The bulldozers would slowly move centerward. The change of speed and direction would be directed by me stationed above. One of the sheets I planned to have two hundred feet long. The resultant shape I planned to suspend in 1967 in front of the Toronto City Hall between high towers and supported by steel cables and a mass of different colored rubber cables (grouped to create the impression of clouds) in constant motion and tension.

At night they would be illuminated by reflectors. Color and light projections would be played over the shapes at night and I also planned to employ sound. Too bad, that dream, that big dream, was not realized."[108] As a board member of the Center, Zach was particularly interested in promoting international participation, and wrote to the embassies of France, Austria, Iran, Ecuador, and other countries asking for the names of sculptors who might be available to represent the various nations at the conferences. At the 1976 conference in New Orleans, Zach introduced and in some cases acted as translator for sculptors from India, Italy, Colombia, Mexico, and other countries.

Zach's involvement in the activities of the National Sculpture Center was just one of many projects that over the years generated an enormous amount of correspondence that would have been impossible for Jan without Judith's skills as stenographer, typist, and writer. Beginning in Brazil, Judith assumed a life-long role of serving as Jan's secretary, publicist, and editor, translating his dictation or scribbled notes into cordial business English that masked his limitations in writing and speaking the language. Some of his long-hand drafts contain short-hand notations by Judith, suggesting that he orally elaborated on his written remarks as she finalized the letters. She kept carbon copies of all correspondence so that his papers provide a remarkably complete archival record from the late 1940s forward.

Zach's involvement with the Sculpture Center provided him with national and international contacts that complemented his own multinational background and career, took advantage of his outgoing personality, and extended his activities to an arena much larger and more cosmopolitan than Oregon and the Pacific Northwest. The opportunity to show a major mature work outside the region came at the National Sculpture Center's conference in 1976 in New Orleans, where he showed his *Flower of Freedom*, No. 7: *Freedom of Expression* (1976) in the International Competition for Sculpture. The juror, Joshua Taylor, director of the National Collection of Fine Arts (now the National Museum of American Art) of the Smithsonian Institution, awarded Zach first prize for this work, a variation of one in his 1968 *Flower of Freedom* series (see Figure 54).

1972

Envisioning the Oregon International Sculpture Symposium

Contacts that Zach made with other sculptors through the National Sculpture Center and its conferences helped him envision and plan a major cultural event in the Pacific Northwest–the Oregon International Sculpture Symposium in Eugene in the summer of 1974. Of all his projects and plans to introduce members of the public to art and promote their engagement with it, none was more ambitious and, indeed, herculean than this symposium, which brought six internationally renowned sculptors to Eugene to make large scale works of art in on-going dialogue with the public. Zach came up with the idea as early as 1970, immediately following his triumphant exhibition at the Portland Art Museum and the installation of his beautiful *Can-Can*, Eugene's most glamorous work of public art, at the Valley River Center. Zach's successes were coming thick and fast, and he was thinking big, as always. His experiences with the National Sculpture Center and its conferences had convinced him that symposia, the gathering of artists to talk about their work and, if possible, demonstrate how they make it, were of incalculable value–to fellow artists, to students, and, he believed, to the public in an era when works of modern public art were proliferating in virtually every American city. His idea for a symposium in Eugene was to identify a panel of internationally recognized experts in the arts who would select the sculptors and invite them to participate. The sculptors would come to Eugene, spend about six weeks creating a large public sculpture in a medium they did not ordinarily employ, and conduct their creative work on site in public, speaking with interested observers and giving at least one talk during their stay. The public works would remain in Eugene or elsewhere in Oregon.

In 1972, Hope Hughes Pressman of Eugene was appointed project director. Francis Newton, director of the Portland Art Museum, was named chair of the selection committee. The other committee members were Fabio Baracloph, publisher of *Sculpture International*; Frank J. Malina, founder and editor of *Leonardo*; Thomas Messer, director of the Guggenheim Museum; David Rhoten, chair of the Oregon Arts Commission; Jacques Schnier, sculptor, professor of art emeritus at the University of California, Berkeley, and chair of the advisory board of the National Sculpture Center; Elden Tefft, director of the National Sculpture Center; and Joshua Taylor, director of the National Collection of Fine Arts. After a thorough process, the committee selected ten sculptors, of whom six were funded to come to Eugene. All were big names in the world of sculpture: Bruce Beasley, California; Roger Bolomey, New York; John Chamberlain, New York; Dimitri Hadzi, New York and Italy; Bernard Rosenthal, New York; and Hugh Townley, Rhode Island. Elza Mayhew, Zach's former student in Victoria who represented Canada in the Venice Biennale in 1964, was one of the original ten but did not participate because of lack of funding, so it was an all-male slate of artists who participated–"a serious oversight," according to the project report. Major funding came from the City of Eugene, the Eugene Urban Renewal Agency, Lane County, the University of Oregon, and the National Endowment for the Arts. The National Endowment, indeed, helped fund several such symposia in cities around the country in an effort to put communities and sculptors in contact and collaboration with one another and to promote the creation of American art for public places.[109]

The Eugene symposium was deemed a success despite problems in publicizing the event, discomfort on the part of some of the artists at working before the gaze of the public, a disappointingly low participation by Oregon and Northwest artists, and the refusal of the City of Bend to accept Townley's concrete abstract forms for its park.

"The lapses and disappointments, however, should in no way diminish the lustre of the project nor the tribute due the man who originated the idea, sculptor Jan Zach," Hope Pressman wrote in the project report, published eleven years later. "Without a doubt, the symposium made a pervasive, creative contribution to the functioning community scene and activity of life in Oregon."[110]

1972

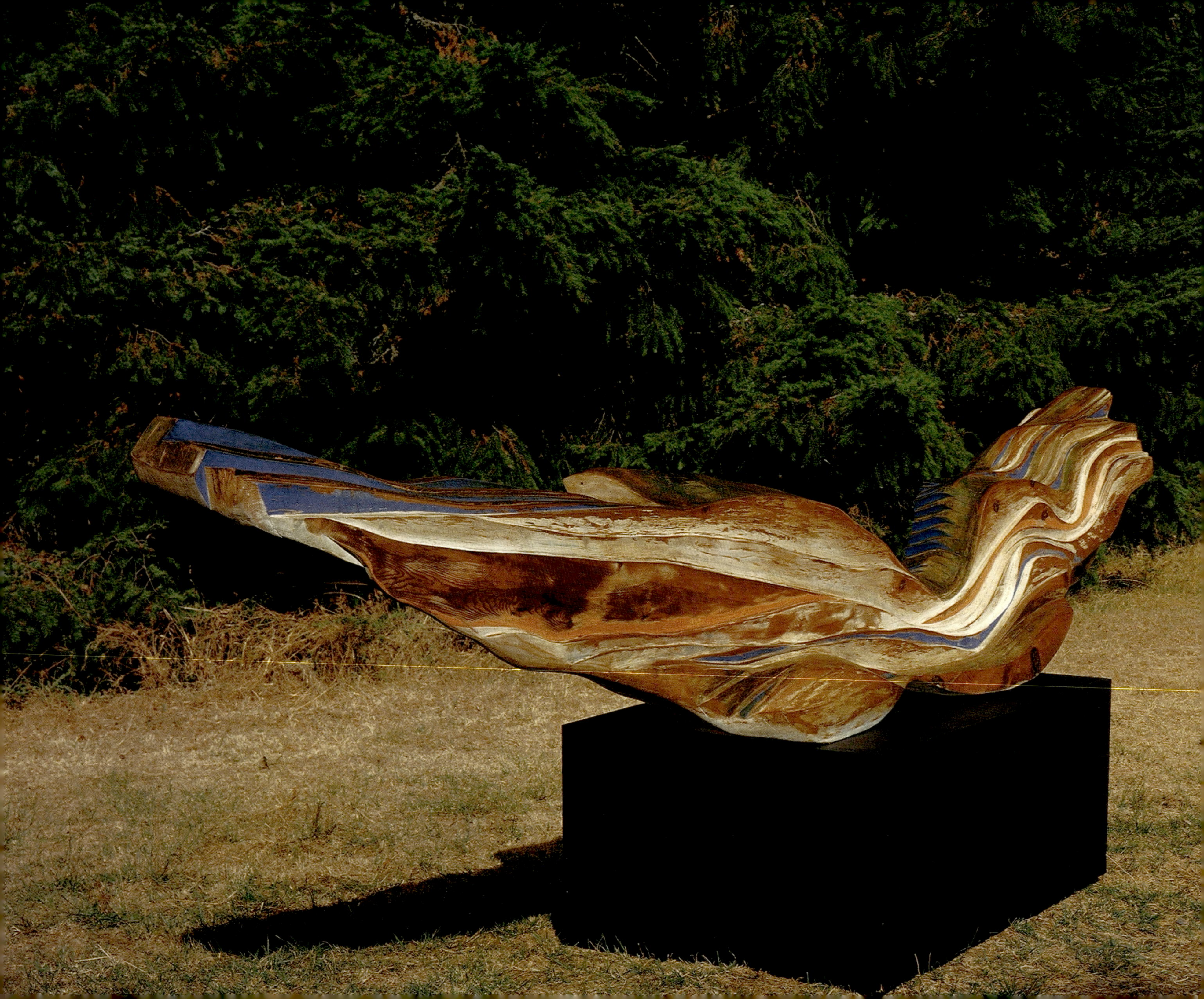

The 1970s and Experiments in Laminated Wood

At about the time that Zach first envisioned the Eugene symposium, he and Judith were buying their property in Elmira and building the new house and studio. In July 1970, they moved from Eugene to the country. If some of Zach's work such as *Sculpture in Suspension* suffered from the move, the stage was set for yet another chapter in his career, and an important element of this chapter was his renewed interest in wood. Such pieces as *Ondine* (1973) and *Drapery of Memory* (1975-1976) are among the major works of Zach's career because of their scale, dramatic forms, and innovative methods of working with wood. Different from his earlier beach log sculptures, the new work in wood incorporated visual and metaphoric elements of the cast aluminum and stainless steel works of the 1960s.

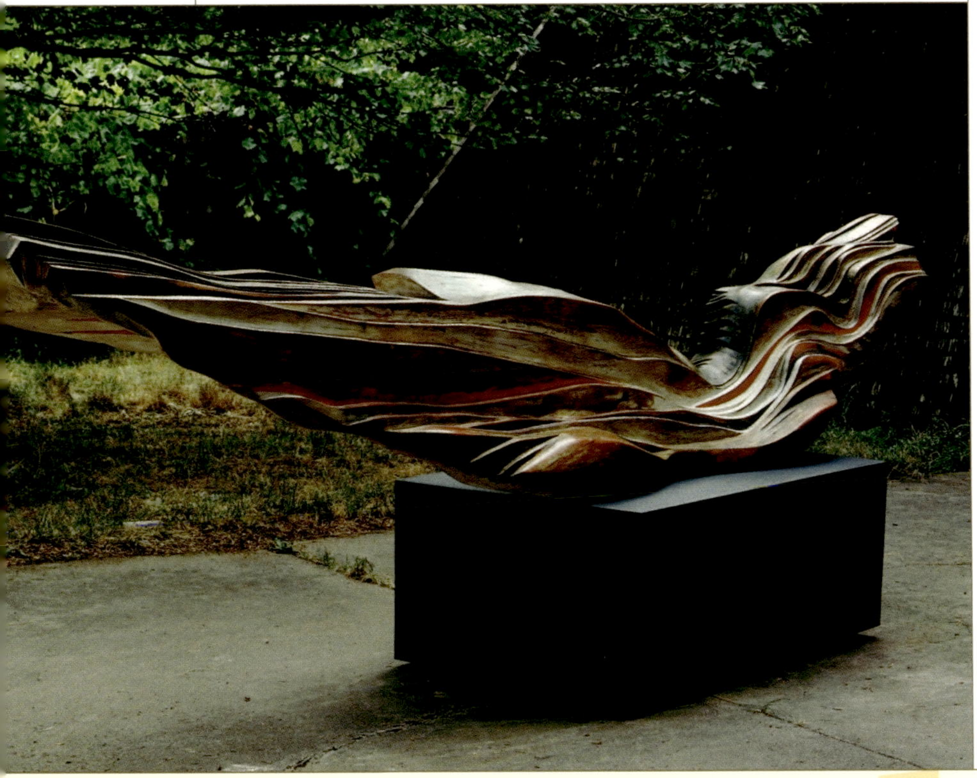

Ondine (Figures 60, 61), with its dramatic fourteen-foot horizontal sweep, is made of long, irregularly contoured pine boards that are laminated to attain the thickness of a log and then carved in order to smooth the transitions between the layered boards. The piece clearly shows the evidence of how it was made, yet appears weathered and time worn in the manner of the beach logs used in Zach's earlier sculpture. In a radical departure from his earlier emphasis on natural effects, he painted traces of blue, red, and white paint onto portions of *Ondine*'s irregular surfaces and then rubbed and sanded the painted areas to enhance the effect of age and patina. *Ondine* floats. While her two wings cantilever upward from a central node and one can imagine this massive thing in flight, in mythology Ondine is a water sprite who cavorts in the sea, and so the floating in question is of the oceanic kind. In the manner of Zach's cast aluminum pieces of the previous decade, *Ondine* is simultaneously the creature and the water she lives in. *The Three Rivers* are the *Three Graces* (Figure 45); *Mermaid* (1960-1961; Figure 46) is both a sinuous female form and a relentless ocean current. The beach log *Venus* (Figure 26) and *Aphrodite* (see Figure 27) made in Victoria also convey the sense of the flowing water that literally helped form the wood and from which, in myth, Venus/Aphrodite had been born. *Ondine* continues Zach's fascination with the world of water as a source of form and meaning in sculpture.

The cast aluminum river figures and mermaid are the cousins of *Ondine* in technical ways, too. The first step in casting the aluminum forms is carving the figures in Sytrofoam; the second step in creating the laminated wood sculptures such as Ondine is carving the surface of the glued-together boards. Both processes involve cutting tools, and both types of work are characterized by the planes and edges that result from carving. The cast aluminum and the laminated wood sculptures share the visual effect of meandering parallel grooves that speak of similar carving processes and imagery of flowing water. Zach created in virtually all media (except, he pointed out, plastic), but a unified vision pervades much of his work, so that materials as different as cast metal and laminated wood result in works of visual affinity and coherence.

Figures 60, 61

Jan Zach. *Ondine.* 1973. Laminated pine, carved and painted. 14' wide.
Collection of Judith Zach, Elmira, Oregon.
Photograph by Sean Poston, 2002.

1973

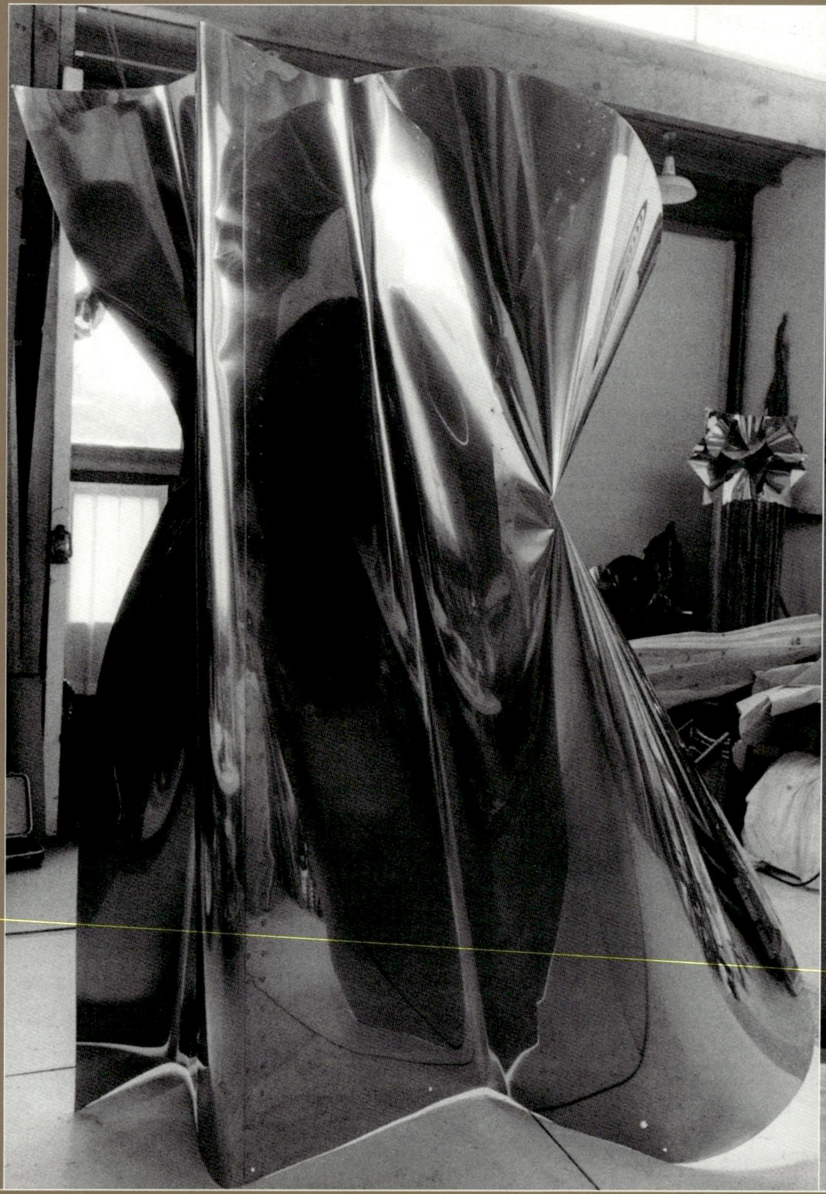

Figure 62

Jan Zach. *Drapery*. 1970-1971. Stainless steel. 10′. Collection of Margaret and David Lederer, Los Angeles, California. Photograph Hallie Ford Museum of Art, Willamette University, Salem, Oregon. Judith and Jan Zach Archives.

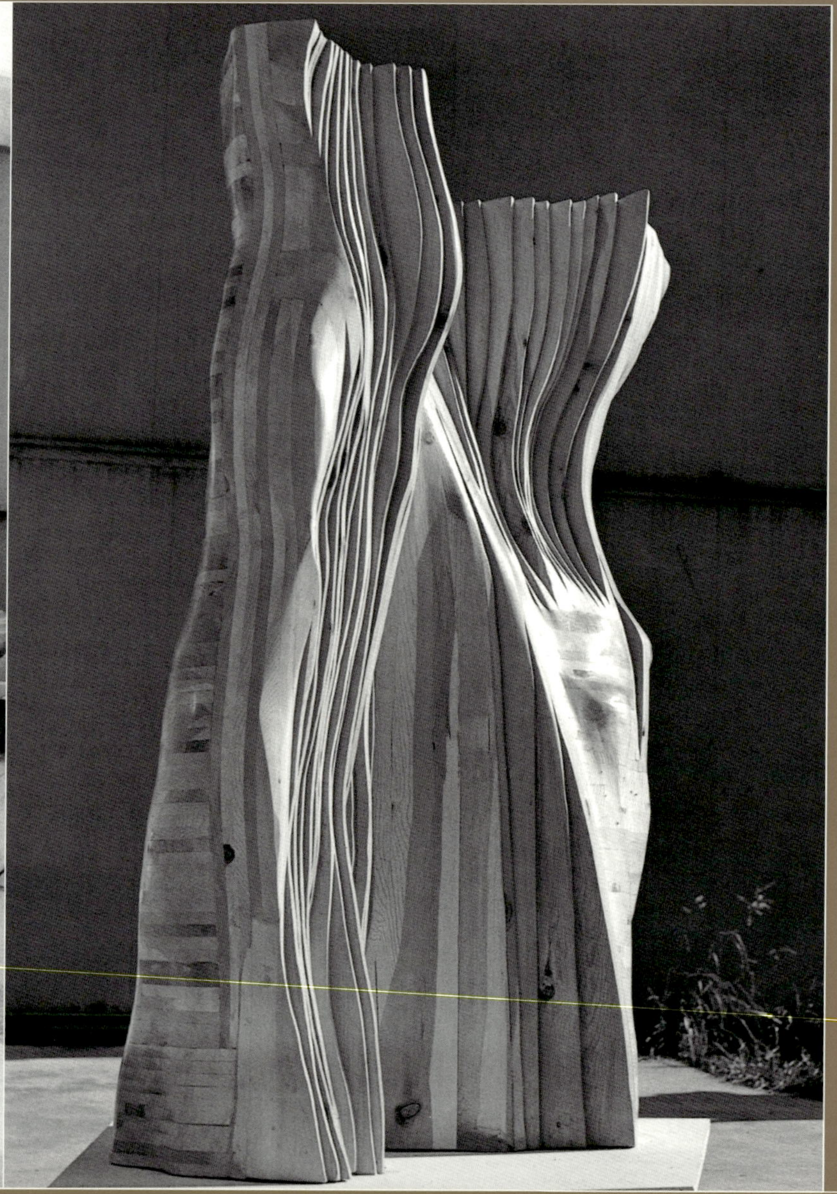

Figure 63

Jan Zach. *Drapery of Memory*. 1975-1976. Laminated and carved pine. 7′. State of Oregon, State Capitol Collection, Salem. Photograph Hallie Ford Museum of Art, Willamette University, Salem, Oregon. Judith and Jan Zach Archives.

This coherence is also apparent in a comparison of Zach's stainless steel and laminated wood sculptures. Consider, for instance, the resonance between *Drapery* (1970-1971; Figure 62), a single sheet of stainless folded to suggest the rush of wind against the gown of a modern Victory of Samothrace, and *Drapery of Memory* (1975-1976; Figure 63), a carved and laminated pine screen of rippling pleats and folds. Approximately of the same proportions, these steel and wood sculptures play off one another not only in their suggestions of flowing draperies but also in their animistic energy. The cast aluminum *Mermaid* (Figure 46) is a direct complement of *Drapery of Memory*, as well. In all three works and indeed in much of Zach's production, his experience designing sets and costumes for the theater and ballet seems to apply. As in classical Greek sculpture, drapery conveys the urgency of human movement and human emotion in Zach's metal and wood sculptures.

Ondine's sweeping breadth is complemented by the soaring height of *Aphrodite* (c. 1974; Figure 64), another laminated wood sculpture created by Zach in the 1970s. A slender, brightly painted spire of a work, this latest of Zach's Venus/Aphrodite figures is fourteen feet tall. The range of effects that Zach could obtain in the laminating process is suggested by comparing *Aphrodite* with such a work as *Phoenix* (1977; Figure 65), made of 300 sheets of marine plywood laminated in the shapes of repeating helixes. Painted orange, this coil of a work is the abstraction of some kind of huge cutting machine. Zach made it partly in order to experiment with plywood and, just as he had persuaded Republic Steel to provide stainless, persuaded a Eugene lumber company (aptly named Bohemia Lumber) to donate the plywood. Zach exhibited *Phoenix* with works by other sculptors at Paolo Soleri's Acrosanti in Arizona, and it remains on view there on extended loan.

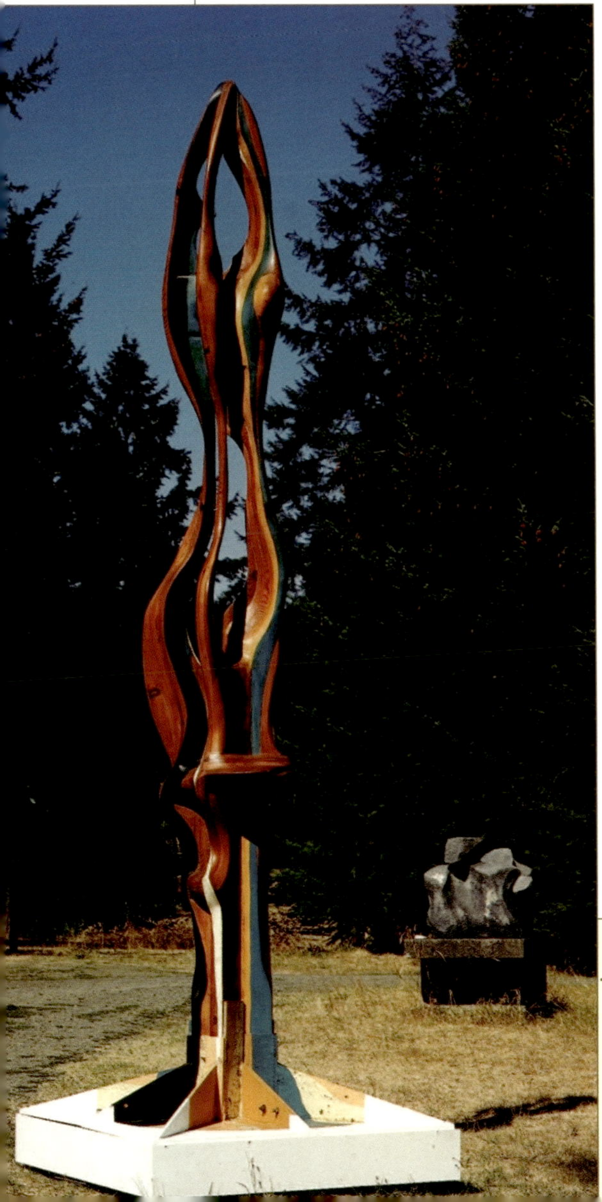

FIGURE 64

Jan Zach. *Aphrodite*. c. 1974. Laminated wood, carved and painted. 14'. Collection of Judith Zach, Elmira, Oregon. Photograph by Sean Poston, 2002.

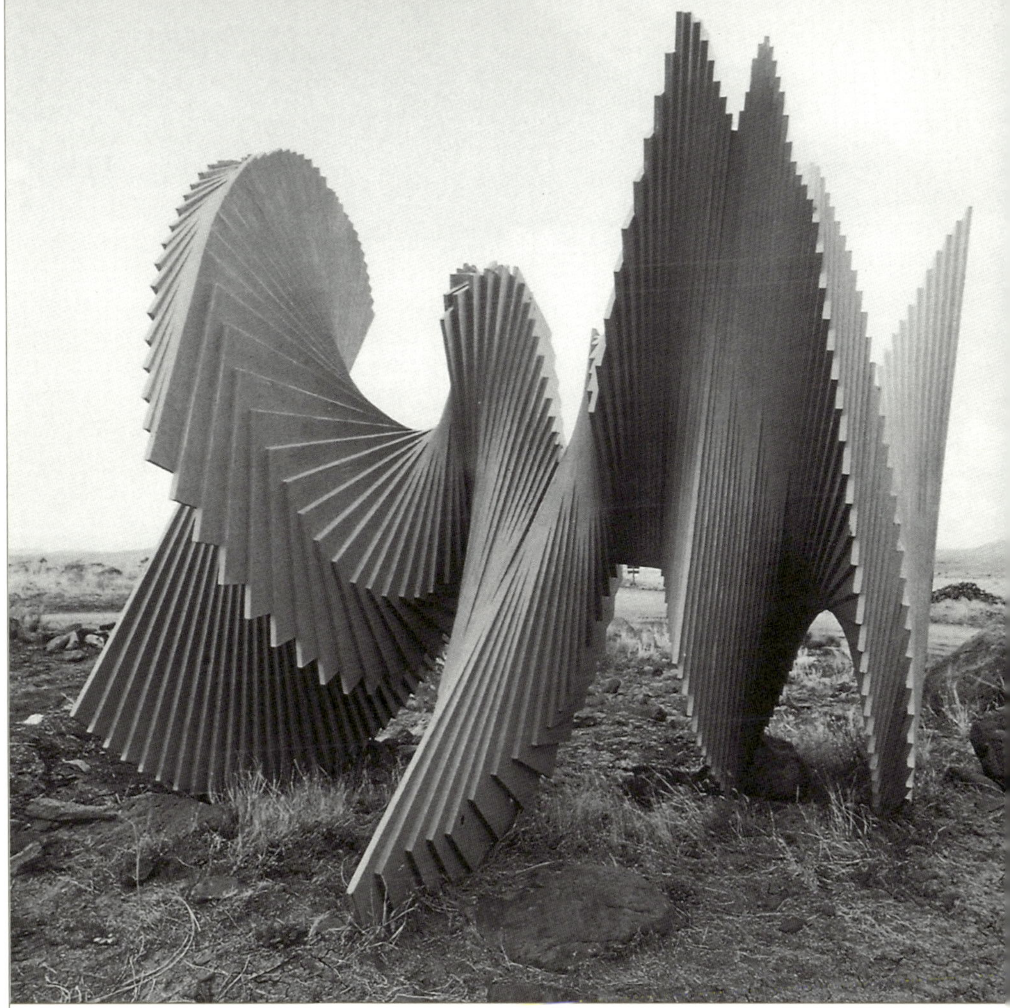

FIGURE 65

Jan Zach. *Phoenix*. 1977. Painted laminated plywood. 11 x 11 x 11'. On permanent loan to Arcosanti, Arizona. Photograph by Jacob B. Brookins. Hallie Ford Museum of Art, Willamette University, Salem, Oregon. Judith and Jan Zach Archives.

1977

Galaxy

Certainly Zach's most ambitious project of the 1970s was *Galaxy* (1977; Figure 66). Commissioned to create a work for the plaza of the new library designed by John Crook for Lower Columbia College in Longview, Washington, Zach took the train to Longview to inspect the site and on the way saw piles of enormous Douglas fir logs. The campus buildings are of low, modern design, and Zach decided to propose a sculpture of great height that would accent the architecture, make dramatic use of Douglas fir indigenous to the Northwest, and honor the Native American totem poles that he had admired since his days in Victoria. His proposal was approved by school officials and by the Washington Arts Commission, which was partly paying for the project with state funds. The Weyerhauser Company of Longview donated three Douglas fir poles each eighty-six feet long, and Zach began his work on site, aided by the Eugene sculptor William Mueller, his former student.

They spent forty-five days preparing the three poles by applying a sealant, painting them black, and banding them at intervals with aluminum (which they painted in bright colors), brass, and stainless steel. The top twenty-one feet of each pole were sheathed in the shiny Endura stainless steel, while the lower zones were banded in differing patterns all based on a seven-foot module. Each pole was unique in its banding but unified by virtue of the module and the identical treatment of the top twenty-one feet. The poles were set at intervals of seven feet, forming a triangular plan. Buried to a depth of six feet, they rose to eighty feet, towering above the campus architecture. "Through the design concept, consistently based on the number 7 and syncopatively alternated between the three poles by varied color intensities and band heights and by the metal bands, I believe I developed a field of tension behind the three poles together to form a 'galaxy.' None of the three poles can exist artistically alone. Only in that 7 x 7 x 7 cohesive triangular field can 'Galaxy' exist as a unit."[111] The poles were hoisted into place, completing *Galaxy*, on July 27, 1977, Zach's sixty-third birthday.

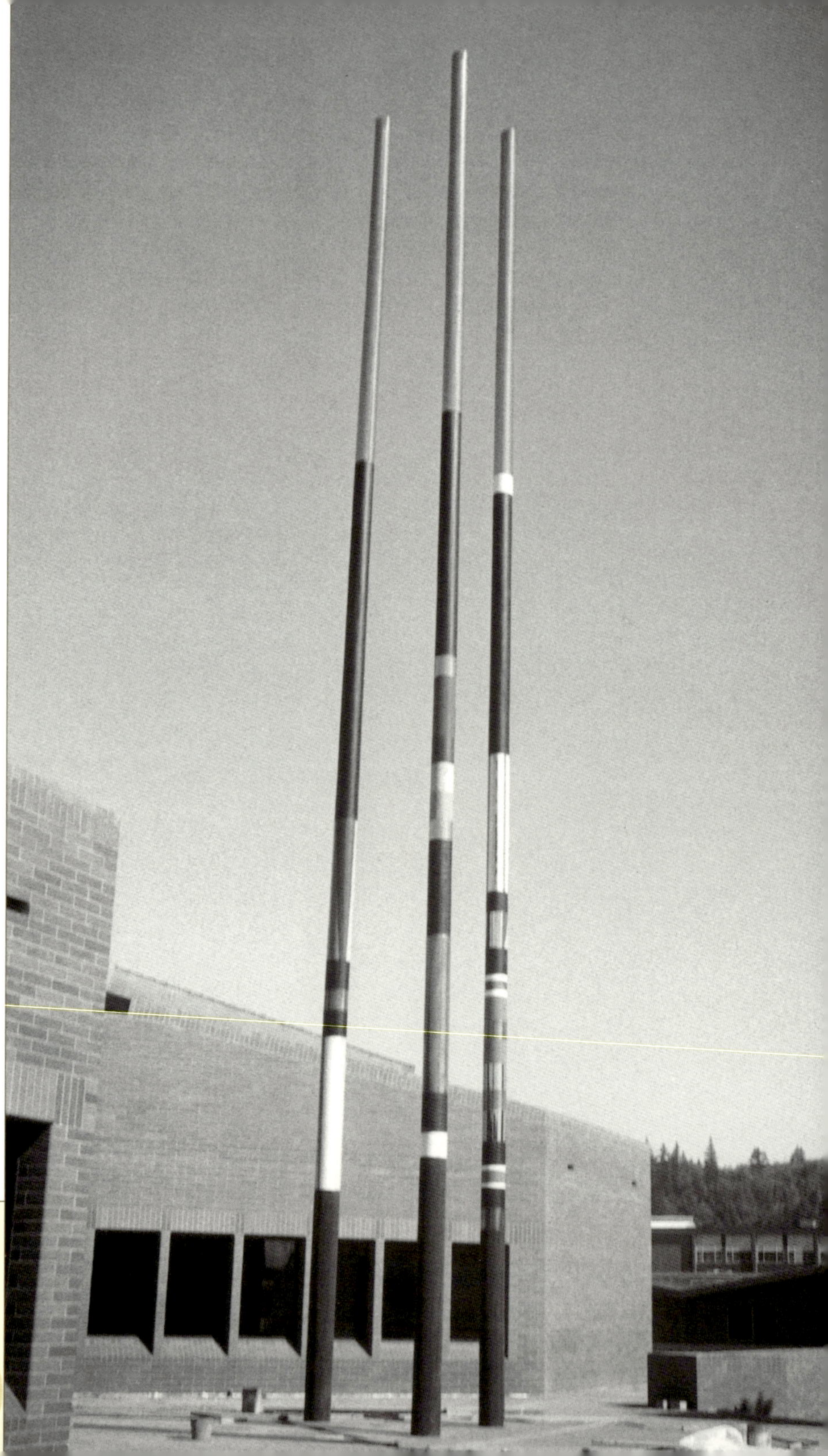

FIGURE 66

Jan Zach. *Galaxy*. 1977. Douglas fir poles sheathed in stainless steel, brass, and polychromed aluminum. Poles 80' spaced at intervals of 7'. Lower Columbia College, Longview, Washington. Dismantled 1980s because of deterioration. Photograph Hallie Ford Museum of Art, Willamette University, Salem, Oregon. Judith and Jan Zach Archives.

1978

"*Through the design concept, consistently based on the number 7 and syncopatively alternated between the three poles by varied color intensities and band heights and by the metal bands, I believe I developed a field of tension behind the three poles together to form a 'galaxy....'*"

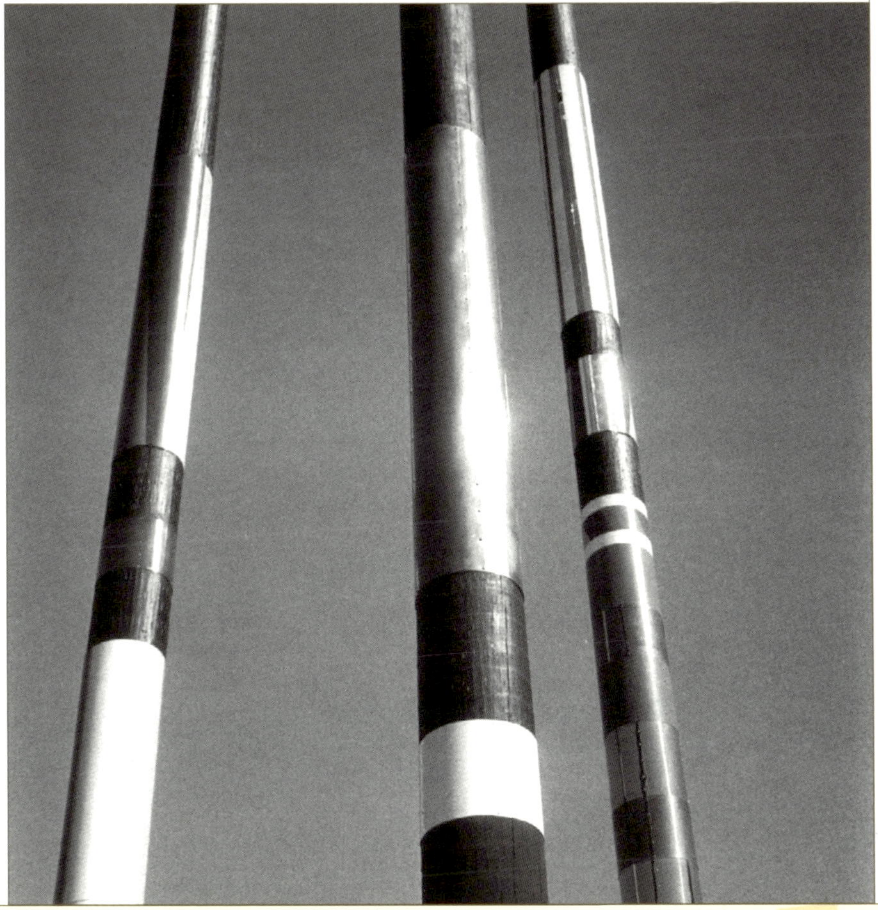

Figure 66 [detail]

Jan Zach. *Galaxy.* 1977. Douglas fir poles sheathed in stainless steel, brass, and polychromed aluminum. Poles 80' spaced at intervals of 7'. Lower Columbia College, Longview, Washington. Dismantled 1980s because of deterioration. Photograph Hallie Ford Museum of Art, Willamette University, Salem, Oregon. Judith and Jan Zach Archives.

1979

Retiring from Teaching

Two years later, in 1979, Zach retired at age sixty-five from the University of Oregon after twenty-one years of teaching. The sculpture program had grown exponentially during these years, and Zach was recognized as an inspirational teacher. Serious art students intending to become sculptors, as well as liberal arts students enrolled in a sculpture class as an elective, found Zach's teaching exciting and stimulating. Zach himself often said that he did not necessarily teach to train sculptors, especially in his elementary courses. One commentator said that "what he does try to do is encourage students to develop imagination, to discover what they want to create, and to create it–in short to use their freedom in a responsible and productive way."[112] Zach noted that "many people are surprised why art is so much involved in education. It is not to produce millions of painters. The more a child or young person expands their imagination–the more space for thinking."[113] Zach taught with flair and drama, sometimes exaggerating his speech patterns for theatrical effect. Zach could choose to speak a "rare, hybrid language known only to himself. Its elements are Slavic syntax and pronunciation, some English words–mostly adjectives–and a sprinkling of Brazilian and Czech idiom. When he's excited he's likely to slip in and out of Slavic, Portuguese, or simply Zach. And though Zach's astonished listeners may not know what he says, they usually understand what he *means*."[114] Polyglot language was Zach's natural speech, but he sometimes played it up in classes as a skillful teacher's way of amusing and sustaining the interest of students. The practice made him a "character" but at the same time an Old World sage who represented for Eugene students a link to European traditions and modernist roots.

Zach assembled a large collection of slides for teaching and showed numerous examples of historic and contemporary sculpture, stressing that in making art students joined an ongoing discourse and practice. Especially in introductory classes, he made his assignments broad and sometimes ambiguous, intentionally leaving the parameters wide to force students to think about concepts new to them in their own exploratory ways. One student was paraphrased as saying, "You are impressed by the novelty of the man, but more importantly you return home, to yourself, viewing your environment and its suppositions from new perspectives."[115] Tommy Griffin, who studied with Zach as a graduate student and became his close friend, remembers the electrifying discussions about sculpture and its place in life and culture that Zach would conduct in seminars at his studio in Elmira. "He was always charging you with such an inspired feeling, even though you couldn't necessarily nail it down to any one thing. You just felt this immense purpose. He saw the purpose in all of us and helped us find our spot."[116]

On the occasion of Zach's retirement, Tommy Griffin, who was then the exhibition curator at the University of Oregon Museum of Art, organized a major retrospective of Zach's life work as a sculptor. Entitled "Jan Zach Sculpture: A Retrospective," it was on view from July 1 through August 12, 1979, at the Museum of Art. The exhibition spanned the period 1952-1979 and included such early works as *Venus* (1952), *Resistance* (1955), and *Persistence* (1960-1962), key examples of Zach's sculptures based on driftwood forms; cast aluminum works from the early 1960s; stainless steel sculptures including *Flower of Freedom*, No. 7: *Freedom of Expression* (the 1976 variant of the 1968 *Flower of Freedom*, No. 7); and the laminated wood *Ondine* (1973) and *Drapery of Memory* (1975-1976). Also on view were drawings, models, and photographs for such works as *Sculpture in Suspension* (1968), *Can-Can* (1968-1969), and *Phoenix* (1977). His model for a proposed *Shrine of Freedom* (1978; Figure 67), envisioned as a monument soaring seventy feet at the nation's capital, indicated Zach's plans for new work. (Although Senator Mark Hatfield expressed interest in *Shrine of Freedom*, it was not funded or built.)

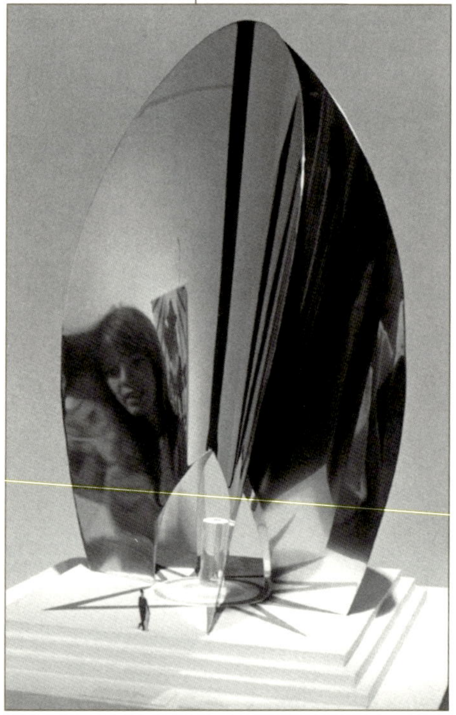

Reviewing the exhibition in *Artweek*, Mike Walsh called it "long overdue" and instructive in the view it provided of Zach's development as a sculptor working in a variety of media. Walsh found the aluminum cast pieces such as *Three Rivers* (*Three Graces*) to be the strongest work; he noted that "the folded, bent metal skins" of the stainless steel sculptures "become extraordinary, light-reflective surfaces" but criticized their "flimsy, awkward construction" that made it impossible to permanently install them outdoors. "Yet, in retrospect," Walsh concluded, "he must be recognized as one of the Northwest's most significant sculptors."[117]

Overall, the retrospective exhibition was a milestone in documenting, presenting, and interpreting Zach's career. It was accompanied by a sixty-page catalogue with an essay by Becky Slade based on Tommy Griffin's taped conversations with Zach, an informal "Introduction" that stands as an important historical document of scholarship on Jan Zach. In the foreword to the catalogue, Griffin describes Zach as a "vortex of creative energy with a limitless imagination. He visualizes even the smallest fragment of nature in monumental scale, and now many of his fantastic dreams are being realized in his sculpture. His influence will undoubtedly be to Northwest sculpture what Mark Tobey's influence is to Northwest painting."[118] In a recent amplification of this comparison, Griffin said that both Zach and Tobey "drew inspiration from the Northwest environment but interpreted it through a much broader view of art–historical art and art's spiritual and human dimensions." Griffin observed that Zach and Tobey did not involve themselves with trends or regionalism, and as a result their art is "enduring, timeless, and universal" and yet completely original, unlike the art of any other.[119]

Accolades and Final Works

Following retirement, Zach traveled to Brazil in 1979 for the first time in twenty-eight years to see art and old friends and to visit Brasilia, the new capital. In 1980, he was invited by the editor Frank Malina to join the honorary editorial board of the magazine *Leonardo*, for which Zach had written articles about *Can-Can* and *Galaxy*. In the preface to the catalogue for Zach's retrospective in 1979, Malina had praised his "dedication to international cooperation among sculptors." In 1981, Zach was the recipient of the Oregon Governor's Arts Award,

FIGURE 67

Jan Zach. Model for *Shrine of Freedom*. 1978. 3'. Location unknown. The artist envisioned a stainless steel, plastic, and wood construction 70' high to be installed in Washington, D.C. Photograph Hallie Ford Museum of Art, Willamette University, Salem, Oregon. Judith and Jan Zach Archives.

1980

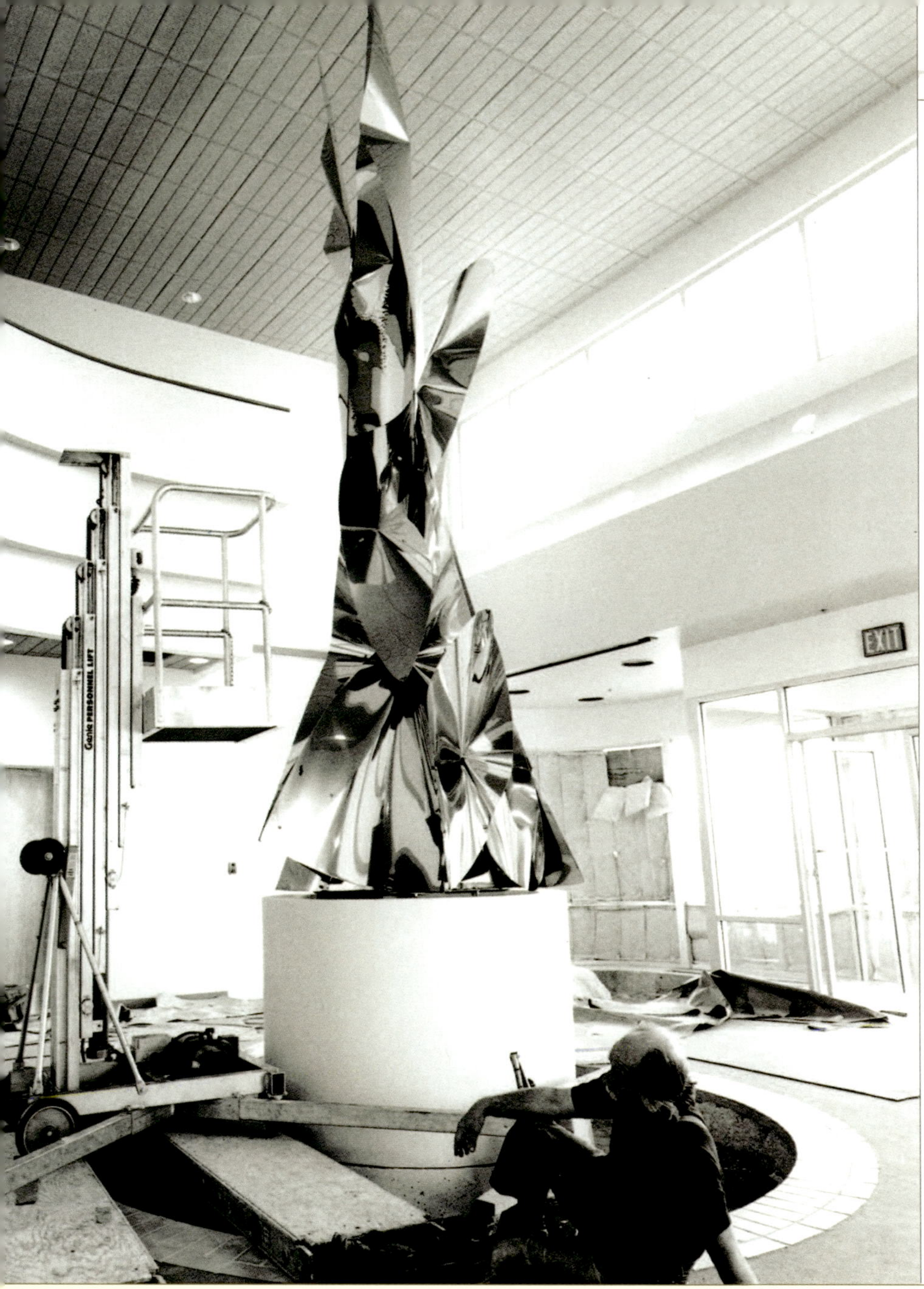

FIGURE 68

Jan Zach. *Frost's Brilliance*. 1985. Stainless Steel. 17'. Commissioned for the lobby of First Interstate Bank, Anchorage, Alaska (relocated to University of Alaska, Anchorage). In the foreground is Jan Zach. Photograph by Michael Besh. Hallie Ford Museum of Art, Willamette University, Salem, Oregon. Judith and Jan Zach Archives.

presented by Victor Atiyeh.[120] In 1984, Zach received a Eugene Arts and Letters Award from the Eugene Arts Foundation.[121] It was a period of honors and accolades and, with the trip to Brazil, a period of reminiscence. But retirement from regular teaching was bracing to Zach, and he welcomed new projects. His interest in travel and the world of international sculpture resulted in his teaching at Banaras Hindu University in Varanasi, India, as a Fulbright Visiting Lecturer for the winter term (November-February) of 1982-1983 at the invitation of a former University of Oregon student. He left the sculptures he made there as gifts to Banaras Hindu University.

In his studio at Elmira in the 1980s, Zach continued his work with stainless steel and laminated wood. Expanding on the *Flower of Freedom* series, he made a number of works in the 1980s entitled *Frost's Brilliance*. Like the flowers, these are compositions of folded stainless steel components assembled to create dazzling compositions that seem to be enlargements of natural forms–in this case the crystalline formations of frost. Some in this series he expanded to a large scale; in 1985 he was commissioned to make a seventeen-foot high *Frost's Brilliance* (Figure 68) for the lobby of the First Interstate Bank branch at the Tudor Center in Anchorage, Alaska (later relocated to a building at the University of Alaska in Anchorage).

Zach's last major laminated wood project was *Marching Women* (1981; Figures 69, 70), a set of sixteen ten-foot high headless figures striding in groups of two, three, four, and five. The female figure had been central to Zach's sculptural imagination since his days at the *Fazenda Penedo* in Brazil, where he made female figural abstractions in concrete. In Victoria, the logs he found on the beaches were made into Venuses and Aphrodites. Working with cast aluminum in Eugene, he made female personifications of rivers and the sinuous *Mermaid* of 1960-1961. His stainless steel *Drapery* of 1970-1971 evoked the image of a rushing female Niobid, and his laminated wood pieces of the 1970s, whether *Ondine* or *Drapery of Memory*, were also concerned with female energy and myth. Zach saw *Marching Women* as a "monument to women's achievement." With their long legs, thin waists, upright postures, and coordinated forward stride, they speak of shared convictions and purposes among women, a will to succeed at some important mission.

Given Zach's life-long commitment to political and personal freedom, the mission of the marching women may well be the attainment of world peace. The sculptor William Mueller, who worked closely with Zach during the last years of his life, helped him make the large-scale laminated *Women* figures, which Zach apparently planned to also cast in bronze.

Zach's last project, left unfinished at his death, was the monumental *Lady* (see Figures 71, 72), an abstract figure fourteen feet tall to be fabricated in welded steel and finished with an impervious coating. It had been commissioned, perhaps somewhat informally, by his old friend Inacio Peixoto for a park in Cataguases, in memory of his wife Amelinha. As a form, it recalls some of Zach's stainless steel "flowers," especially the vertically oriented *Flower of Freedom*, No. 7 (Figure 54), but is made of flat planes to be welded into a rigid monolith. Thematically, it is Zach's final invocation of the female presence and spirit. (*Lady* was fabricated in 1996 by Zach's former student Jerry Harpster, and he and Tommy Griffin planned to ship it to Brazil. But costs and other factors made that impossible. In 2002, it is installed at a site on Demming Road in Elmira.)

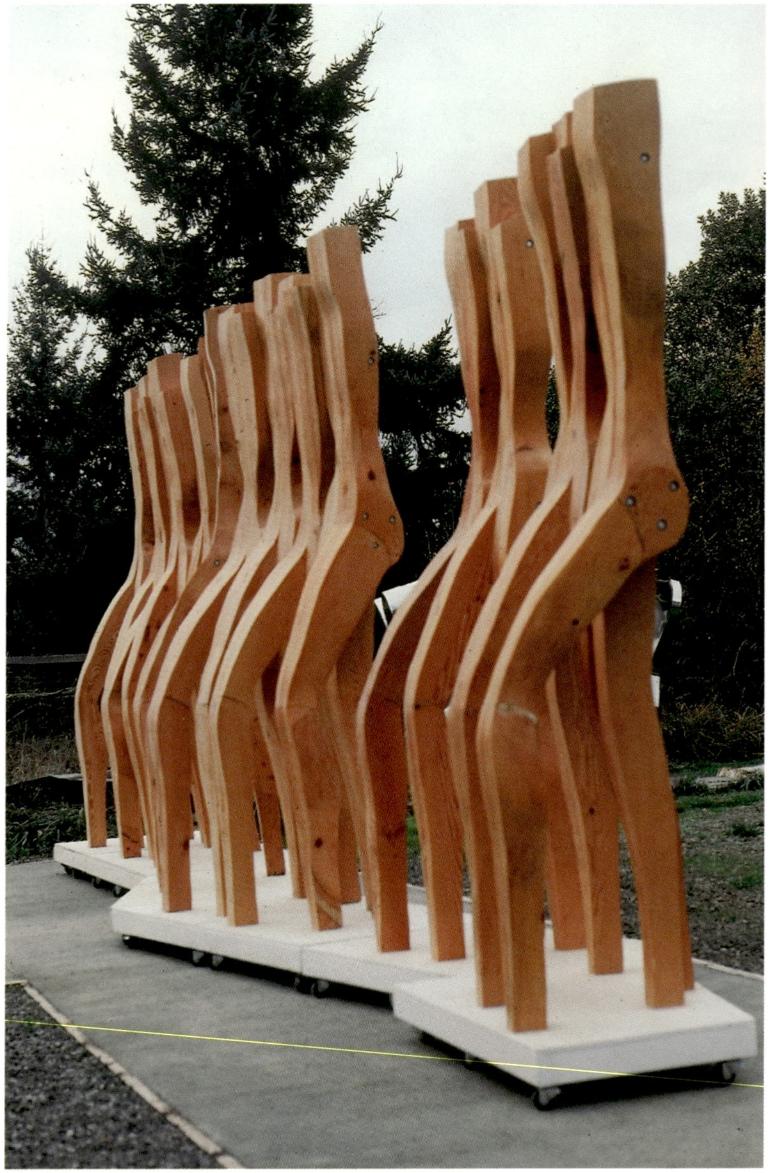

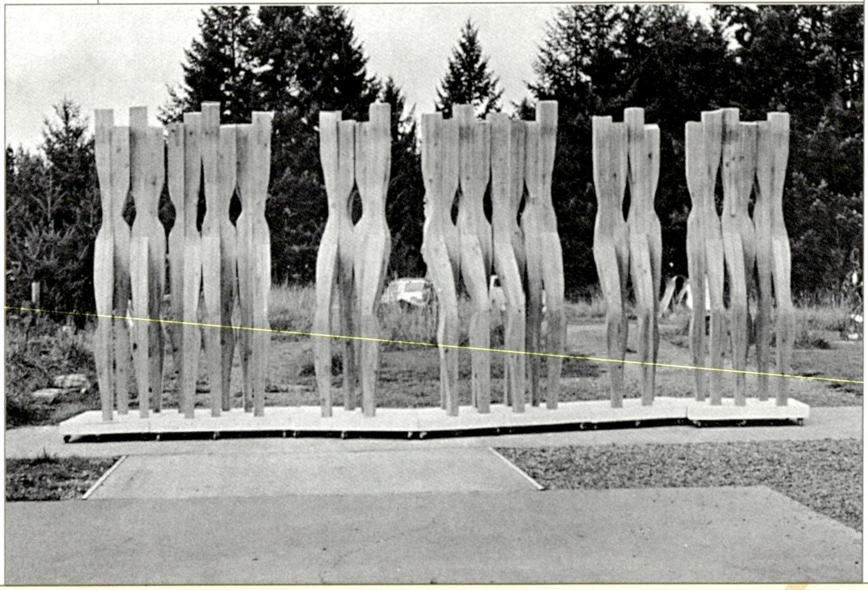

FIGURES 69, 70

Jan Zach. *Marching Women*. 1981. 16 Figures each 10' high. Laminated wood (intended to be cast in bronze). Collection of Judith Zach, Elmira, Oregon. Photograph Hallie Ford Museum of Art, Willamette University, Salem, Oregon. Judith and Jan Zach Archives.

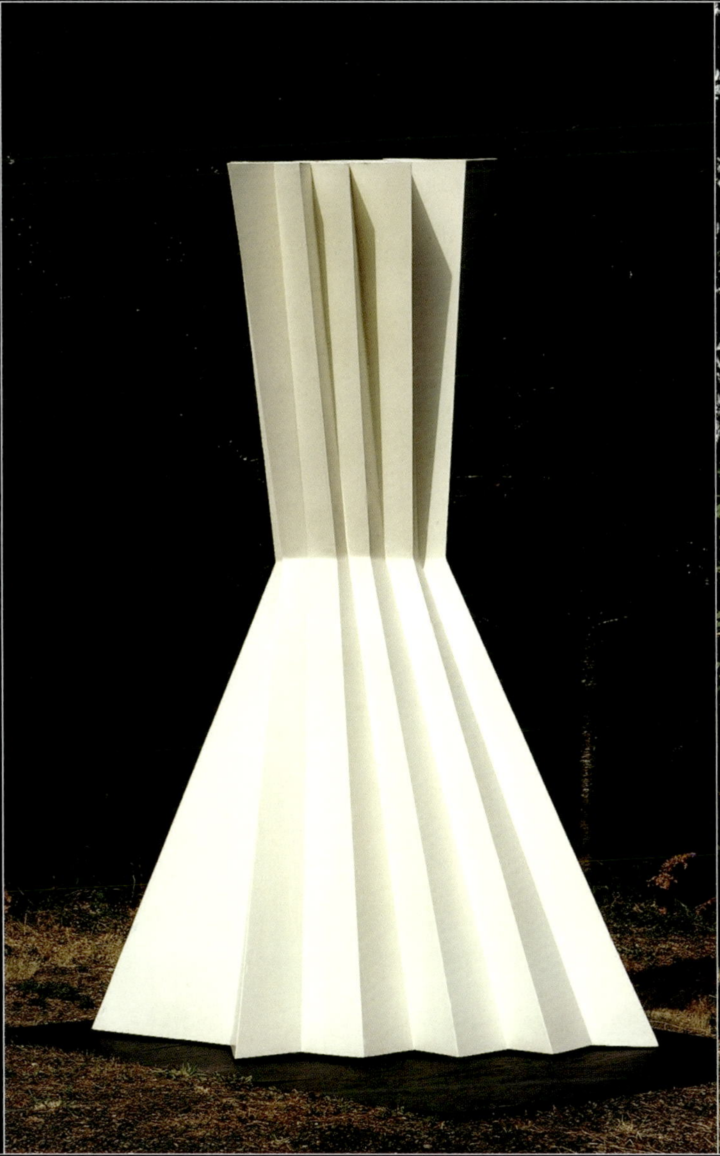

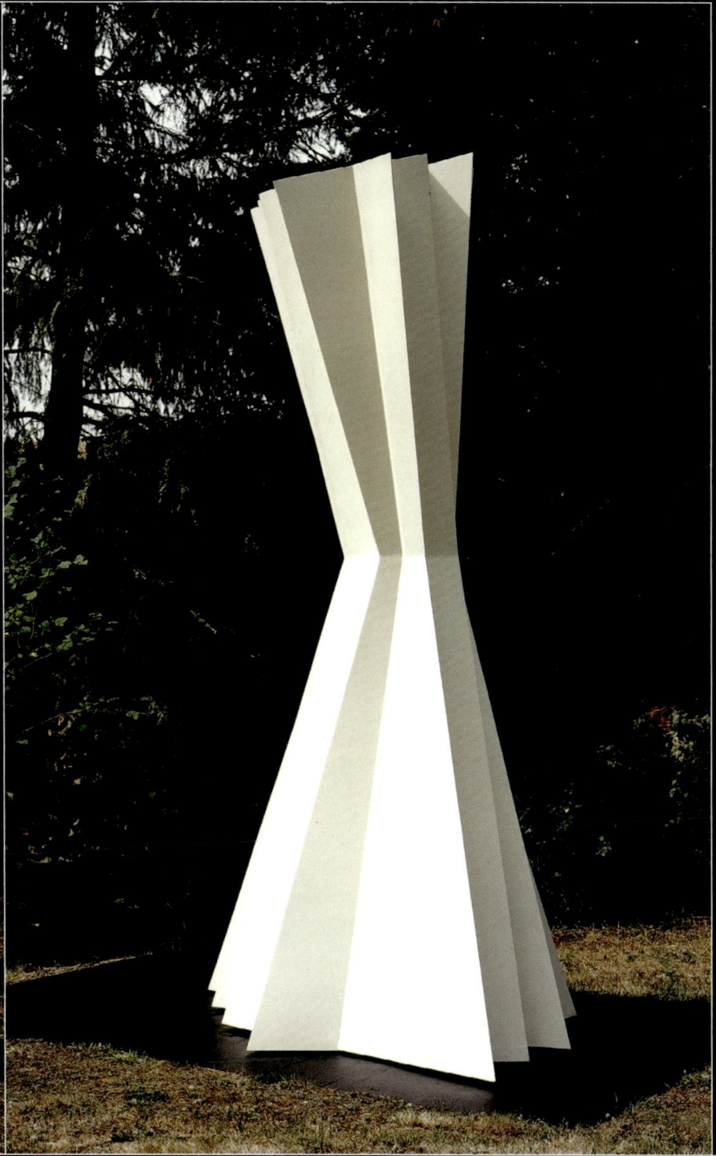

FIGURES 71, 72

Jan Zach. *Lady*. Fabricated Sept. 1996 by Jerry Harpster. 14'. Welded steel sealed with white catalyzed polyurethane. Collection of Judith

Death

In late August of 1986, Zach was vacationing at Crater Lake Lodge with his sister Marta Židlická, who was visiting from Czechoslovakia. The Zachs' neighbors, Carol and David Coleman accompanied by their young daughter, were along on the trip to do the driving. During the night, a fire alarm forced the evacuation of the lodge. In fact there was no fire, but Zach became agitated and concerned about the well-being of his elderly sister. Amid the confusion in the parking lot, he suffered a heart attack and died. The date of his death was August 27, 1986, and Zach had celebrated his seventy-second birthday only one month earlier. For a man so fully in the middle of things, he died young. The Jan Zach Memorial Graduate Award was established immediately at the University of Oregon to encourage students to pursue advanced work in sculpture and embrace international experience. In 1988, the Jan Zach Memorial Fellowship in Fine Arts was established at the University of Oregon by an anonymous donor "in tribute to a man who was not only an internationally renowned sculptor, a devoted citizen of these United States, and a distinguished teacher, but also an admired friend."

Judith Zach and a family friend, the sculptor Olinka Broadfoot, traveled to Prague in 1988 to bury Zach's ashes in the family plot in Bubeneč Cemetery. They placed Olinka Broadfoot's bronze bust of Jan Zach at the grave.[122] This was Judith's only visit to Prague, of which she had heard so much over the years. Zach himself had never returned. His remains were there by the time of the "Velvet Revolution" of 1989, which set the stage for Prague resuming its role as an international artistic center with a vital contemporary art scene. Zach would have found the legacy of Pešánek, however, only in documentary photographs and copy models made in the 1980s and 1990s. Of his own work, Zach would have located his painting *Stefanik Bridge*, his *Self-portrait* (*Remembering Europe*), painted in Brazil but sent to Czechoslovakia as part of an exchange exhibition in 1946, and at least one other portrait of a fellow student in Prague. If he searched long enough, he might have found his painting *Country Road* (or *Lane*) and another work purchased by Prague museums in the 1930s. New Prague would have fascinated him, but in life he would have returned to his actual home of Oregon where he had developed his full powers as an artist. And he would have had much to say about the removal of *Can-Can* from the Valley River Center.

A month before Zach died, he asked Tommy Griffin to help Judith preserve his artistic legacy. His studios were filled with finished works and hundreds of drawings and studies. His papers, documenting much of his career and such chapters in the history of modern sculpture as the formation and development of the International Sculpture Center, were intact. He worried that the sheer volume of artwork and materials would overwhelm efforts to stabilize and preserve them. After Zach's death, Tommy Griffin, Judith Zach, Zach's niece Ruth Gilombardo, Zach's former students Jerry Harpster and Lin Cook, and others met to plan ways to preserve the collection and archives. The demolition of *Can-Can*, the deterioration of *Galaxy* and its dismantling in the 1980s, and the near-loss of the cast iron grills from the Equitable Savings and Loan Association building in Roseburg were events that increased the urgency of their efforts. In 1991, William Mueller, who at that time lived in Bellingham, Washington, organized a large memorial exhibition of Zach's sculpture, along with work by sculptors who were his students and friends, at the Gardens of Art (George F. Drake, director) in Bellingham. On the occasion of this exhibition, Judith shipped *Flower of Freedom*, No. 4 to Prague as a gift to the city in memory of Jan Zach. In 1998, with the advent of the Hallie Ford Museum of Art at Willamette University in Salem, Griffin suggested that it might be possible to arrange a gift of Zach's artwork and papers to the new museum. On February 9, 2000, Judith Zach made a major donation of her husband's work in all media, together with an extensive collection of his papers, exhibition catalogues, and photographs. The Judith and Jan Zach Collection and Archives are remarkable additions to the holdings of the Hallie Ford Museum of Art. The publication of this book and the presentation of the retrospective exhibition "Intersections: The Art of Jan Zach" (February 1-March 29, 2003) are the inaugural projects honoring these collections and the legacy of Jan Zach.

JAN ZACH [1914 1986]

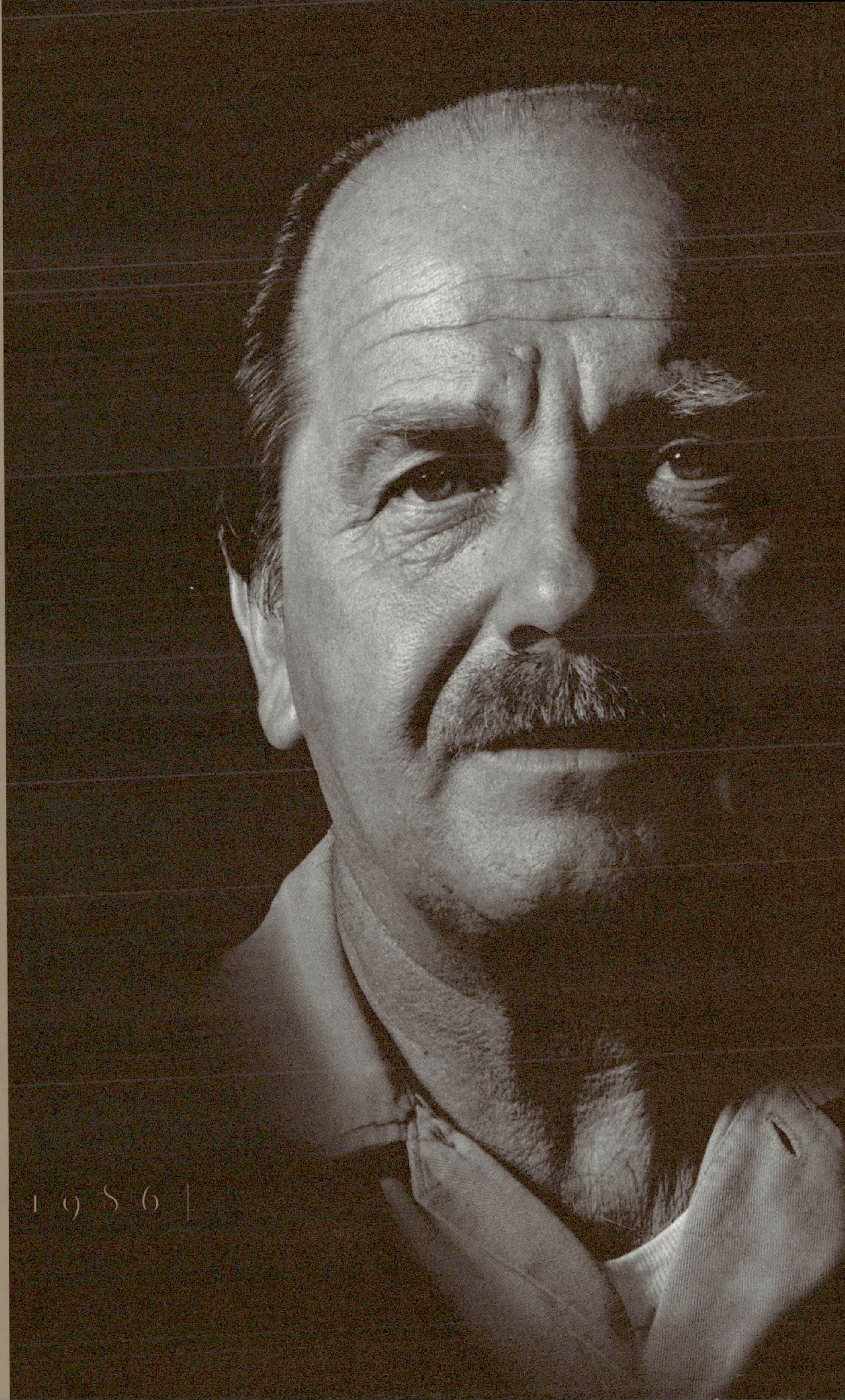

CONCLUSION

Jan Zach's life provided in its own dramatic terms an example of the twentieth-century displacement of an individual from a European homeland to more or less safe havens in the New World. In Zach's case, the displacement took the form of a years-long odyssey that included only briefly New York, the preferred destination of many European artist exiles in the late 1930s and early 1940s. After extended stays in the exotic but artistically problematic cities of Rio de Janeiro and Victoria, Zach spent the last twenty-eight years of his life and his most productive period as a sculptor in the relatively remote locale of Eugene, Oregon. This gradual move from the center to the margins of the world of culture and art makes Zach's story different from otherwise parallel cases – of the painter Arshile Gorky, the Armenian immigrant who became a founding father of the New York School or, to name a figure who crossed paths with Zach, the photographer Yousuf Karsh, another Armenian who found himself in Canada and calculatedly situated himself in Ottawa to intercept the celebrities who passed through. An early death ended Gorky's odyssey. Karsh traveled the world late into his long life in pursuit of famous personages to photograph but always remained Karsh of Ottawa. Circumstances kept Zach moving on, a man without a country who, by the end, could claim to have been a citizen of three (he became a United States citizen on February 11, 1971; Judith, born in Canada, remains a Canadian citizen). Zach's story is about repeated reinventions–the young Czech painter and designer making a name for himself in Prague becomes the immigrant who can't speak the language in New York, who becomes a dashing celebrity of sorts in romantic Rio, who becomes the European "modern artist" in conservative Victoria, who in turn becomes the eccentric, beloved, incomprehensible professor with the funny way of talking in Eugene.

As the settings and roles changed, so did Zach's art. A modern but not particularly *avant-garde* painter became, in a series of stages that commingled memories and new experiences, a remarkably original and inventive sculptor. The memories were of Prague–the city of Gothic and Baroque architecture and sculpture (architecture of space and light, sculpture of movement) and the city of electricity, artificial light, motorized movement, and Pešánek's harnessing of these old and new elements in his amazing kinetic structures. The new experiences were the exuberance and scale of New York, the tropical lushness, intense sunlight, and black shadows of Brazil, the stumps and rocks of the beaches along Dallas Road in Victoria, and the commissions for major sculptures that came to him during his artistic maturity in Eugene.

The history of Oregon art, as generally told to date, is the history of Portland art. Like Carl Hall of Salem, Jan Zach of Eugene has figured less prominently in the narratives than the artists who called Portland home. The seminal exhibition entitled "Art of the Pacific Northwest," presented in 1974 at the National Collection of Fine Arts of the Smithsonian Institution, the Seattle Art Museum, and the Portland Art Museum, focused on "Portland and Its Environs" and "Seattle and the Puget Sound." Accordingly, "The Art of the Pacific Northwest" did not include works by Zach, and Rachael Griffin's catalogue essay did not mention him. In terms of "Oregon art" of the period, towns like Eugene and Salem were separate, marginal places. On the other hand, Rachael Griffin had curated a one-person exhibition of Zach's sculptures at the Portland Art Museum five years earlier (in 1969), and Zach was one of thirty-two Northwest sculptors represented in the exhibition "Works in Wood by Northwest Artists" curated by Griffin at the Portland Art Museum in 1976. But no sculptures by Zach made their way into the collection of the Portland Art Museum (it contains none to this day), and Zach was never commissioned to make a public sculpture for a Portland site, though his work is on permanent public view in Roseburg, Eugene, Salem, Seattle, Bellingham, Anchorage, and in British Columbia.

Zach was an anomaly in many ways. He was "foreign" and eccentric, and to a degree he played on this identity to charm students, beguile potential clients, and get things done. Never forgetting Pešánek, he was hugely and sometimes wildly inventive, opening himself to dismissal because his ideas struck some as preposterous and ego-maniacal. He worked in virtually all sculptural media making his art difficult to categorize, even though his aesthetic vision was remarkably unified, based on the fundamental concepts of light and movement in nature.

From his position in Eugene, he garnered numerous major commissions, especially during the 1960s, and pushed his sculptural ideas to new levels of sophistication in cast metal works, sheet metal constructions, and laminated wood sculptures. Zach, always a newcomer (to Rio, to Victoria, to Eugene), remained something of an outsider within Oregon despite his talk of stumps, boulders, and finding home and himself in the Northwest. His identity as newcomer and yet his urge to belong to a community help explain his loyal membership in the Rotary Club; Zach attended Rotary meetings wherever he found himself–from India to Eugene–using them for access to new communities and community involvement at home. He was proud of his affiliation with Rotary because it provided him with a civic base, and he believed that the artist should be a civic figure like other professionals, whether doctors, lawyers, or business people. Zach understood that Rotary was a site for establishing contacts, brokering deals, and contributing to the community.

In being an internationalist in the era of the Cold War, Zach was atypically political for an "Oregon artist" or a "regional artist" of any sort. His art can be discussed in purely formal and aesthetic terms (Zach often discussed his work and other sculpture in formal ways and was well aware of his historic and contemporary sources), but the expressive throb inherent in Zach's work is his passionate call for freedom. Titles such as *Resistance* and *Persistence* are to be taken quite literally, as is the convulsive energy of the sculptures with these titles. *The Flower of Freedom* series is, in fact, about freedom and its flowering. Zach's entire life as an artist after he left Czechoslovakia was conducted against the memory of Prague as a dream city of movement and light and the fact that Prague had been darkened by fascist and totalitarian regimes. He grieved for Czechoslovakia and other oppressed peoples. He urged his students never to take freedoms for granted. The call for liberation that suffused his art made of it something quite different from characteristically "modern sculpture," whether of the Northwest or elsewhere. This different language, this different inflection, paralleling his own difference in background, personality, and speech, in itself set his work, and him, apart. Artistically and expressively, he was of a broad European tradition of sculpture. But Zach was European, too, in his *joie de vivre*: he was "jolly, very vibrant, alive, excited about life," his niece recalled; he was a person who "just loved everything, always smiling, a wonderful, wonderful person. He loved to fix drinks."[123] Tommy Griffin recalled that he loved champagne and sausages.[124]

Jan Zach as a sculptor is to be remembered for his natural wood carvings, which reveal his expressionistic powers at their most potent; his cast metal sculptures, especially his aluminum casts of the carved polystyrene core forms; his stainless steel shapes and constructions; and his laminated wood structures. He himself seemed to think of wood as his fundamental medium. "Wood was my primary material in sculpture and even though I work in a variety of media . . . I always return to wood," he stated.[125] His wood sculptures in Canada marked his first phase as a mature sculptor; his laminated assemblages such as *Ondine* and *Drapery of Memory* are among his most stunningly gorgeous late works. I have suggested that the laminated wood pieces owe something to the earlier experiments with cast aluminum. Such aluminum sculptures as *Three Rivers* are endlessly intriguing for their reference to the flow of mighty yet graceful rivers, for their evocation of Baroque energy, and for Zach's process of making them–carving Styrofoam and then vaporizing it with molten aluminum by means of ingenious procedures he devised at commercial foundries in Eugene. For me, the glory pieces are the stainless steel works, especially the constructions–sheets of metal riveted together into fantastical entities. The *Flower of Freedom* and the *Frost's Brilliance* series are dazzling both in the sense that they gleam and in the sheer adroitness of their making. They are about lightness in a number of ways: they are luminous, they are light in weight (and thus do not hold up well outdoors, it is true), they reveal a lightness of artistic touch.

The work that was the true culmination of Zach's production in any medium was the stainless steel *Can-Can*, so stylish and elegant, in which Zach held nothing back and brought everything into intersection: the urban modernity of Pešánek's works in civic, commercial settings; the height and graceful canopy of Brazilian trees; reflections of light on the bays and rivers of the Canadian and American Northwest as clouds pass on their slow overhead way; petals from the *Flower of Freedom* series expanded to something stunning and monumental and yet light as a tutu. For *Can-Can* alone, Zach warrants a place in the history of modern sculpture. His surviving *oeuvre* provides the context for understanding the origins and significance of that lost masterpiece while demonstrating the contributions he made to the traditions of wood and metal sculpture and to our understanding of the expressive function that sculpture can have in modern emotional and political life.

1. Anne Mayhew in conversation with David Roberts at Anne Mayhew's home in Victoria, British Columbia, 28 Jan. 2002.

2. Jan Zach was not given a middle name. When a bank stipulated that he list one, he adopted his father's name, Vincent, as his middle name, according to Judith Zach (letter to the author, 1 Apr. 2002).

3. Marta Židlická, sister of Jan Zach, in conversation with JoAnn Elizabeth Seibert, 21 July 2001, at Marta Židlická's home in Hradec Králové, Czech Republic (hereafter cited as Židlická, Conversation).

4. Judith Zach, widow of Jan Zach, in conversation with the author at Judith Zach's home in Elmira, Oregon, 12 Oct. 2001 (such conversations hereafter cited as Judith Zach, Conversation).

5. Fred Crafts, "Freedom's Messenger," *Register-Guard* [Eugene, Oregon] 14 Apr. 1977: B3.

6. Tommy Griffin and Becky Slade, "Introduction" (based on Griffin's taped conversations with Jan Zach), in *Jan Zach Sculpture: A Retrospective* (catalogue for an exhibition at the Museum of Art, University of Oregon, Eugene, 1 July-12 Aug. 1979), (hereafter referred to as Griffin/Slade, "Introduction").

7. Židlická, Conversation.

8. Judith Zach, letter to the author, 1 Oct. 2001.

9. Judith Zach, Conversation.

10. Luděk Jirásko (Academy of Fine Arts, Prague), letter to David Roberts, 21 Feb. 2002.

11. Jan Zach, "Imagery, Light and Motion in My Sculptures," *Leonardo* Summer 1970: 285.

12. Jaromír Fiala, "On My Work with the Pioneer of Kinetic Light Art, Zdeněk Pešánek (1896-1965): A Memoire," *Leonardo* Summer 1980: 182.

13. *Trade-Fair Palace, 2nd Floor, 1930-2000 Art*, exhibition pamphlet (National Gallery in Prague, 2001) 2.

14. JoAnn Elizabeth Seibert confirmed the whereabouts of this painting in July 2002.

15. Jan Zach, unpublished, untitled essay, 1 May 1979: 1, Judith and Jan Zach Archives, Hallie Ford Museum of Art, Willamette University, Salem, Oregon (hereafter referred to as Judith and Jan Zach Archives).

16. Jan Zach, quoted in Slade/Griffin, "Introduction," 8.

17. "Confirmation," document issued by the Academy of Fine Arts, Prague, 2 Dec. 1938. Judith and Jan Zach Archives. Trans. JoAnn Elizabeth Seibert.

18. Judith Zach, Conversation.

19. According to a discharge document in the Judith and Jan Zach Archives, he served his conscription from 1 Oct. 1937 to 22 Apr. 1938 and was released from service because he was "not qualified for military service." The document states that in the event of war, and physical condition permitting, he would be obliged to serve.

20. Ruth Gilombardo, niece of Jan Zach, in telephone conversation with the author, 17 June 2002 (hereafter cited as Gilombardo, Conversation).

21. *The Czechoslovak Pavilion* (undated brochure, no publisher indicated, seven unnumbered pages) [1].

22. Judith Zach, Conversation.

23. David Gelernter, *1939, The Lost World of the Fair* (New York: The Free Press, 1995) 293.

24. David Gelernter, *1939, The Lost World of the Fair* (New York: The Free Press, 1995) 43.

25. Gilombardo, Conversation.

26. Judith Zach, Conversation.

27. "Jan Zach," *Cataguases* [Cataguases, Minas Gerais, Brazil] 12 Nov. 1950: 1.

28. Jan Zach, quoted in Griffin/Slade, "Introduction," 9.

29. Gilombardo, Conversation.

30. Griffin/Slade, "Introduction," 11.

31. Griffin/Slade, "Introduction," 11.

32. Jan Zach, "Imagery, Light and Motion in My Sculptures," *Leonardo* Summer 1970: 285.

33. Walter Harris, "Jan Zach Exhibits His Latest Paintings," *Brazil Herald* [Rio de Janiero] 10 Nov. 1948: unpaginated clipping, Judith and Jan Zach Archives.

34. Jan Zach, quoted in Griffin/Slade, "Introduction," 11.

35. Judith Zach, Conversation.

36. Gore Vidal, age twenty-two at the time Zach's exhibition, lived in Antigua, Guatemala, in the period 1947-1949.

37. Griffin/Slade, "Introduction," 11.

38. Solange de Sampaio Godoy (Director, Museum of Modern Art, Resende), letter to Becky Slade (Assistant to the Museum Registrar, Museum of Art, University of Oregon) 27 June 1979. Curatorial file, Museum of art, University of Oregon, Eugene.

39. Griffin/Slade, "Introduction," 11.

40. Judith Zach, Conversation.

41. Judith Zach, quoted in "Artist Here From Brazil Proposes Local School," *Daily Times* [Victoria, British Columbia] 31 Aug. 1951: unpaginated clipping, Judith and Jan Zach Archives.

42. Anne Mayhew, e-mail message to David Roberts, 13 Feb. 2002.

43. According to Anne Mayhew, the house was built by the Carr sisters' father for Alice to use for a kindergarten. Late in life, the sisters lived there together but in separate quarters with separate entrances (Anne Mayhew, "218 St. Andrews St., Victoria, B.C.," typescript, Mar. 1987). The Zachs rented the half of the house that Emily had occupied until her death in 1945.

44. Colin Graham in conversation with David Roberts at Colin Graham's home near Victoria, British Columbia, 28 Jan. 2002 (hereafter cited as Graham, Conversation).

45. Tony Emery, "The Community and Artist – Victoria's Loss," *Daily Colonist* [Victoria, British Columbia]: undated, unpaginated clipping, Judith and Jan Zach Archives.

46. Audrey St. D. Johnson, quoted in *Art Gallery of Greater Victoria, A History*, undated brochure published in the 1980s, 3-4.

47. Audrey St. D. Johnson, "Jan Zach's Exhibition In Broad, Modern Idiom," *Daily Times* [Victoria, British Columbia] 6 Feb. 1952: 10.

48. Graham, Conversation.

49. "Artist Here From Brazil Proposes Local School," *Daily Times* [Victoria, British Columbia] 31 Aug. 1951: unpaginatd clipping, Judith and Jan Zach Archives.

50. Graham, Conversation.

51. "Famous Teacher for One-Man School of Arts," undated clipping, Judith and Jan Zach Archives.

52. Patricia E. Bovey, *A Passion for Art: The Art and Dynamics of the Limners* (Victoria, British Columbia: Sono Nis Press, 1996) 17.

53. Moncrieff Williamson, "City's Art Climate Cools As Two Visionaries Depart," *Daily Times* [Victoria, British Columbia] 23 Aug. 1958: unpaginated clipping, Judith and Jan Zach Archives.

54. Graham, Conversation.

55. Colin Graham, quoted in Bovey, 16-17.

56. Graham, Conversation.

57. Jan Zach, "Creation, Not Imitation as Modern Art Breaks Documentary Limitations," *Daily Times* [Victoria, British Columbia] 7 Feb. 1953: 13.

58. A.M. Thomas, "Bright Murals Grace Newsroom at Times," *Daily Times* [Victoria, British Columbia] 12 Mar. 1953: 15.

59. *Exhibition of Murals Illustrating the Historical Development of the Automobile*, brochure for an exhibition at the Vancouver Art Gallery, 9 Nov.-5 Dec. 1954, Judith and Jan Zach Archives. The artists of the murals were Lillian Rogers, Margaret Longridge, and Robert Pravda.

60. Jan Zach, quoted in Griffin/Slade, "Introduction," 12.

61. J. Škvára, "Jan Zach," catalogue essay for the exhibition "Jan Zach USA" at the Gallery of Plastic Arts, Litoměřice, Czechoslovakia, in 1996.

62. Stuart Keate, "Two Kinds of Art," *Daily Times* [Victoria, British Columbia] 13 Oct. 1954: 5.

63. Colin Graham, "Art in Review," *Daily Times* [Victoria, British Columbia] 23 Oct. 1954: 9.

64. Jan Zach, "Imagery, Light and Motion in My Sculptures," *Leonardo* Summer 1970: 286-287.

65. Henri Gabriel, "The Hanging Mobile: A Historical Review," *Leonardo* 18, 1 (1985): 39-44. Gabriel mistakenly identifies the medium of *Dancer* as brass. He lists "contemporary mobile artists" as Bruno Munari, George W. Rickey, Lyn Chadwick, Kenneth Martin, Ken Lye, Georges Vantongerloo, Gyula Kosice, Willy Anthoons, Gregorio Vardanega, and Jan Zach together with several younger artists.

66. Jan Zach, *Foreword by the Artist* (brochure for the exhibition "Jan Zach Sculpture, Paintings, Drawings," Arts Center of Greater Victoria, Victoria, British Columbia, Oct. 1954), Judith and Jan Zach Archives. Judith Zach has stated (September 2002) that these are the words of Colin Graham, writing for Jan.

67. Jan Zach, "Imagery, Light and Motion in My Sculptures," *Leonardo* Summer 1970: 287.

68. Michael D. Hall, in telephone conversation with the author, 7 Oct. 2002 (hereafter cited as Hall, Conversation). I am grateful to Michael Hall for this point and other helpful observations about Jan Zach and his work as a sculptor.

69. Jan Zach, "WRESTLERS, Drawings for project," typed portfolio board #19, July 1952, Judith and Jan Zach Archives.

70. Jan Zach, letter to James F. Mathias at the John Simon Guggenheim Memorial Foundation, 8 Oct. 1953, Judith and Jan Zach Archives.

71. Griffin/Slade, "Introduction," 16.

72. Zach's exhibition in October 1954 at the Arts Centre of Greater Victoria included thirteen portraits in cast stone, among them portraits of Stuart Keate, publisher of the *Victoria Daily Times* and a supporter of Zach and his ideas about art, and of Kenneth McAllister, the photographer. The exhibition also included three painted portraits and two portrait drawings.

73. Zach's charcoal drawings of Victoria's beaches, parks, and docks were reproduced in the *Victoria Daily Times* regularly in 1955.

74. Graham, Conversation.

75. Mark Sponenburgh in conversation with the author at Mark Sponenburgh's home, Seal Rock, Oregon, 16 Aug. 2000.

76. Zach's University of Oregon employment contacts (Judith and Jan Zach Archives) show that his official title was Visiting Assistant Professor of Art through the academic year 1958-1959. The same title appeared in his contract for 1959-1960 but was corrected to Assistant Professor in accordance with the minutes of the State Board meeting of 28 July 1959. Beginning with the academic year 1960-1961, his rank was Associate Professor. He was promoted to the rank of Professor in 1966.

77. Mark Sponenburgh in conversation with the author at Mark Sponenburgh's home, Seal Rock, Oregon, 6 Aug. 2001.

78. Tony Emery, "The Community and Artist – Victoria's Loss," *Daily Colonist* [Victoria, British Columbia] 1958: undated, unpaginated clipping, Judith and Jan Zach Archives.

79. Tony Emery, among modern sculptors in Oregon during that period, on the other hand, Zach was a latecomer. The closest parallel to Zach biographically was Frederick Littman (1907-1979) who was born in Budapest, studied and worked as an artist in Paris, and arrived in Portland, Oregon, in 1941, the year Zach settled in Rio. Hilda Morris (1911-1991) also came to Portland in 1941. Like Zach, Littman was a long-time teacher, in his case at the Museum Art School. His students there included Manuel Izquierdo (born in spain in 1925, he is another example of an artist displaced and repositioned by the circumstances of a troubled century), Charles Kelly (born 1931), and Lee Kelly (born 1932). These sculptors and others such as James Lee Hanson (born 1925) were Zach's younger contemporaries on the Oregon scene when he arrived in 1958. The wood carver LeRoy Setziol (born 1916), two years Zach's junior, had settled in the state in 1952. At the University of Oregon, Zach filled the position in sculpture that Mark Sponenburgh (born 1916) had held since 1946; Paul Buckner (1933-1997) would join Zach on the sculpture faculty at the University in 1962.

80. Wallace Baldinger, "The Prometheus of Jan Zach," typescript, Judith and Jan Zach Archives.

81. "Sorority Gives Sculpture to University," *Register-Guard* [Eugene, Oregon] 7 June 1958: unpaginated clipping, Judith and Jan Zach Archives.

82. Hall, Conversation. According to Hall, the interest in casting "spread like wildfire" among American sculptors of the 1960s.

83. "The Iron Trees of Jan Zach," one-page statement printed on the occasion of the dedication of the installation of three of the grills at Umpqua Community College, Roseburg, Oregon, 9 Sept. 1997.

84. Jan Zach, "The Influence of Experiment, Accident and Design on Sculpture Casting," *Proceedings of the Fourth National (International) Sculpture Conference*, 5–7 May 1966, University of Kansas, Lawrence.

85. The remaining eight grills were being stored at Double A Metal Fabricators in Roseburg in 2002. For an account of earlier discussion about the fate of the grills, see: Tricia Jones, "Arts Center wants its 'donated' sculptures," *News-Review* [Roseburg, Oregon] 26 Oct. 1993: 1, 9.

86. *Reclining Form* has weathered considerably in the course of nearly forty years on the grounds of City Hall. Like Mark Sponenburgh's wooden bird located in the gardens of Salishan Lodge on the Oregon coast since the early 1960s, it is in danger of eroding entirely away and possibly was intended, over time, to do so.

87. Hall, Conversation.

88. Hall, Conversation. According to Hall, the process yields noxious gases that can be fatal.

89. Jan Zach, "The Influence of Experiment, Accident and Design on Sculpture Casting," *Proceedings of the Fourth National (International) Sculpture Conference*, 5–7 May 1966, University of Kansas, Lawrence.

90. Kenneth Patecky in conversation with the author, 31 July 2001.

91. *Abstracts of the First Congress of the Czechoslovak Society of Arts and Sciences in America, Inc.*, 34-35. The congress was held 20-22 Apr. 1962 in Washington, D.C.

92. Jan Zach, "Imagery, Light and Motion in My Sculptures," *Leonardo* Summer 1970: 288.

93. Jan Zach, letter to Jose Chavez Morado, 7 Mar. 1965, Judith and Jan Zach Archives.

94. Hall, Conversation. According to Hall, American heavy industry in the 1960s and 1970s was open to collaboration with individual sculptors, providing materials and sometimes facilities for fabricating large public works, and "artists learned to beseech industry for materials."

95. Zach listed the graduate students as R. Cross, T. Rieste, M. Hondo, and J. Burton in his article "Imagery, Light and Motion In My Sculptures," *Leonardo* Summer 1970, 290.

96. Robert G. Christenson (Coordinator for Special Projects, University of Oregon, Eugene), letter to Byron Price, Jim Larson, and Alvin Reed, 22 July 1968, Judith and Jan Zach Archives.

97. Jan Zach, untitled typescript, 29 Jan. 1968, Judith and Jan Zach Archives.

98. Jan Zach, "Imagery, Light and Motion in My Sculptures," *Leonardo* Summer 1970: 291.

99. Rachael Griffin, Curator's statement in *Jan Zach, Recent Works* (catalogue for the exhibition at the Portland Art Museum, Portland, Oregon, 2-27 Apr. 1969) np.

100. Beth Fagan, "Zach's Distinguished Sculpture Show Now in Art Museum," *Sunday Oregonian* [Portland, Oregon] 6 Apr. 1969: 20 (Arts section).

101. Jan Zach, "Imagery, Light and Motion in My Sculptures," *Leonardo* Summer 1970: 291-292.

102. Jan Zach, "Imagery, Light and Motion in My Sculptures," *Leonardo* Summer 1970: 291-292.

103. Ken Paul, typescript of letter to the *Register-Guard* [Eugene, Oregon] 18 May 1989, Judith and Jan Zach Archives.

104. Jackman Wilson, "'Move it or lose it' philosophy doesn't apply to art," *Register-Guard* [Eugene, Oregon] 28 May 1989: C3.

105. Tommy Griffin, quoted in Dana Tims, "Destruction of sculpture angers art world," *Oregonian* [Portland, Oregon] 26 June 1989: C5.

106. Don Bishoff, "Store destroys huge sculpture," *Register-Guard* [Eugene, Oregon] 18 May 1989: B1.

107. Zachary Hull, editor's note on the manuscript, Sept. 2002. Hull posits the idea that Zach's personality and circumstances made him a performer in life and in artmaking and that on some level he may have intended and preferred performance over permanence in his art, sometimes working with materials (decaying wood or thin, bendable sheets of stainless steel) that could never be expected to last indefinitely.

108. Jan Zach, "Round Table on Metals," *Proceedings of the Sixth National (International) Sculpture Conference*, 23-25 Apr. 1970, University of Kansas, Lawrence.

109. Hall, Conversation. According to Hall, the NEA support of such symposia gradually came to be criticized because it seemed to impose art by established, nationally recognized figures on local communities, limiting opportunities for regional artists.

110. Hope Hughes Pressman, "Report to the National Endowment for the Arts: Works of Art in Public Places Program of the 1974 Oregon International Sculpture Symposium," in *In Retrospect: The Oregon International Sculpture Symposium of 1974* (Eugene: University of Oregon, 1985) 41-44.

111. Jan Zach, "My Sculpture, 'Galaxy,'" *Leonardo* Autumn 1980: 316.

112. Belva Finlay, "Same with Life…Always Changing," *Old Oregon* [Eugene: University of Oregon] July-Aug. 1967: 9.

113. Jan Zach, quoted in Gail Bullen, "Retirement is no escape from sculpting urge," *West-Lane News* [Veneta, Oregon] 4 Dec. 1980: 4.

114. Belva Finlay, "Same with Life…Always Changing," *Old Oregon* [Eugene: University of Oregon] July-Aug. 1967: 7.

115. Richard Lee, "Jan Zach Retrospective," *Old Oregon* [Eugene: University of Oregon] Summer 1979: 17.

116. Tommy Griffin, quoted in Fred Crafts, "Jan Zach cultivated ideas like plants," *Register-Guard* [Eugene, Oregon] 1 Nov. 1996: 4 (Entertainment and Arts).

117. Mike E. Walsh, "Jan Zach, Sculpture Surveyed," *Artweek* 28 July 1979: 16.

118. Tommy Griffin, "Foreword," *Jan Zach Sculpture: A Retrospective* (catalogue for an exhibition at the Museum of Art, University of Oregon, 1 July – 12 Aug. 1979) 7.

119. Tommy Griffin in conversation with the author, 7 Aug. 2002.

120. The other Governor's Award for the Arts recipients for 1984 were Ursula LeGuin, the Summer Festival of Music at the University of Oregon founded and directed by H. Royce Saltzman, and Howard and Jean Vollum.

121. The other Eugene Arts and Letters Award recipients for 1984 were Riley Grannan, Toni Pimble, and Phillip Bayles.

122. The location of Zach's grave is Section 1, Area 4, Plot 28 of Bubeneč Cemetary in Prague.

123. Gilombardo, Conversation.

124. Tommy Griffin in conversation with the author, 7 Aug. 2002.

125. Jan Zach, statement in *Masterworks in Wood by Northwest Artists* (catalogue for an exhibition at the Portland Art Museum, Portland, Oregon, 16 June – 25 July 1976) np.

Sources and Resources

Compiled by David Roberts

Judith and Jan Zach Archives

A large collection of Jan Zach's correspondence, records, manuscripts, exhibition catalogues, photographs, reviews, and interviews is housed at the Hallie Ford Museum of Art at Willamette University in Salem, Oregon, in the Judith and Jan Zach Archives. These materials, currently being organized and catalogued, are the gift of Judith Zach, who also donated a significant collection of her husband's sculptures, paintings, drawings, and other artworks to the museum. The following Bibliography includes both resources culled from the Archives and other materials.

Selected Bibliography

Architectural Craftsmen of the Northwest. Seattle: Architectural Craftsmen, c. 1960.

"Artist Here From Brazil Proposes Local School." *Daily Times* [Victoria, British Columbia] 31 Aug. 1951: unpaginated clipping, Judith and Jan Zach Archives, Hallie Ford Museum of Art.

Bangs, Stephen. "For Jan Zach, Patience Has Always Paid Off." *Oregonian* [Portland] 24 Apr. 1977: 11, 13 (*Northwest Magazine*).

Bishoff, Don. "Store destroys huge sculpture." *Register-Guard* [Eugene, Oregon] 18 May 1989: B1.

Bovey, Patricia E. *A Passion for Art: The Art and Dynamics of the Limners*. Victoria, British Columbia, Canada: Sono Nis Press, 1996.

Bullen, Gail. "Retirement No Escape From Sculpting Urge." *West-Lane News* [Veneta, Oregon] 4 Dec. 1980: 3-4.

Crafts, Fred. "Freedom's Messenger." *Register-Guard* [Eugene, Oregon] 14 Apr. 1977: B3.

—. "A Hint of What's Ahead." *Register-Guard* [Eugene, Oregon] 26 July 1979: B1-2.

—. "Jan Zach Cultivated Ideas Like Plants." *Register-Guard* [Eugene, Oregon] 1 Nov. 1996: 4 (Entertainment and Arts).

Emery, Tony. "The Community and Artist–Victoria's Loss." *Daily Colonist* [Victoria, British Columbia] 1958: unpaginated clipping, Judith and Jan Zach Archives, Hallie Ford Museum of Art.

Endura Era. Cleveland, Ohio: Republic Steel Corporation, 1967.

Fagan, Beth. "Show at UO Art Museum to Honor Retiring Professor." *Oregonian* [Portland] 29 June 1979: E9.

—. "Zach's Distinguished Sculpture Show Now in Art Museum." *Oregonian* [Portland] 6 Apr. 1969: 20 (Arts Section).

Finlay, Belva. "Same With Life...Always Changing." *Old Oregon* [University of Oregon, Eugene] July-Aug. 1967: 6-11.

Gabriel, Henri. "The Hanging Mobile: A Historical Review." *Leonardo* 18, 1 (1985): 39-44.

Graham, Colin. "Art in Review." *Daily Times* [Victoria, British Columbia] 23 Oct. 1954: 9.

Griffin, Tommy, and Becky Slade. *Jan Zach, Sculpture: A Retrospective* (Catalogue of exhibition at the University of Oregon Museum of Art). Eugene, Oregon: University of Oregon Museum of Art, 1979.

"Guide Listing Wide Variety of Sculpture and Art Which Decorates Outdoor Areas in Eugene." *Register-Guard* [Eugene, Oregon] 15 June 1983: D14-15.

Harris, Walter. "Jan Zach Exhibits His Latest Paintings." *Brazil Herald* [Rio de Janeiro] 10 Nov. 1948: unpaginated clipping, Judith and Jan Zach Archives, Hallie Ford Museum of Art.

"Jan Zach." *Cataguases* [Cataguases, Brazil] 12 Nov. 1950: 1.

"Jan Zach (Obituary)." *Leonardo* 20 (1987): 105.

Jan Zach: Recent Works (Catalogue of exhibition at the Portland Art Museum, 2-27 April 1969). Portland, Oregon: Portland Art Association, 1969.

"Jan Zach's Classes Commencing Oct. 7." *Daily Times* [Victoria, British Columbia] 2 Oct. 1952: 21.

Johnson, Audrey St. D. "Jan Zach's Exhibition in Broad, Modern Idiom." *Daily Times* [Victoria, British Columbia] 6 Feb. 1952: 10.

—. "Neglected Art of Sculpture Revives in Butchart Gardens." *Daily Times* [Victoria, British Columbia] 30 July 1956: unpaginated clipping, Judith and Jan Zach Archives, Hallie Ford Museum of Art.

Jones, Tricia. "Arts Center Wants its 'Donated' Sculptures." *News-Review* [Roseburg, Oregon] 26 Oct. 1993: 1, 9.

Keate, Stuart. "Two Kinds of Art." *Daily Times* [Victoria, British Columbia] 13 Oct. 1954: 5.

Lang, Naomi. "Canadian Art Shows Exciting Growth." *Sun* [Vancouver, British Columbia] 16 Aug. 1956: 27.

Lee, Richard. "Jan Zach Retrospective." *Old Oregon* [University of Oregon, Eugene] Summer 1979: 17.

Loughnan, Brian. "Czech Paints and Sculpts in Studio of Emily Carr." *Daily Colonist* [Victoria, British Columbia] 3 Feb. 1952: 5.

Malina, Frank, ed. *Kinetic Art Theory and Practice*. New York: Dover Publications, Inc., 1974. Reprints Jan Zach, "Imagery, Light and Motion in My Sculptures." *Leonardo* 3 (1970).

Matassa, Mark. "Four Get Arts Awards: Eugene Celebration Attracts Crowd of 35,000." *Register-Guard* [Eugene, Oregon] 30 Sept. 1984: 8.

"New City Hall." *Register-Guard* [Eugene, Oregon] 24 Sept. 1964: 2-5.

Palette. "Canadians' Art Display Has Merit." *Province* [Vancouver, British Columbia] 1 Oct. 1953: 24.

—. "Sculpture Enlivens Campus." *Province* [Vancouver, British Columbia] 6 July 1956: 22.

Rebelo, Marques. Foreword. *Álbum de Pintura: Jan Zach*. Rio de Janeiro, Brazil: Editôra Vecchi, 1949.

Redstone, Louis G. *Art in Architecture*. New York: McGraw-Hill Book Company, 1968.

Redstone, Louis G., and Ruth R. Redstone. *Public Art, New Directions.* New York: McGraw-Hill Book Company, 1981.

Roukes, Nicholas. *Plastics for Kinetic Art.* New York: Watson-Guptill Publications, 1974.

Rupp, James M. *Art in Seattle's Public Places: An Illustrated Guide.* Seattle, Washington: University of Washington Press, 1992.

Schmidt, Dan. "A Captivating Sample of a Master's Sculpture." *Oregonian* [Portland] 24 Apr. 1977: 11 (*Northwest Magazine*).

Sculpture '67: An Open-Air Exhibition of Canadian Sculpture (Exhibition catalogue). Ottawa, Ontario: National Gallery of Canada, 1967.

"Sorority Gives Sculpture to University." *Register-Guard* [Eugene, Oregon] 7 June 1958: unpaginated clipping, Judith and Jan Zach Archives, Hallie Ford Museum of Art.

Ten Northwest Sculptors: An Invitational Exhibition (Catalogue of exhibition at the University of Oregon Museum of Art, 15 Nov.-31 Dec. 1961). Eugene, Oregon: University of Oregon Museum of Art, 1961.

Thomas, A.M. "Bright Murals Grace Newsroom at Times." *Daily Times* [Victoria, British Columbia] 12 Mar. 1953: 15.

Tims, Dana. "Destruction of sculpture angers art world." *Oregonian* [Portland] 26 June 1989: C1, 9.

Tuele, Nicholas and Liane Davison. *Art in Victoria* 1960/1986 (Catalogue of exhibition at the Art Gallery of Greater Victoria, 24 July-5 Oct. 1986). Victoria, British Columbia: Art Gallery of Greater Victoria, 1986.

"Walls of Gallery Vibrate With Jan Zach Exhibition." *Daily Colonist* [Victoria, British Columbia] 10 Feb. 1952: 5.

Walsh, Mike E. "Jan Zach, Sculpture Surveyed" (Review of retrospective exhibition at the University of Oregon Museum of Art). *Artweek* 28 July 1979: 16.

Wilhelm, Richard B. "Jan Zach, Sculptor." *Northwest Illustrated Art Paper* [Seattle, Washington] 1, 7 (July-August 1986): 22, 24.

Williamson, Moncrieff. "City's Art Climate Cools as Two Visionaries Depart." *Daily Times* [Victoria, British Columbia] 23 Aug. 1958: unpaginated clipping, Judith and Jan Zach Archives, Hallie Ford Museum of Art.

Wilson, Jackman. "'Move it or lose it' philosophy doesn't apply to art." *Register-Guard* [Eugene, Oregon] 28 May 1989: C3.

Works in Wood by Northwest Artists: An Invitational Exhibition (Catalogue of exhibition at the Portland Art Museum, 16 June-25 July 1976). Portland, Oregon: Portland Art Association, 1976.

Wyant, Dan. "In Mural and Sculpture, City Hall Bears Mark of UO Artists." *Register-Guard* [Eugene, Oregon] 26 Apr. 1964: E8.

"Zach Sculpture Exhibition at Ceramic Studio." *Oregonian* [Portland] 14 May 1961: A12.

Zach, Jan. "My Sculpture 'Galaxy'." *Leonardo* 13 (1980): 315-16.

—. "Creation, Not Imitation as Modern Art Breaks Documentary Limitations." *Daily Times* [Victoria, British Columbia] 7 Feb. 1953: 13.

—. "Imagery, Light and Motion in My Sculptures." *Leonardo* 3 (1970): 285-287.

—. "The Influence of Experiment, Accident and Design on Sculpture Casting." *Proceedings of the Fourth National (International) Sculpture Conference* (5-7 May 1966). Ed. Elden C. Tefft. Lawrence, Kansas: University of Kansas, 1966.

—. "Round Table on Metals." *Proceedings of the Sixth National (International) Sculpture Conference* (23-25 Apr. 1970). Ed. Elden C. Tefft. Lawrence, Kansas: University of Kansas, 1971.

Additional Reading

Blažíček, Oldřich J. *Baroque Art in Bohemia.* London: Paul Hamlyn, 1968.

Bydžovská, Lenka. *Czech Modern Art 1900-1960: The National Gallery in Prague: Modern Art Collection, the Trade Fair Palace.* Prague, Czech Republic: National Gallery of Prague, 1995.

Bydžovská, Lenka, Lahoda Vojtěch, and Karel Srp. *Czech Art 1900-1960 from the Collections at the Prague City Gallery.* Prague, Czech Republic: Prague City Gallery, nd.

Fiala, Jaromír. "On My Work with the Pioneer of Kinetic Electric Light Art, Zdeněk Pešánek (1896-1965): A Memoire." *Leonardo* 13 (1980): 182.

Gelertner, David. *1939: The Lost World of the Fair.* New York: The Free Press, 1995.

Hanzlová, Lidmila. *Otakar Nejedlý.* Prague, Czechoslovakia: Odeon, 1984.

Levy, Sophie. *Prague, 1900-1938.* Paris: Reunion des Musees Nationaux, 1997.

Pešánek, Zdeněk. *Kinetismus.* Prague, Czechoslovakia: Ceška Unie A.S., 1941.

Zemanek, J., ed. *Zdeněk Pešánek: 1896-1965.* Prague, Czech Republic: National Gallery of Prague, 1996.

Selected Exhibitions

The following is a partial listing of exhibitions that presented the work of Jan Zach, many of which were accompanied by published catalogues or lists:

Solo exhibition. International House, New York. 1939. Sketches, monotypes, and prints.

Solo exhibition. Palace Hotel, Rio de Janeiro, Brazil. 1941.

"Exposition of the Czech Painter Jan Zach." National Museum of Fine Arts, Rio de Janeiro, Brazil. Nov. 1943. 66 paintings and pastels.

Salon of the National Museum of Fine Arts, Rio de Janeiro, Brazil. 1944.

"Exposition of the Czech Painter Jan Zach." Prefecture of Belo Horizonte, Belo Horizonte, Brazil. Dec. 1944. Paintings.

"Exposition of Contemporary Paintings." Prefecture of Porto Alegre, Porto Alegre, Brazil. Oct. 1947. Jan Zach: *Self-Portrait* and *Mother.*

"Exposition of Contemporary Paintings." Bahia Public Library, Bahia, Brazil. Mar. 1948. Jan Zach: *Horses* (watercolor) and *Horses* (oil).

Solo exhibition. Institute of Brazilian Architects, Rio de Janeiro, Brazil. 27 Oct. 1948-Nov. 1948. Paintings.

"Inaugural Exposition." Museum of Modern Art, Resende, Brazil. Mar. 1950. Jan Zach: *Caminho Para Penedo* and *Mangueiras* (paintings).

Solo exhibition. Museum of Modern Art, Resende, Brazil. Opened 29 Apr. 1950. 29 paintings and prints.

"The Arts Centre of Greater Victoria, B.C. Presents the Painting of Jan Zach." Arts Centre of Greater Victoria, Victoria, British Columbia. 5-19 Feb. 1952. 37 paintings and prints from 1940-1952.

"Exposition of Oil Paintings, Watercolors, and Engravings" (solo exhibition). Museum of Modern Art, Florianopolis, Brazil. Aug. 1952. 63 works.

"Progressive Painters of Western Canada." University of Manitoba Open House, Winnipeg, Manitoba. Opened 27 Sept. 1953. Jan Zach: *Women* and *Still Life* (both tempera).

"Jan Zach: Sculpture, Paintings, Drawings." The Arts Centre of Greater Victoria,Victoria, British Columbia. Oct. 1954. Portraits.

"British Columbia Society of Artists 45th Annual Exhibition." Vancouver Art Gallery, Vancouver, British Columbia. 26 Apr.-15 May 1955. Jan Zach: *Creation* (sculpture).

"Vancouver Art Gallery 24th Annual Exhibition." Vancouver Art Gallery, Vancouver, British Columbia. 20 Sept.-9 Oct. 1955. Jan Zach: *Torso* and *Swallows' Flight* (sculptures).

"An Exhibition of Outdoor Sculpture by Members of the B.C. Region of the Northwest Institute of Sculpture." University of British Columbia, Vancouver, British Columbia. 1956.

"B.C. Arts Today." Art Gallery of Greater Victoria, Victoria, British Columbia. 24 Sept.-21 Oct. 1956. Jan Zach: *Lament* (two works of this title) and *Construction* (all ink drawings).

"Jan Zach: Sculptures, Paintings, and Drawings." University of Oregon Museum of Art, Eugene, Oregon. 5 May-15 June 1959. Included photographs by Kenneth McAllister.

"Third Pacific Coast Biennial: An Exhibition of Sculpture and Drawings by Artists of California, Oregon and Washington." Santa Barbara Museum of Art, Santa Barbara, California. 9 Oct.- 8 Nov. 1959. Traveling exhibition. Jan Zach: *Standing Figure* (sculpture in alder).

"Ten Northwest Sculptors: An Invitational Exhibition." Museum of Art, University of Oregon, Eugene, Oregon. 15 Nov.-31 Dec. 1961.

"Eleventh Biennial Exhibition of Northwest Ceramics." Oregon Ceramic Studio (later named Contemporary Crafts Gallery), Portland, Oregon. 26 May-20 June 1964. Jan Zach: *Figure* (cast aluminum, painted).

Solo exhibition. National Institute of Fine Arts, San Miguel de Allende, Mexico. Apr. 1965. Sculpture and drawings.

"Paintings and Sculptures of the Pacific Northwest." Portland Art Museum, Portland, Oregon. 13 June-9 Aug. 1965.

"Jan Zach USA: Photographic Exhibition of Sculptures." Gallery of Plastic Arts, Litoměřice, Czechoslovakia. Sept.-Dec. 1966. 13 photographs of sculptures primarily from the period 1958-1963.

"Invitational Northwest Show." Seattle Art Museum Pavilion, Seattle, Washington. 1967. Jan Zach: *Windflower* (stainless steel).

"Jan Zach: Sculpture, Models, and Drawings." Erb Memorial Union Art Gallery, Corvallis, Oregon. 15 Feb.-16 Mar. 1967.

"Sculpture '67." Nathan Philips Square, Toronto, Ontario. June-Aug. 1967. Jan Zach: *Windflower* (stainless steel). 52 Canadian sculptors.

"Oregon Sculpture '68." Equitable Plaza, Portland, Oregon. 1968. Jan Zach: *Windflower* (stainless steel).

"Jan Zach: Recent Works." Portland Art Museum, Portland, Oregon. 2-27 Apr. 1969. Works in sheet metal and a few earlier sculptures in wood or cast metal.

"73rd Western Annual Art Show." Denver Art Museum, Denver, Colorado. 3 Oct.-21 Nov. 1971. Jan Zach: *Flower of Freedom #1* (stainless steel).

"Sculptors of Oregon." University of Oregon Museum of Art, Eugene, Oregon. July-Aug. 1974. Jan Zach: *Ondine* (laminated wood, polychromed and gilded).

"Centennial Art Exhibit." Coos Art Museum, Coos Bay, Oregon. Opened 21 Sept. 1974.

Solo exhibition. Governor's Ceremonial Office, Capitol, Salem, Oregon. 1976.

"Works in Wood by Northwest Artists: An Invitational Exhibition." Portland Art Museum, Portland, Oregon. 16 June-25 July 1976. 32 artists.

"Jan Zach." Maude Kerns Art Center, Eugene, Oregon. 7 Apr.-1 May 1977. Zach's first one-person show in Eugene.

"Jan Zach Sculpture: A Retrospective." University of Oregon Museum of Art, Eugene, Oregon. 1 July-12 Aug. 1979. 48 works from period 1952-1979.

"Oregon Invitational Small Sculpture Exhibition." Lane Community College Art Department Gallery, Eugene, Oregon. 18 Nov.-13 Dec. 1985.

"The 2nd Biennial Sculpture Symposium." Maude Kerns Art Center, Eugene, Oregon. 29 Aug.-27 Sept. 1987. 31 artists.

"Jan Zach: Sculptor." Gardens of Art, Bellingham, Washington. 30 June-30 Sept. 1991. Estate sales exhibition of 42 works by Jan Zach and works for sale by 14 friends, associates, and students of Jan Zach.

"Intersections: The Art of Jan Zach." Hallie Ford Museum of Art, Willamette University, Salem, Oregon. 1 Feb.-29 Mar. 2003. Works in all media 1945-1986.

"Jan Zach: Maquettes and Small Sculptures." Hallie Ford Museum of Art, Willamette University, Salem, Oregon. 1 Feb.-29 Mar. 2003.

Major Commissions

1950-1951

Cataguases, Brazil

In conjunction with architectural projects by Oscar Niemeyer, Zach made a sculpture for the garden at the Hotel Cataguases and another for the residence of Francisco Inacio Peixoto. He also painted murals for the lobby of Hotel Cataguases and designed the lighting and decor for the interior of the hotel. Zach sculpted a monument for the College of Cataguases honoring Antonio Amaro, the college's founder.

1958

University of Oregon, Eugene, Oregon

Prometheus. Cast iron, sand, and cement. 8' 6".

Funded by the University's chapter of the Gamma Phi Beta sorority, this first commission by Jan Zach in the United States is located near the Museum of Art on the campus of the University of Oregon.

1959

Lane County Courthouse Park, Eugene, Oregon

Plant Forms. Cast iron. Heights vary from 26" to 27 1/4".
Three Standing Forms. Cast iron. Each 49" high.

The Lane County Art Advisory Committee commissioned these works for the new public service buildings and related parks renovation in Eugene.

1960-1961

Roseburg Equitable Savings and loan Association, Roseburg, Oregon

Eleven cast iron grills: four 17' and seven 24', all 5' wide.

The grills, each with tree patterns, adorned the building from 1961-1993 through numerous changes of ownership. In 1993, the grills were removed as part of remodeling for the Bank of America by Jerry Griese Construction. Griese became the owner of the grills. In 1995, he and his wife donated three of them to Umpqua Community College. The remaining eight are in the possession of Double A Metal Fabricators, Roseburg, Oregon. Two are in deteriorating condition.

1961-1964

Eugene City Hall, Eugene, Oregon

The eighteen works were finished for the dedication of the City Hall on 27 June 1964. Works included twelve concrete reliefs, five metal sculptures (three of them comprising the ensemble *Three Rivers*), and one wood piece. The 1996 condition assessment by James Taggart of Astoria, Oregon, noted serious condition deficiencies in some of the works, with the concrete reliefs being the least deteriorated.

1967

Temple Beth Israel, Eugene, Oregon

Symbolizing the Eternal Light, this work was dedicated 15 September 1967.

1968-1969

Meier and Frank Company, Valley River Center, Eugene, Oregon

Can-Can. Stainless steel. 50' high.

Zach's most important single work, *Can-Can* was installed in the entrance rotunda of the recently completed Meier and Frank store at the Valley River Center. It was removed and destroyed in 1989.

1971-1972

Pacific Northwest Bell Building/U.S. West Communications/Qwest, Seattle, Washington

Untitled. Four cast aluminum reliefs, each 10' high x 30" wide.

These reliefs are located on the exterior wall of the company's office building at 1122 Third Avenue between Seneca and Spring Streets. They are the only public sculptures that Zach made for Seattle. One component is illustrated in James M. Rupp's book on Seattle public art (see Bibliography).

1977

Lower Columbia College, Longview, Washington

Galaxy. Three Douglas fir poles sheathed in stainless steel, brass, and polychromed aluminum. Poles 80' high, spaced at intervals of 7'.

Commissioned by the Washington State Arts Commission, this work had a very short life on the plaza near the college library. By 1982, the three poles had severe dry rot. Zach repaired and resealed them but was unable to preserve structural integrity. A portion of *Galaxy* was soon removed. In about 1988, the remainder of the sculpture was dismantled. The work was deaccessioned from the Washington State Arts Commission collection in November 1991.

1985

First Interstate Bank, Tudor Center, Anchorage, Alaska

Frost's Brilliance. Stainless steel. 17' high.

Commissioned by the Parkwood Company, this was Zach's last commission. The work is now located in a light and airy entry of an annex building at the University of Alaska, Anchorage. The accompanying plaque reads: "Light, space and form are the key elements of Czechoslovakian-born Jan Zach's vision. The composition reflects the imagery and space/time continuum of nature, and embodies manifestations of the celestial spirit. Dedicated to mankind's free spirit. November 7, 1985."

1986-1996

Intended for a park in Cataguases, Brazil

Lady. Welded steel sealed with white catalyzed polyurethane. 14'.

In maquette stage when Zach died, this work was intended as a memorial to Amelinha Peixoto, wife of Zach's friend Francisco Inacio Peixoto. It was fabricated in 1996 by Jerry Harpster and (in 2002) is installed at 89115 Demming Road, Elmira, Oregon.

Selected Collections

Art Gallery of Greater Victoria, Victoria, British Columbia

Butchart Gardens, Brentwood Bay, British Columbia

Capitol Art Collection, State of Oregon, Salem, Oregon

City of Eugene, Eugene, Oregon

City of Prague, Prague, Czech Republic

Coos Art Museum, Coos Bay, Oregon

Garden Rocks State Park, Bellingham, Washington

Gilombardo, Ruth; Belmont, California

Grabenhorst, Coburn L. Jr.; Salem, Oregon

Griffin, Tommy; Portland, Oregon

Hallie Ford Museum of Art, Willamette University, Salem, Oregon

Hotel Cataguases, Cataguases, Brazil

Lane County Courthouse, Eugene, Oregon

Mayhew, Anne; Victoria, British Columbia

Mayhew, Elza; Victoria, British Columbia

Morris and Helen Belkin Art Gallery, Vancouver, British Columbia

Museum of Modern Art, Rio de Janeiro, Brazil

National Gallery of Prague, Prague, Czech Republic

Peixoto, Francisco Inacio; Cataguases, Brazil

Portland Art Museum, Portland, Oregon

Seattle Art Museum, Seattle, Washington

Sovereign Collection, Portland, Oregon

Umpqua Community College, Roseburg, Oregon

University of Oregon, Eugene, Oregon

University of Oregon Museum of Art, Eugene, Oregon

Western Oregon University, Monmouth, Oregon

Zach, Judith; Elmira, Oregon

Awards and Honors

1937

First prize for glass vase design, Czechoslovak Pavilion, Paris Exposition Internationale des Arts et Techniques dans la vie Moderne

1950

"Key to the city," Resende, Brazil

1968

Grant of $5,000 from Chapelbrook Foundation, Boston, Massachusetts

1974

Honor award, Summer Art Festival, Oregon College of Education (now Western Oregon University), Monmouth, Oregon

1976

First Prize, *Flower of Freedom #7: Freedom of Expression*, International Competition for Sculpture, National Sculpture Center Conference, New Orleans, Louisiana

1981

Governor's Arts Award, Oregon Arts Commission, Salem, Oregon

1982

Senior Fulbright Travel Fellowship to India

1984

Arts and Letters Award, Eugene Arts Foundation (now the Arts Foundation of Western Oregon), Eugene, Oregon

[1986]

The Jan Zach Memorial Graduate Award, University of Oregon, Eugene, Oregon

[1988]

The Jan Zach Memorial Fellowship in Fine Arts, University of Oregon, Eugene, Oregon

Memberships and Affiliations

1958-1964

Regional Secretary, Czechoslovak Society of Arts and Sciences in America, Inc.

1959-1960

President, Northwest Institute of Sculpture, Oregon Chapter

Beginning 1968

Member, Board of Directors, Sculpture Information Center, University of Kansas, Lawrence, Kansas

Beginning 1980

Honorary Editorial Board Member, *Leonardo* magazine

Life-long Member of Rotary International

Intersections:
The Life and Art of Jan Zach

Contributors to the Publication Fund

In-Kind Donations

QSL Print Communications
Acme Graphic Design

$5,000+

Anonymous
QSL Print Communications
Acme Graphic Design
Hon-Ching Lee

$1,000 – 2,499

Coburn L. Grabenhorst, Jr.
Dan and Nancy Schneider

$500 – 999

Lin Cook and Jerry Harpster
Tommy Griffin
David and Mary Grace West

$250 – 499

Bruce G. Dean
Jim and Carol Green
W.W. Mueller
Hope Hughes Pressman

$100 – 249

Cynthia G. Adams

$50 – 99

Virginia L. Conley
Adele Egan
James and Donnie Mattingly
Judy Mazzano
Mason D. McQuiston
Suzanne and Bob Morrison
Doris Helen Nelson
Mr. and Mrs. Kenneth Paul
Joanne K. Peekema
Stan Pickens
Jeffrey Weston